APPLEWOOD'S
MILITARY HISTORY
SERIES

Biographical Sketches of General Nathaniel Massie

Gen. Duncan McArthur, Capt. William Wells, and Gen. Simon Kenton

John McDonald

APPLEWOOD BOOKS
Bedford, Massachusetts

Biographical Sketches of General Nathaniel Massie
was originally published in
1852

ISBN: 978-1-4290-2143-2

APPLEWOOD'S MILITARY HISTORY SERIES

Thank you for purchasing an Applewood book. Applewood reprints America's lively classics—books from the past that are still of interest to modern readers. This facsimile was printed using many new technologies together to bring our tradition-bound mission to you. Applewood's facsimile edition of this work may include library stamps, scribbles, and margin notes as they exist in the original book. These interesting historical artifacts celebrate the place the book was read or the person who read the book. In addition to these artifacts, the work may have additional errors that were either in the original, in the digital scans, or introduced as we prepared the book for printing. If you believe the work has such errors, please let us know by writing to us at the address below.

For a free copy of our current print catalog featuring our bestselling books, write to:

APPLEWOOD BOOKS
P.O. Box 365
Bedford, MA 01730

For more complete listings, visit us on the web at:
awb.com

Prepared for publishing by HP

Battle of the Thames.—Page 143.

BIOGRAPHICAL SKETCHES

OF

GENERAL NATHANIEL MASSIE,

GENERAL DUNCAN McARTHUR,

CAPTAIN WILLIAM WELLS,

AND

GENERAL SIMON KENTON:

WHO WERE EARLY SETTLERS IN THE WESTERN COUNTRY.

BY JOHN McDONALD,

OF POPLAR RIDGE, ROSS COUNTY, OHIO.

———————

DAYTON, O.:

PUBLISHED AND SOLD BY D. OSBORN & SON.
1852.

PREFACE.

In presenting the reader with the following narratives of the distinguished men whose characters are attempted to be delineated, no apology is deemed necessary. The subject is one in which all men, who love to see portrayed from the stump, the rise, and progressive improvements of our country, must feel a lively interest. Is there a man whose feelings are so obtuse, as not to follow General Massie and his compatriots, with intense anxiety, through the wilderness, surveying the country, and forming new settlements in the midst of dangers and difficulties the most appalling ? if such there be, I envy him not his insensible stupidity.

The defects in the composition, none will more sincerely deplore than myself; and I regret, more than any other can, that my attainments as an author are not more fully equal to the subjects on which I have treated.

I have endured more pain, from diffidence and even timidity, in presenting myself to the public as an author, than I have suffered from fear in the most dangerous situation. It must appear novel to see a man over sixty years of age, without any of the advantages of education, having but little leisure, and always hard pressed to secure a living, turn his attention to the labor of composition in the evening of life. Under these disadvantageous circumstances, little eclat is expected; if humble mediocrity is allowed I will be content. I took up my pen to rescue from oblivion the names of men who " have done some service to the state."

In this age of enterprise and intellectual improvement, shall it be said by posterity, that, while the bones of our pioneer fathers are

mouldering into dust, no record of their useful labors shall be preserved to perpetuate their memories? "The man dies, but his memory should live."

There are certain epochs in the history of every country which
indissolubly fix themselves in the memory of its inhabitants, from
generation to generation. The war for independence, and the first
settling of the western country being simultaneous, these were the
starting points, from which we date our national existence. The
brilliant achievements performed by our forefathers to effect these
memorable objects appear to have formed the critical ERA, on which
long hung, in doubtful suspense, the destiny of these United States.
It will be admitted by all, that the old Indian war was a continuation
of the war of the Revolution. And, as Thomas Paine eloquently
said in his Crisis, "these are the times that try men's souls; the
summer soldier and the sunshine patriot will in this crisis shrink
from the service of his country—but he that stands it out now deserves the love and thanks of man and woman."

In many scenes of the grand drama, were tragedies performed
which, for boldness and sublimity of execution, throw romance into
shade. The names and characters of some of the actors have found
a place in the history of the country—but of many, very many, who
in that crisis performed brilliant exploits, the names and memories
are lost forever; whilst the names of others are only remembered in
lingering, changeful, traditionary legends.

In attempting to describe the awful catastrophes and frightful
combats which took place on the western frontier, we sometimes
meet incidents to which language is not equal. "The conception is
too bulky to be born alive, and in the struggle for expression every
finger tries to be a tongue." When we reflect on the bold assaults,
or the ingenious, masterly retreats of the old frontier-men—the
patient fortitude with which they endured fatigue and hunger—it is
evident, that man little knows till he is tried in the school of adversity what calamities and hardships are beyond his endurance.
The dangers from their enemies, though great, were only an item in
the catalogue of their sufferings. They had to travel through thick
woods without road or path, scratched with briars, stung by nettles,
or torn by thorns. When night approached, no shelter to protect
them from the "pitiless pelting of the storm," or comfortable
couch on which to repose their weary limbs; the moist earth was

their bed, the firmament of heaven their covering; tormented with gnats and musquitoes, their nights were sleepless; when morning light returned, their cares and watchfulness were resumed, to guard against the danger of being surprised by their bold, vigilant and dexterous enemy.

It must be remembered that the period is almost at hand, when to speak of the enterprising men who first settled on the banks of the beautiful river Ohio, from personal knowledge, will be closed forever. Who, and what they were, and what they accomplished, if not immediately recorded, can shortly be known only as tradition- ary legends. To cast his mite of information on this subject, to those who may succeed him, is the principal design of the author.

When a retrospective glance is taken of the path pursued by the old frontier-men, and the difficulties and dangers encountered and overcome, all will admit, that they performed their fearful duties with a firmness unsurpassed in the annals of history. Many of them bled under the tomahawk of the red men, and to all their existence was one connected period of toil, privation, and watchfulness.

Having been an humble actor in many of the scenes described, the incidents which I did not witness were communicated by the actors shortly after the events took place, so that the reader can place the fullest reliance in the truth of the narratives related in the fol- lowing pages.

The biography of General Massie I had published in the Western Christian Advocate some time since; and, as herewith presented, it has been revised by Henry Massie, (son of the General,) and I have no doubt is much improved on the original draft. Perhaps the work would have pleased better had his friendly pen revised the other parts of the volume.

It is unnecessary to inform the reader that the author of the fol- lowing pages makes no pretension to the accomplishment of learn- ing—this the learned reader will soon discover. My early life was passed with hunters, boatmen, and soldiers, where there were but rare opportunities of associating with men of learning, or polite ac- quirements. I have the most humble opinion of my literary abilities; and when I engaged in writing and publishing in the newspapers sketches of the lives of some of the old backwoodsmen, with whose history I was well acquainted, it was without the most distant idea of writing a book. The approbation with which my narratives appear to have been received by the public, together with the solicitation of some of my friends, has induced me to adopt my present course.

Having endeavored to present the reader with the manners and customs of the old frontier-men, together with some interesting events which will aid the historian of some future day, in delineating the character of the early settlers as well as the early history of the western country, I now take my leave of the subject.

JOHN McDONALD,

Of Poplar Ridge, Ross County, Ohio.

A SKETCH OF THE LIFE

OF

GENERAL NATHANIEL MASSIE.

CHAPTER I.

THE life of every man, of any distinction, is intimate-
ly connected with many of the events that compose the
general history of his country. It is by his connection
with those events he is made to display his character,
and derive from his companions whatever reputation he
may merit. Nor can we, in writing the biography of
such a man, strictly confine ourselves to the immediate
occurrences of his own time; but we must be permitted
to look back a little, and form a connected chain of
events, in order to make plain what would otherwise appear obscure, and give a just importance to events
which would not otherwise seem to merit attention.
These are the reasons I beg leave to urge as an apology
for the following digression.

A short time previous to, and about the time the Revolutionary struggle commenced, the attention of the
citizens of Virginia was drawn to the Kentucky territory ; which was, at that time, and for many years afterwards, the western portion of that state. This attention
was produced by some hardy hunters of the mountains,
who accustomed to danger, and always seeking some
new and exciting field of enterprize, passed far beyond
the pale of civilization, and pushed their discoveries in
the rich bosom of Kentucky. Returning to the settle-

ments, the fame of the exuberant richness of the soil
was spread throughout the land.   They told, that they
had passed beyond the wide chain of mountains, that
composed, at that time, the middle portion of Virginia,
and had reached the valley beyond, and found a beautifully rolling country, covered by a dense forest of large
trees, the ground beneath them carpeted by the luxuriant
growth of waving cane, and that the soil was rich beyond any they ever beheld.   Besides all this, what gave
the greatest joy to the hunter, was the fact, that game
of different kinds abounded in profusion ; so much so,
that the Indian tribes, from different portions of the West,
had from time immemorial contested, in long and bloody
battles, the occupancy of the soil, during the hunting
season ; and, on this account, the country was known
among the Indians by the name of Kentucky, " the dark
and bloody ground."

Such glowing descriptions, in spite of the many and
embarrassing difficulties under which Virginia, at that
time, labored, soon excited the activity of many of her
citizens.   That state owned an immense landed territory,
and had always been extensively liberal in its disposal.
The legislature foresaw, that the only mode to accomplish the early settlement of their vast unappropriated
lands, was to be effected by the liberal encouragement
to settlers ; and, by an act for that purpose, every one,
who made a settlement by clearing a spot of ground,
erecting a cabin, and raising a crop of corn, on such
lands, was entitled to four hundred acres of land, includ-
ing the settlement, and the preemption right to one thousand acres adjoining thereto.   The settlement claims
were bounties given to settlers by the state ; the preemption claims were rights given by the state to the
settlers, to purchase before others and appropriate one
thousand acres adjoining their settlements.   These claims
to land, in Kentucky, were of high standing and much

respected, and generally prevailed beyond other claims, when difficulties did not arise about the location of them. A large portion of the state was quickly settled by this liberal encouragement extended to settlers; yet a very short time was allowed to them. The unbounded rage for the acquisition of western lands seized the speculators, and the greater portion of the country was soon more than doubly appropriated by the military and treasury warrants, issued in almost as large quantities by Virginia, as continental paper.

The wretched " every one for himself" system of locating lands, at that time, gave rise to more than thirty years continued litigation of the land claims. So much, indeed, were they entangled, that in their adjustment, more brilliancy of talent was displayed, and more abstruse learning brought forward and applied, than it could well be conceived possible such a subject could originate. Happily, however, for the country, the rules of our laws, when applied by great and discriminating minds, are rules of reason, and when directed steadily to some great end connected with human transactions, will finally overcome all difficulties, and accomplish the desired object. In Kentucky, a system of land law was soon erected, abstruse indeed, but founded in justice, as it soon relieved their entangled and much litigated titles. But to return.

For several years after the Kentucky territory was explored, many difficulties were encountered in making permanent settlements. The settlers were placed, as it were, in a gauntlet, continually exposed to the inroads of the Indians from the northwest of the Ohio, and also from the tribes that bordered the southern part of Kentucky. These different tribes of Indians meeting yearly, during their hunting and war season, found the country possessed by the whites, who were looked upon by them as a common enemy, who, they justly suspected, had come to rob them of their possessions. Animated by the wrong which was about to be done them, and also by the thought that they were contending for the country, which had been the glorious field of the warlike exploits of their chiefs and warriors, they fought with that bravery which borders on despair. For these reasons, their warfare with the whites was of an exterminating character on both sides, and the scenes of bloodshed that ensued were most terrific. Another great difficulty, under which the settlers labored, was the distance they were removed from the settlements. Supplies of absolute necessaries were not easily transported so great a distance, as no roads were then known, and the only mode of transportation was the pack-horse, and the only guide the compass and the experience of the woodman. Unfortunately, at that time, no remedy could be applied to remove these difficulties, as Virginia with the other colonies were, at that time, engaged in the arduous struggle for Independence, and no protection could, as heretofore, be afforded to the settlers by troops levied for the frontier service.

Under these and many other difficulties, the pioneers of an early day labored. Is it not surprising that the settlement of the country should have continued to progress? Every returning messenger, too, from the new to the old country, had scenes of horror to relate of the stealthy incursions of the savages, their deadly hatred to the whites, and their indiscriminate and inhuman butcheries of them. The thoughts of such things did not discourage the pioneers. On the contrary, the tide of emigration, year after year, began to swell in larger and more regular streams, and the inhabitants soon commenced a system of offensive, as well as defensive, operations. Hitherto, the hunters and surveyors had adopted, from necessity, the roving habits, the cunning, and hardihood of the savages, and had carried on with them a desultory warfare, in which innumerable instances of personal bravery were displayed, that showed them to be men of more than Spartan courage. Many sad lessons, however, had taught the settlers that their only means of safety could be afforded by combinations of the inhabitants. At their stations, they, therefore, constructed block-houses and walls built of trees, as they were found to be the most secure method of defence, and always afforded a place of retreat from danger. In these stations were placed the wives, the children, and the moveable goods of the settlers, and a sufficiency of land in the immediate vicinity was cleared and cultivated to raise the necessaries of life. The men, during the greater part of the year, were busily employed in locating and surveying land.

This subject is so absorbing as to have carried me beyond my intention. It is impossible, indeed, to reflect on the early settlement of Kentucky without being deeply impressed with interest in its varied scenes, and, at the same time, made to feel an almost unbounded admiration of the character of its early inhabitants. Enterprize and courage gave to each one the knowledge of his own capacity, while sincere friendship, strict confidence, and mutual dependence in times of danger cemented them together like a band of brothers. They lived at a time, when those manly and ennobling qualities were necessary for their well-being, and a continuation of these qualities among their descendants, have rendered them celebrated, in our land, for their open and manly bearing and other qualities connected with true courage.

I have made the above remarks, in order to connect them with the subject of this biographical sketch. It was at an interesting period of the settlement of Kentucky, that he entered upon the active duties of a surveyor, and to a man of capacity in that business an immense field of enterprize was opened.

General Nathaniel Massie was born, in Goochland county, Virginia, on the 28th day of December, 1763. He was the eldest son of Maj. Nathaniel Massie of that county, who was a substantial farmer in easy circumstances. The Major was a man of great plainness, industry, and good practical sense, and although possessed of means sufficient, he chose rather to give his sons such educations as would prepare them to transact the common business of life, than such as would be of no service to them in the employments he intended them to pursue. Besides all this he had a large family of children, and acting rather contrary to the old Virginia system, he thought it better for his sons, that at an early day they should be placed in a situation to gain their own livelihood. So soon, therefore, as they completed their educations, he permitted them to select whatever employment they preferred. Nathaniel, the eldest son, chose for his occupation to learn surveying, and go to the western country, which at that time held out great inducements to enterprizing young men. Previously, however, to this, at the early age of seventeen years (1780), he was sent by his father as a substitute for himself, or some member of the family, in the draft of soldiers, made about that time, to recruit the army during the revolutionary war. What length of time he remained, or at what post stationed, is not known to the author. The fact itself shows the confidence reposed in him at that early age by his father, and the excursion was well calculated to make him better acquainted with men and things, and it is highly probable gave a spring to that latent ambition which distinguished him in after life as a man of uncommon enterprize.

After his return home from the army, he studied surveying, and made himself master of that science. In the fall of the year 1783, in his nineteenth year, he was prepared to set out in the world on his own footing. He has been described by an intimate acquaintance of his, who saw him a short time previous to his departure for the West, " as an uncommonly fine-looking young man. That his form was slender, well made, and muscular, and was calculated, from his good constitution and uncommon activity, to endure fatigue, exposure, and privations in an eminent degree. That his countenance was open and expressive of great energy and good sense, and well suited to gain favor from men of enterprize." His father furnished him with a horse well equipped, and all necessary surveying instruments. A small amount of treasury warrants were also placed in his care, together with a letter of recommendation to Gen. James Wilkinson, who was, at that time, a citizen of Kentucky country, and a man of distinction.

The author, as he is personally unacquainted with the early history of General Massie, has been obliged to depend on whatever information his children could afford him, which was but little, as they have lived far away from the home of his youth and family connections. What information he has derived from them of him, while in Kentucky, is contained in some old letters, from different persons to him. It is well known, however, that very shortly after his arrival there he was actively engaged in locating warrants and surveying lands; and from the property he accumulated, it would appear great success had attended his industry. An extract from a letter of his father, of an early date, is given on account of its antiquity.

" *Goochland, Aug.* 24, 1784.

"Loving Son :—I received yours, per Mr. Underwood, wherein you informed me that you were in good health : likewise that favored by Mr. Parker, dated May 25, 1784, wherein you informed me, that the warrant for two hundred and fifty acres of land was joining the other warrant, and that it was rather dangerous to have it surveyed. I am glad to hear that it is the best quality, equal to James river low grounds," &c.

The following letter, as it shows the manner in which surveying was conducted, at that time, is worthy of an insertion.

"*Hanging-fork, April* 26, 1786.

" DEAR SIR :—I am, at this time, unable to come over on the business that I promised you. For my attending the surveys it will not make the least difference, as you can do it as well as if I was with you. I wish you to divide the land that is surveyed, belonging to the Dutchmen, and survey the entries that lay joining of those lands, and divide the entries also. Survey that land you purchased of Captain Owing, and survey the one thousand and five hundred acre entry, that is located at Logan's old camp on Bird's trace, about one mile from another large camp. The old camp was made on the first campaign, in the year '80, and the other the next campaign. I wish you to survey the entries that are on the heads of Grassy creek, in the name of Howard Lewis. If you find where Creuss was buried at a camp, you can easily find the entries. You must take the marked way from the camp up a ridge, westwardly course, about two miles, and the way is marked all the way of the two miles with a tomahawk ; and then you will turn down a hollow to your left hand, until you cross a branch of Grassy creek, and you will see some stumps, where there has been some fire-wood cut, on the east side of the branch ; and continue the marked way the same course, perhaps two and a half miles, near the heads of said waters, and there you will find some trees marked, as the entry calls for, on the west side of the black oak, and some small trees marked near the said oak ; and you will return down to the same branch to the creek, and

down the creek to the fork, and cross the forks and go a
southeast course about four miles, until you come to a
creek ; then up said creek until you find a camp on said
creek, in the bottom, where you will see trees peeled,
and stumps, and an old camp, and there is Mr. Howard
Lewis's entry of two thousand acres.   You will find the
beginning about fifty rods below the camp in a buffalo
trace, on an ash tree, marked M. black with powder, the
mark is facing down the creek ; I peeled the bark off
with my knife; and survey Stephen's above Meam-
ey's and Young's preemption ; and that, I think, will be
as much as you can do at this time.   Now, my good
friend, if you cannot do it, pray write a letter to me,
and direct it to Mr. Nagle, in Danville.   But I would be
glad if you could do it, and I will give you five pounds
besides your fees.   Promise your chain carriers goods
for their wages, which I will pay on your return ; and
am, sir, your friend and humble servant,

"JOHN MARTIN."

" *Mr. Nathaniel Massie.*"

Who this John Martin was is not known, but this letter of instruction to Mr. Massie shows him to have been
a land speculator and a merchant.   I have introduced
this letter to show the necessity of a surveyor's being,
what is termed, a woodsman, and also the manner in
which surveyors' fees were paid.   Mere surveyors had
their fees regulated by law, and were illy paid for their
trouble, and as they were men of great enterprize and
much information as to good unappropriated lands, they
soon became locators of land on the shares.   The locators who were popular, and in whom confidence could
be placed, would get a fourth, a third, and, sometimes,
half, when locations could be made on first rate land.
Massie, at first, acted as a surveyor, but he soon discovered that it was a small business, and that the pro-

2

fitable land business fell into the hands of the locators.
As he was young and extremely active, and one of the best
footmen in the West, he soon became an expert woodsman, to be which was an indispensable qualification of
a land locator, as the country was then an entire and unbroken wilderness. No roads, or even paths, led from
one part to the other; and besides these difficulties, the
restless Indians were continually on the alert to surprise
and cut off surveying parties. The surveyors, too, had
to explore the country, in order to find the most fertile
lands, and in doing this they were obliged to traverse
the woods in every direction, guess at courses, and judge
of distances. Young Massie soon became an expert surveyor, and it was a matter of astonishment, (as he was
raised in the dense population east of the mountains)
how soon he acquired the science and habits of the backwoodsmen. Although he never practised the art of
hunting, he was admitted by all, who knew his qualifications as a woodsman, to be of the first order. He
could steer his course truly in clear or cloudy weather,
and compute distances more correctly than most of the
old hunters. He could endure fatigue and hunger, with
more composure than the most of those persons who
were inured to want on the frontier. He could live upon
meat without bread, and bread without meat, and was
perfectly cheerful and contented with his fare. In all the
perilous situations in which he was placed, he was always conspicuous for his good feeling and the happy
temperament of his mind. His courage was of a cool
and dispassionate character, which added to great circumspection in times of danger, gave him a complete
ascendancy over his companions, who were always willing to follow when Massie led the way.

The field of young Massie's activity seems not to
have been confined, during this period, to the business
of locating and surveying lands. In the fall of 1786,

we find him interested with Gen. James Wilkinson in
speculations in salt, which on account of its scarcity,
and the absolute necessity of the article, rendered it very
valuable.   There were then few places in the western
country, where salt could be made to any advantage. The
art of boring for salt water was then unknown, and the
few places where salt was made, were where the water
rose to the level of the earth, which from its great
mixture with fresh water, generally required eight hundred or a thousand gallons of the water to make fifty
pounds or a bushel of salt, which sold for two to five
dollars, per bushel.   The principal manufactories in
Kentucky, were Bullitt's and Mann's licks near Louisville, from which the inhabitants of the West were scantily supplied at an enormous price. From two old letters from Gen. Wilkinson to Massie, which are inserted
below, we learn that Massie was about to start for Nashville, on the Cumberland river, with a barge load of salt.
Gen. Wilkinson, as the senior partner, directed the affairs
of the firm, and, from his letters of instruction to Massie,
shows his remarkable cunning, and the means employed,
at that day, to keep from being overreached.   The General, at that time, was one of the largest dealers of merchandize in the West, and one of the most popular men
in the country, and was well known to be a man of the
first order of talents, and great discrimination as to the
character of men.   Whether Massie made or sunk money in the salt speculation is not known, and the subject
is introduced chiefly to show in what articles of trade
the commerce of the country consisted, and the manner
in which it was conducted ; and also to show that Massie,
young as he was, had rendered his name respectable by
his industry and attention to business.   The confidence
placed in him by Gen. Wilkinson shows the light in
which he viewed him. These letters further show the
manner in which business was transacted, and informa-

tion communicated between different parts of the country
This was done, generally, by means of expresses. It
was eight or ten years after that period, before post routes
and post offices afforded their facilities to the inhabitants
of Kentucky.

" *Danville, December* 19, 1786.

" DEAR SIR :—I beg you to proceed with all possible
dispatch to the falls. You will call by the lick, and
urge the provision of the salt; and prepare some way
of conveying it to the river, &c. &c. You will make the
best of your way to Nashville, and there dispose of it
for cotton, beaver furs, racoon skins, otter, &c. You
must always observe to get as much cash as you can.
When you have completed your sales, you will yourself
move with the horses, &c., by land, and commit the
other articles, with the barge, to Captain Alexander,
with directions to him to proceed up to the falls, there
secure the boat and property, and give me the earliest
advice of his arrival, by express or otherwise. The
goods which Captain Alexander carries down to the falls,
I wish you to exchange for horses, or elegant high
blooded mares, if you can get great bargains; otherwise,
sell them for cash, peltry, or cotton. When you receive
the salt, take care to have it measured in a proper honest
way, with a spade or shovel, and no sifting, &c. One
Smith is preparing to go down with two or three hundred bushels from the lower lick. Endeavor to get off
before him, and if you cannot, persuade him to stay for
you; but you must not wait for him a moment, as it will
be your interest to arrive before him. You will remember you are going amongst a set of sharpers, and therefore must take care of yourself. Write to me by every
opportunity, letting me know how you come on. Don't
fail in this. God bless you and give you good luck.

" Yours sincerely,

" J. WILKINSON."

" *Fayette*, 29*th Dec.* 1786, *Friday Morning.*

" DEAR MASSIE :—I approve of your plan to go to the port with two hundred bushels of salt, and sell for cash or furs, but take no deer skins. Be sure and get as many otters as possible. Be cautious in your move-ments, guard against the savages, coming and going, and discharge your men the moment you get to the port. The only thing you have to dread is the ice. To be caught in the ice would be worse than the devil's own luck. Act with decision and despatch in whatever you do. God bless you.

" J. WILKINSON."

CHAPTER II.

As much as could be learned of the life of General Massie, while engaged in business in Kentucky, has been related in the last chapter. We have now arrived at a period in his life, when my own information will serve me, instead of the scanty materials from which the nar-rative of his early life has been gathered. The facts, that I shall relate, will be connected with the exploring and settlement of our own portion of the state, and I hope will interest both the old and young. To the old settlers, it will bring to remembrance the privations and hardships endured, and the difficulties and dangers long since passed through, and now almost forgotten in the lapse of time. To the young of the land, it will be a bright example, as it will place before them the hardy virtues of those men, who by their bravery, enterprize, and industry, have astonished the world by the power with which they wrested our country from its savage inhabitants, and have, within a few years, made it almost the garden spot of the land. Mr. Trumbull, in his history of Connecticut, referring to the early history and settlement of new countries, in his beautiful and appropriate language, says, that "no man of genius, taste, and curiosity, can read the accounts of the origin of nations, the discovery, settlement, and progress of new countries, without a high degree of entertainment.   But in the settlement of his own country, in the lives of his ancestors, in their adventures and heroism, he feels himself particularly interested. He at once becomes a party in their affairs, and travels and converses with them, with a kind of filial delight. While he beholds them braving the horrors of the desert, the terrors of the savage, the distresses of famine and war, he admires their courage, and is pleased with all their escapes from danger, and all their progress in settlements, population, opulence, liberty, and happiness. While he contemplates their self-denials and perseverance, in surmounting all dangers and enduring all hardships, in turning the wilderness into gardens and fruitful fields, and transmitting liberty and religion to posterity, he is struck with a pleasing astonishment. The pious man views a divine hand conducting the whole, gives thanks, adores, and loves."

Many of the western pioneers were warriors by profession and courted danger for danger's sake. These, on account of their daring intrepidity, were welcome guests wherever they went. Others there were, whose views were more enlarged, and who with equal courage put danger at defiance, keeping a steady eye to push forward the bounds of civilization in the vast wilds of the west. Such were the leaders of the hardy woodsmen, who were engaged in making new settlements on the borders of the river Ohio, and its tributary streams. Some one of these master spirits led the way in each settlement which was made, in spite of the Indians, whose restless and continual incursions caused every cabin to be raised at the risk of life, and every settlement to be made under the most

trying and perilous circumstances. The rapidity of the
advance of arts and improvements seems so great in later
years, that the few weather-beaten pioneers who yet linger amongst us look around them with surprise and wonder. The change seems so great and so sudden, that it
appears to them like the work of supreme creating power.
In a few years they beheld the country all laid out in
farms and under a high state of cultivation. Instead of
the log cabins, splendid mansions glitter in the sun;
roads made, over which the traveler glides along in his
coach; towns and cities erected, where the ingenious
mechanic displays his arts, and the busy hum of commerce salutes his ear. Railroads formed over which the
traveler passes with the speed of the wind; and to crown
the whole, artificial rivers are constructed to convey commerce in every direction. The master spirits, who by
their toils prepared the way for changes such as these,
have in the history of their lives a degree of originality
and interest far beyond common men. The ever varied
scenes of their adventures and dangers, will (or should)
always render a narrative of their lives acceptable to
those who can relish a description of men of merit.
Every one should feel an interest to see such names
transmitted to latest posterity, and thereby render " honor
to whom honor is due."

I will borrow a few words from Mr. Doddridge's
notes. " Is the memory of our forefathers unworthy of
historic or sepulchral commemoration? No people on
earth, in similar circumstances, ever acted more nobly or
more bravely than they did. No people of any country
or age made greater sacrifices for the benefit of their posterity, than those which were made by the first settlers
of the western regions. What people ever left such noble
legacies to posterity, as those transmitted by our forefathers to their descendants ?"

As the scene of the adventures of General Massie and

his companions, is confined to that part of our state, known as the Virginia military district, I thought a brief account of its history would be useful and interesting.

The state of Virginia, during the progress of the Revolutionary war, in order to engage the active services of her citizens, and give an ample compensation to those hardy officers and soldiers, who were devoting their lives and fortunes to the good of their country, by several acts of her legislature, granted them liberal bounties in new unappropriated lands for their services. To satisfy these bounties, a large tract of land was reserved in the Kentucky territory.

Shortly after the close of the war, in order to avoid the confusion heretofore attendant on the careless locations of lands, and also to do ample justice to those interested, an act of the legislature was passed, authorizing certain deputations of officers therein named, or a certain number of them, from both the continental and state lines, to appoint superintendents on behalf of their respective lines ; and also nominate two principal surveyors, to be commissioned as other surveyors; and to contract with the surveyors for their fees, who were authorized to select their own deputies with the consent of the superintendents. By a further provision of this act, the holders of warrants were required to place them in the hands of the surveyors of their respective lines by a specified day, and that then, the priority in the location of their warrants should be decided by lot. The surveyors, after these preliminary arrangements, were authorized to proceed to survey all the good land in that tract of country lying between Green and Cumberland rivers, as set apart by law for the officers and soldiers, and then to proceed to survey on the northwest side of the river Ohio, between the rivers Scioto and Little Miami, until the deficiency of lands to satisfy all military bounties should be fully and amply made up.

Pursuant to this act of the legislature, the deputation of the officers of the continental line, consisting of Major General Charles Scott, Brigadier General Daniel Morgan, Colonel William Heth, Lieutenant Colonel Benjamin Temple, and Captain Mayo Carrington, elected Colonel Richard C. Anderson to the office of principal surveyor of the bounties of lands to be entered for the officers and soldiers of that line. A contract dated the 17th day of December, 1783, was also entered into between Col. Anderson and the deputation of officers, regulating the fees of the surveyor, and other matters connected with the business. A copy of that contract, in the hand writing of Col. Anderson, is now before me, and as an old document, of much importance in its time, deserves notice, and is accordingly inserted.*

* COL. ANDERSON'S CONTRACT.

Be it remembered this seventeenth day of December, in the year of our Lord one thousand, seven hundred and eighty three, that Richard Clough Anderson, of the state of Virginia, for and on the part of himself, his heirs, executors and administrators of the first part, and Major General Charles Scott, Brigadier General Daniel Morgan, Colonel William Heth, Lieutenant Colonel Benjamin Temple, and Captain Mayo Carrington, a deputation on the part of the officers and soldiers of the Virginia continental troops, for this purpose duly appointed; for and on the part of the said officers and soldiers, for themselves and their successors in such deputation of the second part, have covenanted, promised, contracted and agreed, and do by these presents, covenant, contract, promise, and agree; to and with each other in the manner and form following, that is to say;

First :—The party of the first part being elected the principal surveyor for the purpose of locating and surveying the several bounties of lands which have been given and granted by the General Assembly of this state to the said officers and soldiers, shall forthwith proceed to obtain the legal qualifications for effectually executing his said office of principal surveyor, and having obtained such qualification shall proceed as early as may be on the business of locating and surveying the bounties of land aforesaid, for the several officers and soldiers entitled thereto, as original grantees of the said state, and for their heirs agreeable to their respective warrants, according to such modes and regulations as have been, or shall hereafter be, established by the General Assembly; faithfully, and effectually, doing and performing at every stage of the business, whatever it is customary for surveyors to do and perform. *Secondly :*—The said party of the first

In the spring or summer of the year 1784, Colonel Anderson moved to Kentucky, and purchased a fine farm near Louisville, where he finally established his residence, and gave to it the appropriate name of the " Soldier's Retreat." On the 20th day of July of the same year, he opened his office for the purpose of having entries and surveys made of the lands in the Kentucky reservation. Previous to this, however, on the 1st day of March, 1784, Virginia, by her delegates, had ceded to the United States her territory northwest of the Ohio, as a common fund for the benefit of all the states, reserving the country lying between the Miami and Scioto rivers to be appropriated for the purpose of satisfying the continental line warrants, in case the land reserved in Kentucky, would not be sufficient for that purpose. The deficiency of good land in Kentucky was soon discovered, and the attention of the holders of warrants and the

part shall carry with him, and keep in service during the time of his being on the said business, or until discharged by the superintendents, four effective men for chain carriers, markers, and hunters, armed and furnished with ammunition, and also equipped with the necessary utensils for performing the duties aforesaid, for each deputy or assistant surveyor, he shall employ; whose pay shall not exceed three shillings per day to be paid by the said surveyor, and he to be reimbursed therefor by the parties of the second part. *Thirdly :*—The party of the first part shall, out of his own fees, pay the college dues which shall arise on this business, exonerating the said officers and soldiers therefrom. *Fourthly :*—The parties of the second part, that is to say, the said officers and soldiers, their heirs, executors, or administrators, respectively pay, or cause to be paid to the party of the first part, his heirs, executors, administrators or assigns, the usual surveyor's fees, as by law established; three shillings whereof for every thousand acres to be paid down at the time of lodging the warrant or warrants, on which the said surveys are to be made.

In witness whereof the said parties have hereunto interchangeably set their hands the date above written.

(A copy.)　　　　RICHARD C. ANDERSON.
　　　　　　　　DANIEL MORGAN, B. G.
　　　　　　　　WILL. HETH, Col.
　　　　　　　　BENJAMIN TEMPLE, Lt. Col.
　　　　　　　　M. CARRINGTON, Capt.

land speculators was turned towards the reservation north-
west of the Ohio.

This fine portion of our state, known and called as before stated by the name of the Virginia military district,
possesses from its situation and soil many advantages.
On the east and north, its boundary is the Scioto river;
on the west, the greater part of the district is bounded
by the Little Miami, while the entire southern boundary
is washed by the Ohio, for upwards of one hundred miles.
The soil of this tract of country presents for its extent, a
greater variety than probably any other of the like extent in the United States.   In the southeastern portion,
the uplands extending thirty or forty miles below the
mouth of the Scioto, and thirty miles north from the
Ohio, are hilly and the land poor, and at this time the
greater part of it is vacant.   Below the mouth of Brush
creek, the hills along the Ohio, for a short distance from
the river, are rich and heavily timbered.   Farther down
the river, the extent of rich land increases to the mouth
of the Little Miami.   The bottoms of the Ohio, Scioto,
Miami, and the large tributary streams, composed of a
rich and dark loamy soil, are celebrated for their fertility,
and the heavy crops annually taken from them, for a succession of upwards of thirty years without rest or re-
newal in any way, show that their celebrity is not without foundation.   The middle portion of the country presents, however, the greatest variety of soil.   Although
the extent of bottom land along the streams is considerable, yet the greater portion is upland of good quality, on
which wheat is raised in great abundance.   A portion of
it is level land timbered with beech and sugar trees, which
at the first settlement of the country was considered
rather too flat and wet for cultivation, but since it has
been cleared and cultivated it is justly considered first
rate land, alone surpassed by the rich alluvial bottoms.
A part of the middle portion consists also of prairie or

barren land, the value of which has been lately discovered to be greater than ever was expected, as it presented, at the first settlement of the country, a marshy appearance, which it was not supposed could be overcome by cultivation. The industry of our inhabitants has overcome this obstacle; and the barrens are fast becoming very valuable land. The other part of the district consists of barrens, and also of wet and flat land, timbered with sugar and beech trees, and is at this time quite unsettled. From this variety of soil great advantages arise. In our bottoms, we raise corn in great abundance; in our uplands, wheat and other small grain; while our barrens, or prairies, furnish most desirable pastures for grazing. We have thus a soil, in which an equal portion of the inhabitants are engaged in raising different articles of produce, and greatly assist each other by furnishing a home market for different kinds of stock and the produce of the soil. But to return.

In the winter and spring of the year 1787, Major John O'Bannon and Arthur Fox, two enterprising surveyors in Kentucky, passed over into the district to obtain a knowledge of the country, for the purpose of making entries of the land, so soon as the office should be opened for that purpose. They explored with their companies the whole extent of country along the Ohio, and passed some distance up the Scioto and Miami rivers, and some of their tributary streams. On the 1st day of August, 1787, Colonel Anderson opened the office for receiving the entries of lands in the district, at which time entries of the bottoms of the Ohio were made, and also a large portion of the bottoms of the Scioto and Little Miami rivers. About that time, or shortly before, several expeditions from Kentucky made excursions into the district, for the purpose of destroying the Indian towns. Simon Kenton, a name celebrated among backwoodsmen, was along in almost all of these expeditions, and returning home attempted some entries of lands, in which he was not successful, on account of his want of sufficient skill in making them.

So soon as it was made known to Congress, that entries had been made in the district northwest of the Ohio, by virtue of the continental warrants, an act was passed in July, 1788, by which it was resolved, that Congress would consider all locations and surveys made on account of the troops, between the Scioto and Little Miami as invalid, until the deficiency on the southeast side of the Ohio should be ascertained and stated to Congress ; and the Executive of Virginia was requested to inform Congress of the deficiency, if any, and the amount of it. This act, together with the danger apprehended from the Indians, obstructed further entries and surveys in the district until an act of Congress, passed in August 1790, repealed the act of July 1788, which removed all difficulties as to the entries and surveys, previously made or subsequently to be made. This act also regulated the mode of obtaining patents, and was amended by the act of 1794, and other subsequent acts.

The difficulty about the early locations of lands northwest of the Ohio in this district, arose from the ignorance of those engaged, as to the extent of jurisdiction acquired over those lands by the United States, from Virginia, by her cession in March, 1784. This is shown from the fact that the governor of Virginia issued patents on a number of surveys in the district. These patents were of course void, and were subsequently cancelled, and patents issued by the President, under the seal of the United States. We will now return.

The first excursion made by General Massie into the interior of the district northwest of the Ohio, was in the year 1788 ; but no account of the particulars of this expedition or his companions is now known. He was probably in company with Arthur Fox, who was at that time engaged in surveying lands in the district, and a particular friend and companion of Massie. A letter from his father, about this time, refers to this expedition.

" *Goochland Co. Oct.* 4, 1788.

LOVING SON :—I received yours, favored by Mr. Underwood, wherein you inform me that you had made a trip over the Ohio ; that you had tarried there but a few days. I am afraid that you venture too much. Should you escape after doing what you have engaged, I would advise you to drop venturing too much, &c. By your last, you say that you can finish all you have undertaken by spring. God send you a safe return, &c. I will keep a cask of cider till the first of April expecting to see you, if God is willing.

" I am your loving father,

" NATHANIEL MASSIE."

For some time, during the prohibition of entries made by the act of Congress, of the lands of this district, Massie was engaged in writing in Col. Anderson's office, in order to acquire a complete knowledge of the business of locating and surveying. His character for dispatch in business and enterprize gained him the friendship and confidence of Col. Anderson, who had the control of the warrants, placed in his hands by his brother officers and soldiers. A very large amount of these, so soon as the act of Congress of August, 1790, removed all further obstruction, he placed in the hands of Massie, to enter and survey on such terms as he could obtain from the holders of them. As the risk of making entries was great, and as it was desirable to possess the best land, the owners of warrants, in most cases, made liberal contracts with the surveyors. One fourth, one third, and sometimes as much as one half acquired by the entry of good lands were given by the proprietors to the sur-

veyors. If the owners preferred paying money, the
usual terms were ten pounds, Virginia currency, for each
thousand acres entered and surveyed, exclusive of chain-
men's expenses. These terms cannot appear extrava-
gant, when we consider, that at that time the danger encountered was great, the exposure during the winter was
severe, and that the price of first rate land in the west
was low, and an immense quantity in market.

The locations of land warrants in this district prior to
1790, were made by stealth. Every creek which was
explored, every line that was run, was at the risk of life
from the savage Indians, whose courage and perseverance
was only equalled by the perseverance of the whites to
push forward their settlements. It was a contest for
dominion : and the bravery, the stratagem, and the boldness displayed by the Indians in executing their plans,
could only be equalled by their fearless onsets in attacks
and their masterly retreats when defeated.

The Indians, at this time, had among them a number
of master spirits, and it is greatly to be regretted that the
history of their exploits is lost forever. The patient resolution and fortitude with which they contended against
superior discipline and numbers, the wiles and stratagems
displayed by them during their long and bloody wars,
proved that they possessed intellectual qualities of the
first order. Their fortitude in enduring pain, fatigue,
and starvation, was unequalled, except by such of the
whites as were long disciplined in the Indian school.

Besides exposure to the Indians while surveying, the
surveyors in the district had other difficulties to encounter. By passing the Ohio, they placed that river between
them and their place of retreat, in case they were defeated and pursued. The season of the year, too, chosen
by them for surveying was the depth of winter, as they
were then more secure from interruption ; as the Indians
were at that time of the year in their winter quarters, and

when hunting were found in small bodies. Against danger and exposure, the surveyors were without shelter in the district.

CHAPTER III.

IT is now believed by many persons, that the men who effected our independence and those who first settled the western country, were more robust and hardy than the present race of men. This is a mistaken notion. It was their constant exercise of mind and body, which braced and invigorated their constitutions to endure the constant draught that was made upon them, that rendered them so hardy. The weak and feeble, and all such as were predisposed to disease, who ventured on the frontier in those days of peril and privations, soon fell by sickness, or in sudden retreats lost their lives by the Indian's tomahawk, and were no more heard of. The remnant of those pioneers, who still linger amongst us, are the gleaning of the most hardy of the original stock. Their long lives prove much in favor of activity and hardihood, yet for both qualities they were indebted to the circumstances by which they were surrounded: the occasion made them what they were. It is believed that man is, and has been, the same in all ages of the world. He is civilized or barbarous, strong and active, or weak and indolent, as are his companions. The habits and manners of the old frontier-men were a perfect state of nature, where every one was his own judge, and righted his own wrongs and was his own dependence in difficulties. It cannot now be conceived or believed, how soon an active, lively, and enterprizing young man would unlearn to practice the artificial rules of civilized life, and acquire the customs and habits of the frontier-men, or even the more ferocious

habits of the Indians. This fact shows how much we
are formed by custom, and also that it is only in a dense
population, that the arts of civilized life unfold their protecting and salutary beauties.

With men, such as these, hardy, robust, and daring,
and in the situation of the district as described in the
last chapter, Massie, in the winter of the year, 1790, determined to make a settlement in it, that he might be in
the midst of his surveying operations and secure his party
from danger and exposure. In order to effect this, he
gave general notice in Kentucky of his intention, and offered each of the first twenty-five families, as a donation,
one in-lot, one out-lot, and one hundred acres of land,
provided they would settle in a town he intended to lay
off at his settlement. His proffered terms were soon
closed in with, and upwards of thirty families joined
him. After various consultations with his friends, the
bottom on the Ohio river, opposite the lower of the
Three Islands, was selected as the most eligible spot.
Here, he fixed his station, and laid off into lots a town,
now called Manchester; at this time a small place, about
twelve miles above Maysville, (formerly Limestone)
Kentucky.

This little confederacy, with Massie at the helm (who
was the soul of it,) went to work with spirit. Cabins
were raised, and by the middle of March, 1791, the
whole town was enclosed with strong pickets, firmly fixed in the ground, with block houses at each angle for
defence.

Thus was the first settlement in the Virginia military
district, and the fourth settlement in the bounds of the
state of Ohio, effected. Although this settlement was
commenced in the hottest Indian war, it suffered less
from depredation, and even interruptions, from the Indians, than any settlement previously made on the Ohio
river. This was no doubt owing to the watchful band

of brave spirits who guarded the place—men who were reared in the midst of danger and inured to perils, and as watchful as hawks. Here were the Beasleys, the Stouts, the Washburns, the Ledoms, the Edgingtons, the Denings, the Ellisons, the Utts, the McKenzies, the Wades, and others, who were equal to the Indians in all the arts and stratagems of border war.

As soon as Massie had completely prepared his station for defence, the whole population went to work, and cleared the lower of the Three Islands, and planted it in corn. The island was very rich, and produced heavy crops. The woods, with a little industry, supplied a choice variety of game. Deer, elk, buffalo, bears and turkeys, were abundant, while the river furnished a variety of excellent fish. The wants of the inhabitants, under these circumstances, were few and easily gratified. Luxuries were entirely unknown, except old Monongahela double distilled. This article was in great demand in those days, and when obtained, freely used. Coffee and tea were rare articles, not much prized or sought after, and were only used to celebrate the birth of a new comer. The inhabitants of the station were generally as playful as kittens, and as happy in their way as their hearts could wish. The men spent most of their time in hunting and fishing, and almost every evening the boys and girls footed merrily to the tune of the fiddle. Thus was their time spent in that happy state of indolence and ease, which none but the hunter or herdsman state can enjoy. They had no civil officers to settle their disputes, nor priests to direct their morals; yet amongst them crimes were of rare occurrence. Should any one who chanced to be amongst them, prove troublesome, or disturb the harmony of the community, his expulsion forthwith would be the consequence; and wo be to him if he again attempted to intrude himself upon them.

[Face 33.]

That " there is a nobility above birth, and riches above
wealth," was clearly manifest in the lives of the old
pioneers. A distinguished Roman said, "the bravest
man was the noblest man." If this position be true, the
nobility of the frontier men remains unrivaled. That
there "are riches above wealth," was evidenced in the
lives of the citizens of the frontier stations. There were
no rival grades or castes in these small communities, to
create envy : in their society all stood on a par. Their
minds were buoyant with hope; and when danger was
not apparent, they were the happiest, and of course the
richest people on earth.

The manners of the frontier men among themselves,
were affectionate and familiar. They addressed each
other by their Christian names only; which custom still
appears to them, the most friendly and courteous mode
of intercourse. To one who looks back on what the
world was then, it seems as if "money-making and sel-
fishness had frozen up the avenues to the heart. That
frank, friendly intercourse, which was the delight and
honor of this land, is gone, it is feared, for ever; and
the cold, calculating spirit of accumulation, or the worth-
less emulation of show and splendor, has succeeded."

When this station was made, the nearest neighbors
north-west of the Ohio, were the inhabitants at Columbia, a settlement below the mouth of the Little Miami,
eight miles above Cincinnati, and at Galliapolis, a French
settlement, near the mouth of the Great Kenhawa. Look
at the map of the State of Ohio, reader. You will
there see the long and dreary waste, Massie and his companions, during their exploring expeditions through the
wilderness of the present State of Ohio, had to travel,
without roads or paths. They could not hear the agreeable
sound of the plowman's gee - haw, nor the keen crack of
the wagoner's or coachman's whip, nor the clink of the
blacksmith's hammer, nor the pleasant clitter-clatter of

the mill. All was the lonely and solitary gloom of the dark forest. Then, too, could be seen the wide spread prairie, dressed in nature's gayest herbage, where the most beautiful and sweet scented flowers mingled in wild confusion, where neither bush nor tree could be seen, and where the blue sky appeared, in sublime grandeur, to lean on the outer edge of the earth, like an immense crystal bowl inverted. Here silence reigned with the stillness of death, except when broken occasionally by the cries of wild animals, and the appalling yell of the Indian.

Massie having permanently established himself in his station, continued to make locations and surveys of land in every direction. It was during this period that many interesting events transpired, connected with the surveying parties. Great precaution was used while surveying, and the invariable rule with Massie was, to keep spies around him ; and if they came across fresh Indian signs, and the enemy appeared to be numerous, then to desist from surveying, and, like the terrapins, return to their cover. This precaution, though vigilantly adhered to, did not always prevent the surveyors from meeting with disasters, as will appear by the following incident.

Early in the spring of the year 1792, Massie proceeded to make some surveys on a small creek, which empties into the Ohio four miles above Manchester, accompanied by Israel Donalson, and two others. They meandered up the river to the mouth of the creek, and sat down on a log, not far from the bank of the river, to eat some junk. As they were eating and amusing themselves with chit-chat, they were not a little startled to see seven or eight Indians walk up the bank of the river without their arms, having left them in their canoe at the mouth of the creek. Massie and his party fled. The Indians, yelling horridly, pursued them. When the surveying party reached the foot of the hill, they had a deep ravine to cross, about ten or twelve feet wide, and as many in depth. Massie, and two others of his companions, leaped the ravine; but poor Donalson, being less active in making the leap, plunged into the ditch. Massie, and the two others, soon ran to Manchester, and gave an account of their misfortune. He was ignorant whether or no Donalson was killed. Early next morning he collected twenty men, and went to the ravine, and found that Donalson must have been taken. The trail of the Indians was pursued for some distance, when it was concluded, that if the pursuit was continued, and the Indians were aware of it, they would immediately kill Donalson; but that if they were permitted to go off unmolested, they would, in all probability, save his life. The pursuing party immediately returned to Manchester, permitting the Indians to pursue their course.

Some time passed before the fate of Donalson was known at the station, and that was made known by his own sudden appearance. From his account of the affair, it appears the Indians had been trapping up Big Sandy River, and were on their return to Wapatomaka town (now Zanesfield), on Mad river. That the Indians had passed from the mouth of Big Sandy, down the Ohio, until they reached the mouth of the creek where they landed, with their canoes, and had given pursuit to the party. The foremost Indian, pursuing them closely, saw Donalson make his unfortunate plunge, and before he could recover, leaped upon him tomahawk in hand. Donalson instantly surrendered, and was made a prisoner. It was late in the evening when they took him, and they immediately loaded him with their peltry, and made a rapid march homeward. In a few days they reached the Chillicothe town, on the Little Miami. At this time, he began to think about effecting his escape, although the difficulties against which he had to contend were great, owing to the extreme caution and watchfulness of the

Indians. At night they confined him in the following
manner. They took a strong tug (a rope made of the
raw hide of the buffalo or elk), and fastened it around his
body, each end of the tug being tied around the body of
an Indian. The tug was tied so tightly, that it could not
be slipped, nor could he move to the one side or the other
without drawing the Indian after him. It was from such
a situation he had to extricate himself. One night, while
the Indians were tying him after the usual manner, he
puffed up his body to its full extent, by drawing in his
breath; and when they had completed the process, he
found that there was a good deal of play in the noose of
the tug. He laid very still until the Indians were fast
asleep. Then, having partly undressed himself, he
began slowly and cautiously to slip from the noose.
After a long trial he succeeded in slipping himself out,
and found himself once more a freeman. He instantly
rushed to the thickets. The night was clear, and he
could steer his course by the stars. Striking off in a
southern direction, he traveled all night. The next day
he fell on Harmer's old trace, and followed its course to
the South. In two days he reached Fort Washington,
now Cincinnati. Here he remained a few days to recruit
himself, and then returned to his friends at Manchester,
where he was most joyfully received, as there had been
with them great anxiety as to his fate. The creek, at the
mouth of which he was taken, was called after him
" Donalson's Creek ;" which name it still retains, and
will retain when the event which gave birth to its name,
will be forgotten. Mr. Donalson is still living, the
patriarch of Manchester, and is, I believe, the only one
of the first settlers who lives there at this time. He held
many public offices. He was a member of the convention which formed the constitution for the State of Ohio,
and uniformly preserved the character of an honest and
useful man.

In the early part of the winter of 1791–92, Massie was engaged in locating and surveying the lands on Brush creek, as far up as the three forks, intending, as soon as there was less danger from the Indians, to proceed on a larger scale. It was in the spring of the same year, that he was engaged in surveying the bottoms of the Little Miami. He had advanced up the river as far as the spot where the town of Xenia is now situated, without molestation. Early one morning, the party started out to perform the labors of the day. Massie was walking in advance of the party, when an Indian was perceived by General William Lytle, with his gun pointed at Massie, and in the act of firing. Lytle, with uncommon quickness, fired, and killed the Indian. After this occurrence they advanced cautiously, and soon found themselves near an encampment of about one hundred and fifty Indians. The party commenced a rapid retreat, and were closely pursued by the Indians. The retreat and pursuit continued without relaxation, until the party safely reached Manchester, or, as it was then called, Massie's station.

During the winter of 1792–93, Massie continued to locate and survey the best land within a reasonable distance of the station. As the Indians were always more quiet during the winter, he employed two men, Joseph Williams and one of the Wades, to accompany him to explore the valley of Paint creek, and part of the Scioto country. He found the bottoms rich beyond his expectations, and made entries of all the good land on that creek. During that expedition, Kenton, Helm, and others, who had accompanied the various detachments from Kentucky, which had invaded the country, made a few entries, but the large bulk of rich land was still vacant.

In the spring of the year 1793, the settlers at Manchester commenced clearing the out-lots of the town;

and while so engaged, an incident of much interest and excitement occurred. Mr. Andrew Ellison, one of the settlers, cleared a lot immediately adjoining the fort. He had completed the cutting of the timber, rolled the logs together and set them on fire. The next morning, a short time before daybreak, Mr. Ellison opened one of the gates of the fort, and went out to throw his logs together. By the time he had finished this job, a number of the heaps blazed up brightly, and as he was passing from one to the other, he observed, by the light of the fires, three men walking briskly towards him. This did not alarm him in the least, although, he said, they were dark skinned fellows; yet he concluded they were the Wades, whose complexions were very dark, going early to hunt. He continued to right his log-heaps, until one of the fellows seized him by the arms, and called out in broken English, "How do? how do?" He instantly looked in their faces, and to his surprise and horror, found himself in the clutches of three Indians. To resist was useless. He therefore submitted to his fate, without any resistance or an attempt to escape.

The Indians quickly moved off with him in the direction of Paint creek. When breakfast was ready, Mrs. Ellison sent one of her children to ask their father home; but he could not be found at the log-heaps. His absence created no immediate alarm, as it was thought he might have started to hunt after the completion of his work. Dinner time arrived, and Ellison not returning, the family became uneasy, and began to suspect some accident had happened to him. His gun-rack was examined, and there hung his rifle and his pouch in their usual place. Massie raised a party, and made a circuit around the place, and found, after some search, the trails of four men, one of whom had on shoes; and as Ellison had shoes on, the truth, that the Indians had made him a prisoner, was unfolded. As it was almost night at the time the trail was discovered, the party returned to the station. Next morning, early preparations were made by Massie and his party to pursue the Indians. In doing this they found great difficulty, as it was so early in the spring that the vegetation was not of sufficient growth to show plainly the trail of the Indians, who took the precaution to keep on hard and high land, where their feet could make little or no impression. Massie and his party, however, were as unerring as a pack of well trained hounds, and followed the trail to Paint creek, when they found the Indians gained so fast on them, that pursuit was vain. They therefore abandoned it, and returned to the station.

The Indians took their prisoner to Upper Sandusky, and compelled him to run the gauntlet. As Ellison was a large man and not very active, he received a severe flogging as he passed along the line. From this place he was taken to Lower Sandusky, and was again compelled to run the gauntlet, and was then taken to Detroit, where he was generously ransomed by a British officer for one hundred dollars. He was shortly afterwards sent by his friend, the officer, to Montreal, from whence he returned home before the close of the summer of the same year.

Another incident connected with the station at Manchester, occurred shortly after this time, which, although somewhat out of order as to time, I will take the liberty to relate in this place.

John Edgington, Asahel Edgington, and another man started out on a hunting expedition towards Brush creek. They camped out six miles in a northeast direction from where West Union now stands, and near where Treber's tavern is now situated, on the road from Chillicothe to Maysville. The Edgingtons had good success in hunting, having killed a number of deer and bears. Of the deer killed, they saved the skins and hams alone. The bears, they fleeced; that is, they cut off all the meat which adhered to the hide without skinning, and left the bones as a skeleton. They hung up the proceeds of their hunt on a scaffold, out of the reach of the wolves and other wild animals, and returned home for pack horses. No one returned to the camp with the two Edgingtons. As it was late in December, no one apprehended danger, as the winter season was usually a time of repose from Indian incursions. When the Edgingtons arrived at their old hunting camp, they alighted from their horses and were preparing to strike a fire, when a platoon of Indians fired upon them, at the distance of not more than twenty paces. Asahel Edgington fell to rise no more. John was more fortunate. The sharp crack of the rifles and the horrid yells of the Indians, as they leaped from their place of ambush, frightened the horses, who took the track towards home at full speed. John Edgington was very active on foot, and now an occasion offered which required his utmost speed. The moment the Indians leaped from their hiding place, they threw down their guns and took after him. They pursued him screaming and yelling in the most horrid manner. Edgington did not run a booty race. For about a mile the Indians stepped in his tracts almost before the bending grass could rise. The uplifted tomahawk was frequently so near his head, that he thought he felt its edge. Every effort was made to save his life, and every exertion of the Indians was made to arrest him in his flight. Edgington, who had the greatest stake in the race, at length began to gain on his pursuers, and after a long race, he distanced them, made his escape, and safely reached home. This, truly, was a most fearful and well contested race. The big Shawnee chief, Captain John, who headed the Indians on this occasion, after peace was made and Chillicothe settled, frequently told the writer of this sketch of the race. Captain John said, that " the white man who ran away was a smart fellow, that the white

man run and I run, he run and run, at last, the white
man run clear off from me."

CHAPTER IV.

A PERSON engaged in writing upon a particular subject
will, as a matter of course, within the range of his information, collect a mass of materials, from which it will
be his duty to select the most useful and interesting. To
do this, however, with skill sufficient to please the majority of his readers, is a difficult task. A person usually writes upon subjects about which he has bestowed
much thought, and in which he feels a deep interest.
Of course, matters which appear to him of great importance, he will discover frequently to be overlooked by
the generality of readers. Of such treatment he must
not complain, but, on the contrary, he must strengthen
himself by a large share of independence, which will
make him write with a consciousness, that his narrative
will meet with a kind reception from the intelligent, and
that it will be found useful for the future.

Such is my situation in writing this sketch. I know
that many things I have written may not entertain, yet I
believe them to be useful facts and have inserted them.
From this cause, and as I am writing the life of the most
extensive surveyor and land speculator with us in early
times, I shall take the liberty to describe the method by
which the titles to lands in the Virginia military district
were acquired and perfected, and also the method by
which surveying was actually conducted in our wild
country.

I have said above, that the lands in this district were
entered and surveyed by virtue of military land warrants
issued by the state of Virginia to her officers and sol-

diers of the continental line. These warrants were issued to satisfy bounties, promised by various acts of her legislature to these officers and soldiers, and prescribed the amount of land to which each person should be entitled, according to rank in the army and the time of actual service. Each person after the expiration of the time of service, received from the governor and council a certificate of his rank in the army, the length of time of service and the number of acres to which he was entitled, which certificate was filed with the register of the land office, and a warrant on printed paper and under the seal of the office, was issued to the owner. In many cases, warrants issued by virtue of special acts or resolutions of the Assembly, and were usually known, on this account, as resolution warrants. A warrant is merely a direction and authority given to the principal surveyor of land to survey and lay off, in one or more surveys for the person entitled, his heirs, or assigns, the given quantity of acres specified in the warrant. These warrants when issued were delivered to the owners, who were required to file them with the principal surveyor, and pay him a certain fee for receiving them. When filed they at first took their legal order in location.

The holders of warrants were at liberty to locate them, yet as they were unacquainted with the vacant land, they usually employed the deputy surveyors, as their agents, to enter and survey them, on certain agreed, or well known terms.

The first step taken towards the acquisition of land by a warrant is by means of an entry. An entry is the appropriation of a certain quantity of vacant land by the owner of the warrant. It is made in a book kept by the surveyor for that purpose, and contains the quantity of acres intended to be appropriated, the number of the warrant on which it is entered, and then calls for some specific, notorious, and permanent object or objects by which the locality of the land may be known, and usually concludes with a general description of the courses to be pursued in a survey of it. This particularity was required, that every person holding a warrant might be enabled, without interfering with the prior locations of others, to locate his own warrant, and this could not be done with safety in a wild country, unless prior entries were made with sufficient certainty as to their notoriety. The defect of entries, in this particular, has given rise to a greater amount of litigation in land titles, than any other cause whatever.

Next, in order, came the survey, which is intended to give a certain and regular form to the entry, by metes and bounds actually marked, and established by the surveyor. The great requisite with the survey was a conformity to a just and reasonable construction of the entry, as to the land intended to be appropriated by it. A want of conformity, in this respect, rendered the survey defective as to all lands without the calls of the entry. Surveys, when made, were returned to the general surveyor with a fair plat of each particular tract of land, and a description of the same by metes and bounds, and was signed by the deputies who executed them, together with the names of the chain-men and markers annexed, who made each survey. The surveys were then recorded, and the plats, with a certificate from the surveyor under his seal of office delivered to the owner, together with the original warrant and the assignments, if any, if the warrant was satisfied; if it was not, then a copy of the warrant and certificate from the surveyor of the fact that the warrant was still unsatisfied. The owner of each survey could then obtain a patent for his land from the President of the United States.

The system of entering and surveying lands, in the irregular manner we find in this district, was adopted from the Virginia and Kentucky land system. In these

states, great inconvenience and litigation, have been the
result of it. The unsettled situation of the country, the
unbounded rage for speculation, and the immense quantity of land warrants afloat, and the little value attached
by Virginia to her lands, all combined to make land titles
hazardous in the extreme, and was the cause of much
innocent suffering. In this district, although much litigation has resulted from this system, yet the surprise is,
when we consider the unsettled state of the country at
the time entries and surveys were made, that it has not
been greater. This may, in a great measure, be attribu-
ted to the minute attention, the uniformity, and ability of
Col. Anderson in the discharge of his duties, and the experience of his deputies, and their great confidence in
each other. Yet, under all circumstances, this may be
called a defective system, especially when we compare it
with the simple, the regular, and admirable system adopted
by the United States, in their surveys of public lands.

The plan adopted by Massie, in his various surveying
excursions at that time, was such as to secure safety to
the party. Three assistant surveyors, with himself making the fourth, were generally engaged at the same time
in making surveys. To each surveyor was attached six
men, which made a mess of seven. Every man had his
prescribed duty to perform. Their operations were conducted in this manner :—In front went the hunter, who
kept in advance of the surveyor two or three hundred
yards, looking for game, and prepared to give notice
should any danger from Indians threaten. Then followed, after the surveyor, the two chain-men, marker, and
pack-horse men with the baggage, who always kept near
each other, to be prepared for defence in case of an attack. Lastly, two or three hundred yards in the rear,
came a man, called the spy, whose duty it was to keep on
the back trail, and look out lest the party in advance
might be pursued and attacked by surprise. Each man

(the surveyor not excepted) carried his rifle, his blanket, and such other articles as he might stand in need of. On the pack-horse was carried the cooking utensils, and such provisions as could be conveniently taken. Nothing like bread was thought of. Some salt was taken, to be used sparingly. For subsistence, they depended alone on the game which the woods afforded, procured by their unerring rifles. In this manner was the largest number of surveys made in the district. But to return.

In the fall of the year 1793, Massie determined to attempt a surveying tour on the Scioto river. This, at that time, was a very dangerous undertaking; yet no danger, unless very imminent, could deter him from making the attempt. For that purpose, he employed about thirty men, of whom he choose three as assistant surveyors. These were John Beasley, Nathaniel Beasley, and Peter Lee. It was in this expedition, Massie employed, for the first time, a young man by the name of Duncan McArthur as a chain-man or marker. This man had distinguished himself remarkably on several occasions, and particularly in Harmer's unfortunate expedition. He was one of the best woodsmen of his age. He was a large, strong, and muscular man, capable of enduring fatigue and privations, equal to the best trained Indians. His courage was unquestioned, to which was added an energetic mind, which soon displayed its powers. He afterwards became a surveyor, and was one of the most acute land speculators in the western country. Such a man Massie desired to have on an expedition of this character.

In the month of October, some canoes were procured, and Massie and his party set off by water. They proceeded up the Ohio to the mouth of the Scioto, thence up the Scioto to the mouth of Paint creek. While meandering the Scioto, they made some surveys on the bottoms. After reaching the mouth of Paint creek, the sur-

4

veyors went to work. Many surveys were made on the
Scioto, as far up as Westfall. Some were made on
Main, and others on the North Fork of Paint creek, and
the greatest parts of Ross and Pickaway counties in the
district were well explored and partly surveyed. Massie
finished his intended work without meeting with any disturbance from the Indians. But one Indian was seen
during the excursion, and to him they gave a hard chase.
He, however, escaped. The party returned home de-
lighted with the rich country of the Scioto valley, which
they had explored.

During the winter of 1793-4, Massie, in the midst
of the most appalling dangers, explored the different
branches to their sources, which run into the Little Miami river, and thence passed in a northeastern direction to
the heads of Paint and Clear creeks, and the branches
that form those streams. By these expeditions he had
formed from personal observation, a correct knowledge
of the geographical situation of the country composing
the Virginia military district.

During the winter of 1794-5, Massie prepared a party
to enter largely into the surveying business. Nathaniel
Beasley, John Beasley, and Peter Lee were again employed as the assistant surveyors. The party set off
from Manchester well equipped to prosecute their business, or should occasion offer give battle to the Indians.
They took the route of Logan's trace, and proceeded to a
place called the deserted camp, on Tod's fork of the
Little Miami. At this point, they commenced surveying,
and surveyed large portions of land on Tod's fork, and up
the Miami to the Chillicothe town, (now in Clark county) thence up Massie's creek and Cæsar's creek nearly
to their heads. By the time the party had progressed
thus far, winter had set in. The ground was covered
with a sheet of snow, from six to ten inches deep. During the tour, which continued upwards of thirty days,

The Surveying Party's Encampment.

the party had no bread.   For the first two weeks, a pint
of flour was distributed to each mess once a day, to
mix with the soup, in which the meat had been boiled.
When night came, four fires were made for cooking, that
is, one for each mess.   Around these fires, till sleeping
time arrived, the company spent their time in the most
social glee, singing songs and telling stories.   When
danger was not apparent or immediate, they were as
merry a set of men as ever assembled.   Resting time arriving, Massie always gave the signal, and the whole
party would then leave their comfortable fires, carrying
with them their blankets, their fire-arms, and their little
baggage, walking in perfect silence two or three hundred
yards from their fires.   They would then scrape away
the snow, and huddle down together for the night.   Each
mess formed one bed, they would spread down on the
ground one half of the blankets, reserving the other half
for covering.   The covering blankets were fastened together by skewers to prevent them from slipping apart.
Thus prepared, the whole party crouched down together
with their rifles in their arms, and their pouches under
their heads for pillows; laying spoon-fashion, with three
heads one way and four the other, their feet extending
to about the middle of their bodies.   When one turned,
the whole mess turned, or else the close range would be
broken and the cold let in.   In this way, they lay till
broad day light; no noise and scarce a whisper being
uttered during the night.   When it was perfectly light,
Massie would call up two of the men in whom he had
the most confidence, and send them to reconnoiter,
and make a circuit around the fires, lest an ambuscade
might be formed by the Indians to destroy the party
as they returned to the fires.   This was an invariable custom in every variety of weather.   Self-preserva-
tion required this circumspection.   If immortality is due
to the names of heroes who have successfully labored in

the field of battle, no less honors are due to such men as
Massie, who ran equal risk of life from danger with less
prospect of eclat, and produced more lasting benefit to
the country.

Massie proceeded to survey up Cæsar's creek, nearly
to where its waters interlock with the waters of Paint
creek. Late one evening, he came upon the tracks of
Indians in the snow. Some of his men were despatched
to search out the Indian encampment, while others were
sent in pursuit of the assistant surveyors, in order to collect the force into one body, that he might be prepared
to attack or defend as circumstances might direct. A
short time before sun-down, his force was collected. In
a few minutes after, the two men returned who had been
sent to discover the Indian camp. They reported, that
they had proceeded as near the Indian encampment as
they could with safety, and that it consisted of eight or
ten tents, and that from the noise about the camp, they
had no doubt but that there was a large number of Indians. Massie, thereupon, concluded that it would be
too hazardous to attack them while the snow was on the
ground, believing it would endanger the whole party
if they would be compelled to retreat, encumbered with
any wounded. He therefore resolved to desist from surveying, and make a rapid retreat to his own station, not
doubting but that he would be pursued, as the Indians
would have no difficulty in tracking them through the
snow. The line of march was formed for home by the
party, who traveled until ten or eleven o'clock at night,
when they halted and remained until morning, when
they again resumed their march, moving in a southern
direction. About twelve o'clock, they came to a fresh
trail, which was made by four horses and eight or ten
footmen. This trail was crossed diagonally, and was
again struck upon after traveling a few miles. After a
consultation with some of the most experienced of his

men, Massie concluded the Indians, whose trail had been crossed, knew nothing of them, and determined to pursue them so long as they kept the direction in which they appeared then to be going. The pursuit of the Indians was kept up as fast as the men could walk, until dusk without overtaking them. The party then halted to consult as to their future operations. In a few minutes, the Indians were heard at work with their tomahawks, cutting wood and tent poles, within a few hundred yards of the place where the party had halted. It was put to vote, whether the Indian camp should be attacked immediately, or whether they should postpone it to day-light. A majority were for lying by and attacking them in daylight. Two or three men were then sent to reconnoiter their camp and bring away their horses. The horses were brought away, and preparations made to lie by for the night. Massie, who was more thoughtful than the rest of the company, began to reflect on the critical situation of the party. He told them, he did not approve of the idea of lying by until morning, as there was no doubt they were rapidly pursued by the Indians from the head of Cæsar's creek, and that by waiting until morning, the pursuing Indians might come up in the course of the night, and when day-light appeared, they would find themselves between two fires. He said it was true the Indians might be destroyed more effectually in daylight, but that it was dangerous to loiter away their time on a retreat, and advised that whatever they did to the Indians should be done quickly, and the march continued towards home. It was resolved to follow his advice.

It was about two hours in the night when this occurred. The day had been warm, and had melted the snow which was eight inches deep, and quite soft on the top. At night it began to freeze rapidly, and by this time there was a hard crust on the top. In this situation, the crust when broken by a man walking on a calm night could be heard at the distance of three hundred yards. Massie, under these circumstances prepared to attack the Indians forthwith. The men were formed in a line, in single file, with their wiping sticks in their hands, to steady them when walking. They then commenced moving towards the Indian camp in the following manner :—the foremost would walk about twenty steps, and halt ; then the next in the line would move on, stepping in the tracks of the foremost, to prevent any noise when breaking the crust of the snow. In this cautious and silent manner, they crept within about twenty-five yards of the Indian encampment, when an unexpected interruption presented itself ; a deep ravine was found between Massie and the camp which was not perceived by the reconnoitering party. The Indians had not as yet laid down to rest, but were singing and amusing themselves round their fires, in the utmost self-security, not dreaming of danger in their own country, in the depth of winter. The bank of the ravine concealed Massie and his men, who were on low ground, from the light of the Indian fires. After halting a few minutes on the bank of the ravine, Massie discovered, a few paces above him, a large log which had fallen across the ravine. On this log he determined to cross the gully. Seven or eight of the men, on their hands and knees, had crossed, and were within not more than twelve or fifteen paces of the Indians, crouching low, and turning to the right and left, when too many men at the same time got on the log ; and as it was old and rotten, it broke with a loud crash. This started the Indians. The whites, who had crossed over before the log broke, immediately fired into the Indian camp, shouting as they run. The Indians fled, naked, and without their arms. No Indian was killed in the camp, although their clothing and blankets were found stained with blood. No attempt was made to pursue them. Their camp was plundered of the horses and arms, making al-

together considerable booty. The party traveled that
night and until noon the next day, when they halted to
cook some provisions, and rest their wearied limbs.
After taking some refreshments, they loitered about the
fires a short time, and again commenced their march
through snow and brush, and about midnight of the second day, arrived at Manchester, after a fatiguing march
of two days and nights from the head of Cæsar's creek.

On the last day of their march, about a mile north of
where West Union now stands, one of the men who
carried a bag of Indian plunder, and rode one of the
horses, dropped the bag, and did not miss it until they
arrived at Manchester. Sometime in the succeeding day,
two of the men took fresh horses, and rode back on the
trail, to look for the bag. They found the bag some distance south of the brow of the hill, and concluded they
would go to the brow and look over for deer. When
they reached it, they were astonished to find the spot
where a large party of Indians had followed the trail to
the top of the hill, and there stopped to eat their breakfast, leaving some bones and sinewy jirk, that was too
hard to eat. Had the Indians pursued the trail one hundred yards farther, they would have found the bag, and
laid in ambush for the whites to return, and would doubtless have killed or taken the men who returned for the
bag. This was truly a narrow escape.

CHAPTER V.

The winter of 1794–95 was attended by no disturb-
ances from the Indians, as the defeat they had sustained
the summer before from General Wayne, had completely
checked them in their depredations. In the spring of
1795, Massie again prepared a party to return to the

waters of the Little Miami, Paint creek, and the Scioto, for the purpose of surveying. He employed three assistant surveyors, with the usual complement of men. Every man carried, as usual in these surveying tours, his own baggage on his back. No one, indeed, was exempt from this service; and when the weight is taken into consideration, and the encumbrance from it, there seems to be little ground for the complaints, which have latterly been made, about the inaccuracies of early surveys. Indeed, it is really astonishing, how they could be made so accurate as they are found to be.

Early in March the party set off from Manchester. The weather was fine, and the spring appeared to have commenced in earnest. Massie commenced surveying on the west fork of Ohio Brush creek. The woods then furnished game in great abundance, such as turkeys and bears, of the finest quality. A description of the method in which bears were taken, although familiar to the old backwoodsmen, will be perhaps interesting to their descendants, as these animals have become scarce since the settlement of the country. It is well known that bears retire to the hollows of rocks or trees, about the last of December, and remain in a dormant state until the winter breaks, be it early or late. When the weather becomes warm, they will bustle out of their holes to the nearest water, once in two or three days. In walking from their holes to the water, they are careful to step in the same track; and as the earth at that season of the year is soft and spongy, the feet of the bear, in passing and repassing, make a deep impression. These impressions are called by the old hunters, "the bear's stepping-place." When the hunter finds the stepping-place, he can easily follow the track, until he finds the tree in the hollow of which, or in some cave or hole in the rocks, the animal lies at ease. They are then, by various means used, driven from their holes, and shot. During this expedition, a young man, by the name of Bell, who was very active in climbing trees, exhibited great boldness in driving them from their holes. When a bear was tracked to a tree, this man, when the tree was not very large and smooth, would climb up and look into the hole, and punch the bear with a sharp stick until it would come out. Bears at this season are very lazy and difficult to move. By punching them, however, for some time, they will move heavily to their holes, and slowly drag themselves out. As soon as they were clear of their holes, some one or two picked marksmen would shoot them. Bell, so soon as he would provoke the bears to come out, would slip out on a limb, and wait with perfect composure until the marksmen would shoot them. These feats are specimens of Bell's daring. He was, altogether, one of the most hardy, fearless, and thoughtless men of danger, I ever saw. In this way numerous bears were found and killed. The fat part of the meat, boiled or roasted with turkey or venison, makes a very luxurious repast. But to return.

The weather, for some time, continued quite pleasant, while the party surveyed towards the head waters of Brush creek. They thence passed to the Rocky and Rattlesnake forks of Paint creek ; thence crossing Main Paint, they passed up Buckskin, and across to " the old town," on the north point of Paint creek. While surveying in this section of the country, the weather became cloudy, and commenced snowing and hailing. The snow continued to fall and drift for two days and nights ; and when it ceased, the ground was covered between two and three feet deep. The camp was on the ground, at this time the farm of Colonel Adam Mallow, four miles above Old town (or Frankfort, as it is now called.) About the time it ceased snowing, the weather became warm, and a soft rain fell for a short time. Suddenly it became intensely cold, accompanied by a frost, which soon formed a strong crust on the snow, which had been previously softened by the rain. The snow, although somewhat settled by the rain, was at least two feet deep, with a crust that would bear about half the weight of a man. This was the deepest snow I ever saw, before or since, in the western country. The turkeys, and other small game, could run on the crust of snow, which disabled the hunters from pursuing and killing game; and as the party had no provisions with them, the doleful prospect of death by starvation stared them in the face.

This tour was subsequently called the starving tour; and the remnant of those who are on this side of the grave, yet remember with horror their situation at that time. The prudence exercised by them heretofore, of sleeping away from their fires, was not attended to. The party lay around their fires by day and night, anxiously praying for a change in the weather. Some of the strongest and most spirited among the party, several times made ineffectual attempts to kill game. Among these hunters, General Duncan McArthur, of Fruit hill, near Chillicothe, and William Leedom, of Adams county, were conspicuous. On the third day of the storm, they killed two turkeys. They were boiled, and divided into twenty-eight shares or parts, and given equally to each man. This little food seemed only to sharpen their appetites. Not a particle of the turkeys was left. The heads, feet, and entrails, were devoured, as if most savory food.

The fourth morning of the continuance of the snow, Massie, with his party, turned their faces homeward. The strongest and most hardy of the men were placed in front, to break through the snow. This was a fatiguing and laborious business, and was performed alternately by the most spirited and strongest of the party. They thus proceeded in their heavy and disconsolate march the whole day, and at night reached the mouth of the Rattlesnake fork of Paint creek, a distance of about ten miles. In the course of that day the sun shone through the clouds, for the first time since the storm commenced, and by its warmth softened the crust on the snow. This rendered the traveling less laborious. As the party descended the sloping ground towards the bank of Paint creek, they came across a flock of turkeys, and killed several. These were cooked, and equally divided among the men. That night the party lay by their fires without guards or sentinels; and as the night was warm, the snow gradually melted. Early next morning the most of the party turned out to hunt, and killed a number of turkeys, some deer, and a bear. When these were brought to camp, a feast ensued, which was enjoyed with a zest and relish, which none can properly appreciate, but those who have been so unfortunate as to be placed in a similar situation.

The writer of this narrative accompanied General Massie on this tour, and had previously passed through many trying and distressing scenes; but the hardships and privations of this tour were the most trying to the firmness, resolution, and fortitude of men, he ever saw or experienced. Only reflect, reader, on the critical situation of twenty-eight men, exposed to the horrors of a terrible snow-storm in the wilderness, without hut, tent, or covering, and, what was still more appalling, without provision, without any road or even a track to retreat on, and nearly one hundred miles from any friendly aid or place of shelter, exposed to the truly tremendous and pitiless peltings of a storm of four days continuance, and you can fancy to yourself some faint idea of the sufferings of this party.

Although more than forty years have passed, I can scarcely think of our sufferings, even at this length of time, without shuddering. The people of the present time, who now inhabit our western country, and are sheltered from tempestuous storms in comfortable and elegant mansions, and are blessed with peace and plenty, can scarcely appreciate the sufferings and privations of those who led the way in settling our western country. Under all the hardships of this tour, Massie always showed a cheerful face, and encouraged his men to hope for better times. Nothing like despondency ever clouded his brow, nor did his good humor forsake him during the gloom and despair of this trying occasion.

The storm being passed, fine weather and plenty ensued, and the party again went cheerfully to work. Massie surveyed all the land he at first designed, and returned to Manchester without any adventure worthy of relation.

The summer of the year 1795 passed off without any disturbance from the Indians. This was doubtless owing to the check given them, the summer previous, by General Wayne; and also from the fact, that they were at that time stipulating with General Wayne a treaty of peace. Although not much faith was placed in Indian treaties, yet the settlements of the whites began to extend from the town of Manchester into the country. Massie sold a large amount of land to actual settlers upon credit, and many cabins were raised along the Ohio, and on Brush and Eagle creeks; but they were uninhabited from the fear of the Indians.

The fertility of the soil on Paint creek and throughout the Scioto valley, began to attract the attention of many Kentuckians to that quarter of the country. As General Massie had, some years previously, entered and surveyed the land in that section of the country, and was the owner of large tracts of first-rate land, he determined, at all hazards, to attempt a settlement at some spot in the Scioto valley, whether the attempt would result in peace or war. For the purpose of attracting settlers, he issued a notice, that he intended to lay off a town at some ad-

vantageous site on the Scioto river; and offered as a
donation to the first one hundred settlers, one in-lot and
one out-lot of four acres in the town, provided they would
build a cabin on their lot, or otherwise become permanent settlers of the town or its vicinity.

This notice soon attracted the attention of several
respectable citizens of Kentucky. Among these were
Captain Petty, an old soldier, and the Reverend Robert
W. Finley. A party was soon raised to explore the
country and select the situation of the town. A short
and correct description of this expedition is given by an
anonymous writer, over the initials of "F. B." in the
Western Christian Advocate, of June 13th, 1834, which
is in all probability from the pen of the Reverend J. B.
Finley, now or lately a presiding elder of the Methodist
Episcopal church, and the son of the Reverend Robert
W. Finley. I take the liberty of making an extract from
that piece, as it is connected with the subject.

"In the year 1795, while Wayne was in treaty with
the Indians, a company came out from Manchester on the
Ohio river, to explore the north-western territory, and
especially the valley of the Scioto. General Massie was
in this little band. After proceeding several days cautiously, they fell on Paint creek, near the falls. Here
they found fresh Indian signs, and had not traveled far
before they heard the bells on the horses. Some of the
company were what was called *raw hands*, and previous
to this wanted much ' to smell Indian powder.' One of
the company, who had fought in the revolutionary war,
and also with the Indians, said to one of these vaunting
fellows, 'If you do, you will run, or I am mistaken.'
A council was now called. Some of the most experienced thought it was too late to retreat, and thought
it best to take the enemy by surprise. General Massie, Fallenach, and R. W. Finley, were to lead on the
company, and Captain Petty was to bring up the

rear. The Indians were encamped on Paint creek, precisely at what is called Reeve's crossing. They came on them by surprise, and out of forty men, about twenty of them fought. Those fellows who wanted to smell powder so much, ran the other way, and hid behind logs, and Captain Petty reported afterwards that they had the ague, they were so much affrighted. The battle was soon ended in favor of the whites, for the Indians fled across the creek, and left all they had but their guns. Several were killed and wounded, and one white man, a Mr. Robinson, was shot through the body, and died immediately. These Indians had one male prisoner with them, who made his escape to the whites, and was brought home to his relatives. As soon as the company could gather up all the horses and skins, and other plunder, they retreated for the settlement at Manchester, on the Ohio river. Night overtook them on the waters of Scioto Brush creek, and as they expected to be followed by the Indians, they made preparation for the skirmish. The next morning, an hour before day, the attack was made with vigor on the part of the Indians, and resisted as manfully by a few of the whites. There being a sink-hole near, those bragging cowards got down into it, to prevent the balls from hitting them. Several horses were killed, and one man, a Mr. Gilfillan, shot through the thigh. After an hour's contest, the Indians retreated; and the company arrived at the place they started from, having lost one man, and one man wounded. Thus ended the exploring of the valley of the Scioto this year.

" In this expedition, our fellow citizen, the late General James Menury, was present, and sustained throughout his character of a brave man, being one of the first to engage with the enemy. This was the last Indian fight during the old Indian war.

" The fall and winter of 1795 passed off without any thing worthy of note taking place in the settlement.

[Face 58.]

The Paint Creek Fight.

5

General Wayne had concluded a treaty of peace with the Indians, which was looked upon rather as a truce than a permanent peace. Numerous treaties of peace had been made with them during this long and bloody war, which treaties lasted no longer than till an opportunity offered to make some successful assaults upon the whites. Indeed, the whites themselves, at that day, were not very scrupulous of violating the terms of treaties, both parties being exasperated against each other, on account of the many horrid massacres which had reciprocally taken place in a border war of thirty years. But, fortunately for the whites, Wayne seemed to have turned in earnest the spirit of the Indians, as the treaty of Grenville remained inviolate, with a very few exceptions, until 1812."

This was the last Indian fight on the waters of the Scioto river.

Notwithstanding that I was born and raised on the frontier, I am unable to describe to the life, the terror, tumult, and confusion of an Indian alarm. Although I have, when young, repeatedly run clinging to my mother's gown from our cabin, to a place of more safety—the confusion and distressing scene of a family in flight, their cabins in flames, their all destroyed, the thousand restless cares and tender sorrows, to which they were incessantly exposed, language fails in describing. To see whole families wandering from their homes, seeking shelter and safety, was only a common occurrence on the frontier. Such scenes as these tried the worth of men, and proved who were the soldiers. Happily for our country, no repetition of such scenes of distress and terror, are to be anticipated in future.

CHAPTER VI.

The failure of the expedition to select the situation of a town on the Scioto river, as related in the last chapter, did not deter Massie from making a further attempt. About the last of February or first of March, 1796, a party was again collected at Manchester. Some of the party went by water up the Ohio and Scioto, and others by land, and met at the mouth of Paint creek, at a place afterwards known as the "Station prairie." The party who arrived by water, brought in their boats, besides a few of the necessaries of life, farming utensils, and other articles necessary to make a permanent settlement.

On the first day of April of that year, they landed their goods, commenced the construction of their cabins, and prepared for planting corn. Three hundred acres of rich prairie were quickly turned up by thirty ploughs; and the land for the first time resounded with the cheerful sound of the plowman's voice.

That season was attended by great prosperity to the settlers. Although they suffered, at one time, greatly for the want of some of the necessaries of life, yet in this they were soon relieved by the luxuriant crops of their plantation. No disturbance ensued from the Indians, who mixed with the whites in the most friendly manner, showing every disposition to preserve inviolate, the conditions of their treaty of peace. Indeed, the behavior of the Indians was entirely peaceful for many years, unless they were excited by the cupidity of the whites, in selling them ardent spirits.

While these things were transpiring at the settlement, Massie was engaged in making a selection for the site of a town, which was at last located on the Scioto river. That stream (the greater part of it) runs in very regular channel from the north almost due south.　About four or five miles, however, above the mouth of Paint creek, the river suddenly makes a bend, and runs a short distance east, thence southeast to the mouth of Paint creek.　That stream, the largest tributary of the Scioto, for four or five miles above its mouth, runs almost parallel with the Scioto.　Between these two streams there is a large and beautiful bottom, four or five miles in length, and varying from one to two miles in breadth, and contains within the space upwards of three thousand acres.　This bottom, (as also the bottoms of the Scioto and Paint creek generally,) is very fertile ; the loam, of alluvial formation, being from three to ten feet in depth.　These bottoms, when first settled, were generally covered by a heavy growth of timber, such as black walnut, sugar tree, cherry, buckeye, hackberry, and other trees which denote a rich soil.　A portion of them, however, were found destitute of timber, and formed beautiful prairies, clothed with blue grass and blue sedge-grass, which grew to the height of from four to eight feet, and furnished a bountiful supply of pasture in summer and hay in winter, for the live stock of the settlers.　The outer edges of these prairies were beautifully fringed around with the plum tree, the red and black haw, the mulberry and crab apple. In the month of May, when these nurseries of nature's God were in full bloom, the sight was completely gratified, while the fragrant and delicious perfume, which filled the surrounding atmosphere, was sufficient to fill and lull the soul with ecstasies of pleasure.

The western boundary of this valley, between the two streams, is a hill, two or three hundred feet in height. Its base to the south is closely washed by Paint creek, and when this stream first enters the valley, it terminates in an abrupt point, and then extends up the valley of the Scioto, in a north-west and north course, for many miles, and forms the western boundary of the bottoms along that stream. From the point where the hill abruptly terminates at Paint creek, running north-north-east, at the distance of about one mile across the valley, you reach the bank of the Scioto, at the sudden bend it makes to the east. The valley between this bend of the Scioto and Paint creek, immediately below the point of the hill, was selected as a site for the town. This part of the valley was chosen, as it consisted of high and dry land, not subject to the floods of the river, which frequently inundated the valley towards the mouth of Paint creek.

The town was laid out on a large tract of land owned by General Massie, and contained two hundred and eighty-seven in-lots, and one hundred and sixty-nine out-lots. The in-lots were six poles in width in front on the street, and ran back twelve poles to the alleys; except the in-lots on Market or Front street, which ran with the river, and extended back irregularly. The out-lots adjoined the in-lots, and contained four acres, almost in a square. The streets were laid out of uncommon width, two of them being six poles wide; two, five poles; and the others, four poles.

After the necessary steps had been taken to run off the lots, streets, and alleys of the town, by blazing and marking the trees of the thick woods, the proprietor held a consultation with his friends, and gave to the town the name of Chillicothe. This name was derived from among the many names, given by the aborigines of our country to different objects. In their language, it was a general name for " town." They had two towns, called alone by this general name; " The Old Town," on the north fork of Paint creek, and " New Chillicothe, or Town," on the head of the Little Miami river.

One hundred in and out-lots in the town, were chosen by lot, by the first one hundred settlers, as a donation, according to the original proposition of the proprietor. A number of in and out-lots were also sold to other per-

sons, desiring to settle in the town. The first choice
of in-lots were disposed of for the moderate sum of ten
dollars each. The town increased rapidly, and before
the winter of 1796, it had in it several stores, taverns,
and shops for mechanics. The arts of civilized life soon
began to unfold their power and influence in a more
systematic manner, than had ever been witnessed by
many of its inhabitants, especially those who were born
and raised in the frontier settlements, where neither law
nor gospel were understood or attended to.

In the sales of lands, his policy showed great foresight
in reference to the rapid and permanent settlement of the
country, which seemed to be his constant aim. He divided off large bodies of land into small tracts of one and
two hundred acres each, and by low prices, and liberal
terms of payment, every one, as well those with, as
those without the means, were induced to purchase, as
time was granted them to pay for their land by means of
their own industry. In the settlement of a new country,
no other course pursued in the disposal of lands will induce a rapid settlement. Every farm in a new country,
always enhances in value, in proportion to its actual improvement, and the value is sometimes more than ten-
fold the cost of the original purchase. Besides this, farms
of small dimensions, in a free country, are always cultivated with more care, neatness, and actual profit, than
large farms, and add far more to the population and in-
trinsic wealth of a country. This observation can be
made by any one who will look at the situation of our
country. In those parts where the land is divided into
small and well cultivated farms, the prosperity of the inhabitants is greater, and the country more intrinsically
rich, than where the land is held in large bodies.

Large quantities of fine bottom land, on the Scioto
river and Paint creek, were sold by General Massie, at
the sum of one and two dollars per acre. These lands

quickly rose in value, and at this time, not quite
forty years since first sold, the owners would be unwill-
ing to dispose of them at forty dollars per acre. Such
has been the unparalleled prosperity of our country !

Gen. St. Clair, governor of the northwestern territory,
placed great confidence in General Massie, and through
him transacted most of the business with the settlements
above the little Miami. Through him, as Colonel Massie,
the militia of that part of the northwestern territory were
first organized.

In the year 1800, General Massie was married to a
daughter of Colonel David Meade of Kentucky, formerly
of Virginia. In 1802, Congress passed a law, authorizing the people of that portion of the northwestern territory, comprising the state of Ohio, to form a constitution and state government. Members were elected to
compose that convention, which met at Chillicothe, on
the first day of November 1802, and after a session of
about three weeks, the present constitution of our state
was formed. General Massie was a very efficient member of this convention. He was elected a member with
great unanimity, as he was by far the most popular man
between Limestone and Zanesville. Indeed his good
offices to the first settlers of the country were so numerous, that it would be risking a good deal, to speak irre-
verently of the man, who made most of them by his indulgence freeholders.

General Massie was elected to the senate from Ross
county, the first session the assembly met under the new
constitution, and was elected speaker during the session.
This duty he performed to the entire satisfaction. of the
body over which he presided.

Under the constitution, a new organization of the militia was to be made. Massie was elected the first Major
General of the second division of the militia of Ohio,

having held the office of colonel under the government of the northwestern territory.

General Massie was, at this time, one of the largest landholders in the state of Ohio, and as he was now married, he began to think about selecting a suitable place for a residence. Around the falls of Paint creek, in Ross county, he had a large body of excellent land, consisting of several thousand acres. The advantage of this situation on account of the fine water privileges, and the excellent situation of the farm for raising stock, induced him to select it as a place of residence. Here, he built a large and comfortable mansion.

This country, at that time, was very much visited by the citizens of Virginia, as they owned large quantities of land in this section. General Massie's residence was the usual resort, where they always met with a welcome reception and were hospitably entertained. In his hospitality, indeed, he rather bordered on extravagance, especially when visited by any of his old war-worn and woods companions. No gratification, which he could afford, but was freely extended to those who followed him in times of danger. His lady although raised in polished and fashionable life, took great pleasure in rendering his awkward woods companions easy and at home. I well remember it was in Mrs. Massie's room I first saw tea handed around for supper, which I then thought foolish business and still remain of that opinion.

There is no better evidence of the truth, " that a free people are capable of self-government," than the fact, that the first settlers of this country transacted their business, and discharged the ordinary duties of life, with the greatest decorum and punctuality, without the intervention of magistrates to enforce laws. It was expected that every one would act with due regard to the well being of society, and whenever any one was disposed to act otherwise, the lovers of good order would instantly

put things to right. Early, however, in the year 1797,
the governor of the northwestern territory, appointed
Thomas Worthington, Hugh Cochran, and Samuel
Smith, as justices of the peace for the settlement at
Chillicothe. The last mentioned justice transacted the
principal part of the judicial business. His prompt and
decisive manner of doing business rendered him very
popular. His docket could be understood only by himself. Scarcely was a warrant issued by him, as he preferred always to send his constable to the accused to
bring him forward to have prompt justice executed. No
law book was of any authority with him. He always
justified his own proceedings by saying, " that all laws
were intended for the purpose of enforcing justice, and
that he himself knew what was right and what was
wrong, as well as those who made the laws, and that
therefore he stood in need of no laws to govern his actions." In civil and criminal cases, he was always
prompt in his decisions, and sometimes amusing in his
mode of executing justice, as will be seen from the following case, which was brought under his cognizance.
A man, by the name of Adam McMurdy, cultivated some
ground in the station prairie below Chillicothe. One
night, some one stole, during his absence, his horse collar. McMurdy, next morning, examined the collars of
the plowmen then at work, and discovered his collar in
the possession of one of the men and claimed it of him.
The man used towards him abusive language, and threatened to whip McMurdy for charging him with the theft.
McMurdy went immediately to Squire Smith, and stated
his case. The Squire listened until his story was told,
and then despatched his constable with strict orders to
bring the thief and collar forthwith before him. The
constable quickly returned bringing with him, in the one
hand, the collar, while with the other he grasped tightly
the accused. The Squire immediately arraigned the ac-

cused in his court, which was held in the open air, on
the bank of the Scioto.   It was then asked of the accus-
er, how he could prove the collar to be his ?   McMurdy
replied, "If the collar is mine, Mr. Spear, who is present can testify."   Mr. Spear was then called to testify.
Before he was sworn, he came forward and said, " that
if it was McMurdy's collar, he himself had written Mc
Murdy's name on the inner side of the ear of the collar."
The Squire turned up the ear of the collar, and found accordingly McMurdy's name written there.   " No better
proof could be given," said the Squire, and ordered the
accused to be immediately tied up to a buckeye, to receive five lashes well laid on, which was accordingly
done.   Thus ended the case to the satisfaction of all, except the culprit.   The trial did not occupy five minutes
of time.   Such was the Squire's summary manner of
dispensing justice.   Squire Smith was an honest and
impartial man, with a vigorous and discriminating mind,
always disposed to do justice in his own way.

The settlement in and round Chillicothe, was, I believe, the first made in peace west of the mountains.
The progress of improvement in the town and country
was rapid, and the country was soon filled with a dense
population.

This was the second settlement General Massie had
the honor of forming in the western wilderness, an honor
that reflects much credit on him, as his labors and energy have added greatly to the wealth and strength of
the nation, and the comfort and prosperity of the people
of the land.   Had it not been for him and a few other
daring spirits sent by Providence to prepare the way,
our country might have remained a wilderness, the abode
of " wild beasts and men more wild and savage than
they."

From the time of the settlement at Chillicothe, Gen.
Massie lived alternately, as his business demanded at-

tention, in the state of Kentucky and the northwestern territory. His knowledge of the situation, the quality, and the owners of land in the Virginia military district, gave him great advantages as a speculator. On his own account, and as a partner of several land companies formed in Virginia, he purchased and sold a large quantity of the most valuable land in the district.

In the year 1807, General Massie and Col. Return J. Meigs were competitors for the office of governor of Ohio. They were the most popular men in the state. Col. Meigs received a small majority of votes. The election was contested by Massie on the ground that Col. Meigs was ineligible by the constitution, in consequence of his absence from the state, and had not since his return lived in the state a sufficient length of time to regain his citizenship. The contest was carried to the General Assembly, who after hearing the testimony, decided that " Col. Meigs was ineligible to the office, and that Gen. Massie was duly elected governor of the state of Ohio." Massie, however desirous he might have been to hold the office, was too magnanimous to accept it when his competitor had a majority of votes. After the decision in his favor he immediately resigned.

General Messie, after this time, represented Ross county in the Legislature, as often as his leisure from other pursuits would admit. In the year 1810, he resigned the office of Major General of the Ohio militia.

In the spring of the year 1813, when the British and Indians besieged the army, under the command of the brave General Harrison in Fort Meigs, the news of the danger with which our army was threatened, roused Massie from his retreat at the falls of Paint creek. Although now getting in years, a spark of his youthful fire still remained unquenched. As soon as he learned that his countrymen were in danger, he shouldered his rifle, mounted his horse, and rode to almost every house on Paint creek, urging to his fellow citizens every argument that patriotism could suggest to take the field without delay, and relieve our army from its perilous situation. Although he had no legal right to command, this did not deter him from joining his countrymen in arms. Numbers joined him from Paint creek. With these he proceeded to Chillicothe. There, likewise, a number joined him. There was no time to organize, as delay might be fatal to our countrymen, who were cooped up in Fort Meigs, surrounded with thrice their number of white and red savages. The party being on horseback moved rapidly to Franklinton, gathering strength as they went along. At Franklinton, there was a depot of public arms. Arms and ammunition were there distributed to upwards of five hundred men, and Massie was elected commander by acclamation. They left Franklinton without delay, and as the men were all mounted they dashed ahead as fast as their horses could carry them to the scene of action. When they had nearly reached Lower Sandusky, they were met by an express from General Harrison with the news, that the enemy had raised the siege of Fort Meigs and returned to Canada. Massie and his volunteers returned to Chillicothe, where they disbanded themselves and returned every man to his farm. Thus ended the expedition, after the absence of a few days. This was General Massie's last act in public life.

General Massie still resided at his residence at the falls of Paint creek, where he had erected a large furnace for the purpose of manufacturing iron. He had just commenced the business with every prospect of success, and was arranging his much extended land transactions. He had been blessed in the partner of his bosom, and with sons and daughters. His life had hitherto been spent in toils and action in the midst of danger and privations, and he was now preparing to spend the evening of his days in a quiet and happy retirement. We are

never, " but always to be blessed." How inscrutable
are the ways of Providence ! This useful man could not
be exempt from the common lot of humanity. Although
he had uniformly been one of the most healthy of men,
he was suddenly attacked with disease which terminated his mortal career. On the third day of November
1813, he breathed his last and was buried on his farm.

General Massie left a widow, and three sons and two
daughters. These are all grown, and occupy a respectable rank in society. They are just such children as
will make a parent's heart glad; all industrious, tem-
perate and moral.

I have now recorded all the material incidents in the
life of this good and useful man, so far as they have
come to my knowledge. There are doubtless many
interesting events in his life, during his residence in
Kentucky, which are now lost for ever. His character
was well suited for the settlement of a new country ;
distinguished, as it was, by an uncommon degree of
energy and activity in the business in which he was
engaged. His disposition was ever marked with liberality
and kindness.

General Massie's private character, in all the relations
of husband, father, and friend, was worthy of imitation :
but still it is not claimed that he was " one of those fault-
less monsters the world never saw ;" " to err is human, to
forgive divine." So we will permit his frailties to sleep
with him in his grave.

[Face 71.]   Gen. Duncan McArthur

A SKETCH OF THE LIFE

OF

GENERAL DUNCAN McARTHUR.

CHAPTER I.

GENERAL Duncan McArthur was born on the 14th day of January, in the year 1772, in Duchess county, state of New-York. His parents were natives of the Highlands of Scotland. His mother was of the Campbell clan, which is illustrious in Scottish story. General Mc'Arthur had the misfortune to lose his mother when quite a youth.

In 1780, he being eight years of age, his father moved to the western frontier, in the state of Pennsylvania. Our revolutionary war was then in progress. All the energies of our citizens were concentrated to protect themselves from Indian depredations, and to win independence from foreign oppression. Under these trying circumstances, subsistence and clothing were difficult to be procured, and schools in the western country were almost unknown. However, by the time he was twelve or thirteen years of age, he had learned to read and write. Duncan being the eldest child, was, as soon as he was able to work, kept at hard labor, to aid in supporting his father's numerous family of children. His father was in indigent circumstances, and as soon as his crop was laid by, Duncan was either hired out by the day, or month, to the neighboring farmers.

6   71

At the date of which I am writing, there were no wagon roads across the Alleghany mountains. They were a frightful world of rocks and forests. All the merchandise (and many articles were indispensable), such as powder, lead, salt, iron, pots and kettles, and above all, *beloved rum*, then used in western Pennsylvania, were conveyed over the mountains on pack-horses. McArthur, when very young, made frequent trips with packers.

Men who were raised in the western country, and are now over sixty years of age, look back with astonishment at the change which has taken place within their remembrance. The world, as they knew it, has been transformed. At that time it was almost an every day occurrence, to see a long line of pack-horses, in single file, cautiously wending their way over the stupendous Alleghany, on a path scarcely wide enough for a single horse. When surmounting the dizzy heights, they often turned round the points of projecting rocks, where the least jostle, or a slip of the horse's foot, would have precipitated it into the abyss beneath, and crushed it to atoms. So narrow and dangerous were the passes in many places, that a horse loaded with bulky articles could not pass these projecting rocks, without first being unloaded. The difficulties of the road were not the only danger they had to encounter ; the wily Indian frequently lay in ambush to massacre the traveler.

So good judges were they of the easy passes over the mountains, that scientific engineers have selected nearly the same tracks, on which the western packers passed with their brigades of pack horses in single file ; where now are constructed turnpikes and railroads, on which the traveler glides, or rather floats along through air securely, and almost with the rapid speed of the bird of Jove. Such have been the happy results produced by the daring enterprise and useful labors of the western pioneers. Notwithstanding that their lives were con-

tinued scenes of privation, danger, and patriotic devotion
to their country, it is not claimed that they were free
from errors. Not having been fettered by laws, and
each one being the guardian and avenger of his own
rights and wrongs, they grew up in a state of rude independence. Their prejudices were strong, their passions
warm, and they were frequently hurried into excesses.

> " They were as free as nature first made man,
> Ere the base laws of servitude began—
> When wild in woods the noble savage ran."

Their courage in surmounting danger, their fortitude in
enduring hardships and privations, their hospitality, their
patriotism and ardor for fame, were conspicuous in every
period of their history.

The subject of this narrative grew up to manhood on
the western frontier, without fortune, without the aid of
friends, without the advantages of education, without that
society which is essential to mental improvement, until
he was considerably advanced in years. General Mc-
Arthur, notwithstanding he saw as much of the world,
its pageantry, and polished society, as most of those who
have filled the same stations, yet retained the frank
manners of the old backwoodsman. His good sense
always rendered even his frankness, and apparent blunt-
ness of manner, not only acceptable, but agreeable. That
young man is worthy of commendation, who, raised in
poverty, and without education, builds up a reputation by
energy and perseverance. It must be instructive to the
young men of the country, in a land where all must be
the artificers of their own fortunes, to study the history
and character of Duncan McArthur, from his earliest
youth to his honored old age. Political honor, and frequently wealth, are the rewards of energetic devotion to
the good of mankind. In early life McArthur was buried
in a western wilderness ; in maturer years we see him,
a distinguished military officer in time of war, and a skil-

ful legislator in time of peace. The young men of our
country, who read the incidents of his life, will learn
what is to be gained by industry, energy, and firmness
of purpose. Those who have small means, and few
friends in their youth, should not despond : their future
destiny depends much upon themselves. But I must
return to my narrative.

In the year 1790, Duncan McArthur, in the eighteenth
year of his age, left his father's house. The incursions
of the Indians kept the frontier settlements in continual
alarms, and all the force which the stations could command, was constantly kept in requisition for defense.
The government of the United States was then under the
direction of the great Washington, who had used every
means in his power to induce the Indians to live in friendship with their white brethren. But his benevolent efforts were ineffectual, and he determined to employ a
force which, if properly directed, would keep the savages
in awe. The command of the expedition was conferred
on General Harmar, a popular soldier of the revolution.
A requisition was made on western Pennsylvania and
Kentucky for volunteers, a call which was promptly
complied with. Duncan McArthur enrolled himself with
the Pennsylvania volunteers, who forthwith sailed down
the Ohio to Fort Washington (now the city of Cincinnati). At this place they were joined by some regular
troops, and a regiment of volunteers from Kentucky,
commanded by Colonel Hardin.

From fort Washington the army proceeded northwardly, through an unbroken wilderness, carrying their
subsistence with them. When they arrived within thirty
miles of the Indian towns, a detachment of six hundred
men, under the command of Colonel Hardin, were sent
in advance, with orders to make forced marches, and, if
possible, to surprise the Indians and destroy their towns
before they would have time to collect their united forces

for defense. Our young adventurer accompanied this detachment. They proceeded at a rapid march until they arrived at the towns ; but the birds had flown. The wary enemy had been apprised by their watchful spies of the approach of danger, and had fled to the woods and swamps for protection. These towns were situated at the junction of the rivers St. Mary and St. Joseph, where fort Wayne was erected, in 1794, by General Wayne. From this place the river takes the name of Maumee, or Miami of the Lakes.

Four days after Colonel Hardin's detachment took possession of these towns, General Harmar arrived with the main army, and remained several days on the ground, destroying all the Indian property he could find. During this time none of the Indians showed themselves, but permitted their towns to be destroyed. Having completed the destruction of the place, General Harmar turned the face of his army homeward, marching about ten miles the first day, where he encamped for the night. He had left a few trusty spies to linger in concealment about the Indian towns, to observe any movements which they might make. In the evening of this day, these faithful sentinels discovered a number of Indians returning to their ruined towns. The spies forthwith retreated to the camp, and informed the general that the Indians had returned to their towns.

Upon receiving this intelligence, General Harmar again detached Colonel Hardin, with the Kentucky volunteers and a company of regular troops, to the Indian towns. They made a quick march, and arrived near the towns about daybreak. Before making the attack, the detachment was divided into two divisions ; the one commanded by Colonel Hardin, the other by Major Hall. To Major Hall's division young McArthur belonged. Colonel Hardin's division crossed the St. Mary's, and attacked the Indians. A severe battle ensued, in which

Hardin was defeated with considerable loss. Major Hall fell in with another party of Indians ; a sanguinary battle was fought, the Indians were defeated, and driven several miles up the St. Joseph. Major Hall then returned to Harmar's camp, before he was apprised of the total defeat of Hardin. Thus the horrors of this severe fight were divided, but the Indians had the fruits of an entire victory.

Without making any further attempts to gain his withered laurels, Gen. Harmar immediately returned to Fort Washington, and there the army was disbanded. The Kentuckians returned to their homes, and the Pennsylvanians, in detachments, went up the Ohio river in keelboats.

On their return up the river, an occurrence took place which shows the energy and perseverance of our young adventurer in his early life. Between Limestone (now Maysville) and Massie's station (now Manchester), McArthur and another young man left the boat early in the morning, and went back into the country to hunt, intending to head the boat before night. The day was cloudy, and they were total strangers to the country. They missed their direction, and at night when they came to the river, they were lower down than when they left their company in the morning. They stayed that night at a William Brooks', three miles above Maysville. Their boat and companions were one day in advance, and no settlement above them nearer than the mouth of the Big Kanawha, a distance of two hundred miles, and many streams which emptied into the Ohio to cross. In addition to these difficulties, the Indians were constantly on the alert to destroy small parties who might be passing up or down the Ohio river. These difficulties did not deter our young adventurer from making the attempt " to push ahead," to overtake his boat. They left Mr. Brooks' on foot, trailing at times along the foot of the hills, at other times along the margin of the river, till they arrived at the mouth of Big Sandy river, late in the evening. This stream was exceedingly high from recent rains, its current shooting nearly across the Ohio; their boat was in view, and their companions were only two or three hundred yards above its mouth. They hallooed and called at the highest pitch of their voices, but they were not heard on account of the tremendous roaring of the angry waters. Early next morning they had the mortification to see their companions move off with their boat without them. There was no time to be lost in fruitless repining, but with the perseverance common to the backwoodsmen of that time, they set off up the Big Sandy several miles, where they constructed a raft, and with much difficulty crossed the river, and then traveled as fast as they could to overtake their companions; but their efforts were ineffectual. All the streams above Big Sandy had risen, and they were compelled to construct rafts to cross them. In this manner they were so much delayed, that when they arrived at the mouth of Big Kanawha their boat had gained several days on them. Here they gave up the pursuit, and rested their weary bodies a few days, when they again commenced their toilsome journey on foot for Wheeling, where they arrived about the first of December. From thence McArthur returned to his father's home.

CHAPTER II.

THE energy of McArthur's character began to unfold itself in very early life. No danger could appal him, nor fatigue deter him from the pursuit of an enterprise. Let us trace his early history.

In 1791, he was elected an ensign in a company of militia, and received his commission from Governor

Mifflin, of Pennsylvania. Every militia officer in those trying times was expected to be shortly called upon to take his station in the "tented field." Consequently, the citizens were generally careful to select the best men the country afforded. There is no doubt that young McArthur felt more elated at that time, with an ensign's commission in his pocket, than he did in after life, when he was elected governor of Ohio.

In 1792, he joined, as a private, a volunteer company commanded by Captain William Enoch. This company was stationed at Baker's fort, on the river Ohio, some distance below Wheeling. A younger brother of Captain Enoch was lieutenant of the company. Shortly after their encamping on the river, and at a late hour in the evening, a few Indians were discovered across the river from the fort, on the Ohio shore, carelessly walking about. There is no doubt but these Indians showed themselves for the purpose of inviting the whites across the river, and if they could succeed, intended to lay in ambush and destroy them. Early the next morning Lieut. Enoch with fifteen men, amongst whom was Mc-Arthur, crossed the river before day. As soon as it was light enough to distinguish objects at a distance, Lieut. Enoch and his party went to the place where the Indians had showed themselves the previous evening, and found the trail of five or six Indians, and incautiously pursued them over the river hill to Captina creek, about one mile from the river, and not much further from the mouth of the creek. As the party of whites were pursuing the trail, they went down a small drain, with a narrow bottom. On the right of the drain was a steep, rocky bank, fifty or sixty feet high; on this bank thirty or forty Indians lay concealed. The whites passed on till they came in front of the Indian line, when a tremendous fire was opened upon them; the fire was instantly returned by Enoch and his party. Both parties took shelter behind trees, logs, or rocks, and the battle was continued with animation on both sides for some time. Lieutenant Enoch and McArthur were treed near each other, and loaded and shot several times. The hills along Captina creek are steep, high, and craggy, the valleys narrow, so that the keen crack of the rifles, added to the deafening shouts of the combatants, causing the echo to vibrate from hill to hill, made it seem that those engaged in this strife of arms were fourfold the actual number. At length a ball from an Indian's rifle pierced the breast of the brave Lieut. Enoch ; he fell, and immediately expired. Six others of his little band were slain, and some badly wounded.

Their commander being killed, and many of their gallant little band being slain or disabled, the remainder determined upon a retreat. No officer was left to command, and although McArthur was the youngest man in the company, in this time of peril he was unanimously called to direct the retreat. The wounded who were able to walk were placed in front, whilst McArthur, with his Spartan band, covered the retreat. The moment an Indian showed himself in pursuit he was fired upon, and generally, it is believed, with effect. The Indians were so severely handled in the fight, that they soon gave up the pursuit. The same day the remains of the brave Lieut. Enoch's command returned to Baker's fort, the place from which they set out in the morning.

In this engagement, McArthur had several fair shots ; a man of his steady nerve would not often miss his mark. The Indians were commanded in this battle by a Shawnee chief, known to the whites about Chillicothe by the name of *Charley Wilkey*, (the same who took Samuel Davis prisoner). He told the author of this narrative, that the battle of Captina was the most severe conflict he ever witnessed ; that although he had the advantage of the ground and the first fire, he lost the most

men, half of them having been either killed or wounded.
The carnage was indeed most fearful, considering the
small numbers engaged. More than one half of each
party were killed or wounded. I have never seen in
print any account of this severe conflict with the savage
foe.

McArthur's intrepid conduct in the Captina affair rendered him very popular with the frontier men, as far as
the account of this sanguinary conflict extended. Although he had with equal energy and boldness discharged
his duty as a soldier in the battle field on the St. Joseph's,
in the campaign with General Harmar, yet the dexterity
and courage of a private soldier could not be so easily
distinguished where large numbers were engaged.

During the winter of 1792 and 1793, he went down
the Ohio river to the neighborhood of Limestone (Maysville), in Kentucky, his restless disposition not permitting him to tarry long at the stations, which were then
" few and far between," on the banks of the Ohio. Alternately he engaged in the laborious avocations of the
new settlers, or in the toilsome vocation of hunting in the
sequestered and lonely forests. Occasionally he was
employed about thirty miles above Maysville, at a salt
lick, one of those establishments which were all-impor-
tant to the early settlers ; and thus he spent some portion
of his early life, always seeking employment, and rendering himself useful to his fellow men, and promoting
thereby his own advancement. We revert to these employments of the earlier part of young McArthur's life,
with the full conviction that no honest employment is
disreputable, and to show the steps by which industry,
capacity and integrity, may rise to affluence and honorable distinction, from the most humble beginnings.

At this salt establishment he first became acquainted
with *Gen. Joseph Vance,* who was then a mere youth,
but who labored in those days with McArthur in the

same vocations. Unaided by patronage, and self-taught, by the force of his own genius, and by perseverance, he has risen from that humble condition to competence and distinction. When the Indian wars ceased, his father settled on Mad river, near where the town of Urbana was subsequently erected. He has been repeatedly a member of the general assembly of this state, fourteen years a member of the lower house of congress, and is now the governor of the state of Ohio. It is to sterling worth that this tribute of respect is paid. In this country, where the system of entails is cut up by the roots, the persevering poor of one generation may become the rich of the succeeding generation.

In the spring of 1793, General Nathaniel Massie was collecting a party to go to the Scioto country on a surveying tour. McArthur left the salt works and went with Massie as a chain carrier, or marker. Although this was a period of Indian warfare, Massie, and a party of about thirty men, went up the Ohio to the mouth of the river Scioto, and up the Scioto to the mouth of Paint creek. Their baggage was taken by water in canoes, whilst the surveyors leisurely meandered the Ohio and Scioto rivers, making occasional surveys as they went forward. When they arrived at the mouth of Paint creek, they sunk their canoes in deep water for concealment, and went to work with spirit. The country around where Chillicothe was subsequently laid out, was surveyed, and up the Scioto as far as Westfall. Surveys were also made up the north fork of Paint creek, as far as Old Town, with meeting but one Indian, who made his escape. They saw in several places fresh signs made by Indians, but Massie and his party were too vigilant and numerous to be successfully attacked by a few stragglers. The Indians, therefore, sought safety in flight. There is no doubt that if Massie had remained much longer in that part of the country, a sufficient number of Indians would have collected and destroyed them. But his party returned to Manchester after an absence of several weeks, without any loss.

This bold enterprise of about *thirty* men, proceeding more than one hundred miles into the enemy's country, and remaining in the neighborhood of their first encampment, to survey a large scope of country, astonishes us, and indicates the recklessness and daring of the early backwoodsmen.

In the fall of this year, the Indians were very troublesome to the frontier settlements along the Ohio river. The government of Kentucky employed spies, or rangers, to traverse the frontier country in every direction, and to give the alarm to the frontier stations, should Indians be found lurking about their neighborhoods. There was as much competition amongst the bold backwoodsmen of that day, for those posts of honor and danger, as there is now exhibited by office-hunters in seeking " the loaves and fishes." It would seem that every age has some peculiar events which answer to stir up the passions, and keep them in a state of excitement, as if " the passions were the elements of life." On the fidelity of these spies depended the lives, the property, and safety of the frontier settlements. It is not surprising, then, that the eyes of all the citizens were turned towards the conduct of those who were selected as sentinels, to watch the motions of a restless and insidious foe. A young man who had the good fortune to establish and maintain a character for intrepidity and honesty, was a special favorite, not only with the men, but amongst the ladies, no matter how rough his exterior, or uncouth his manners. Even in those trying times of Indian hostility, and the deprivations in settling a new country, to secure the smiles and approbation of the fair was an object of peculiar interest with young ambition.

CHAPTER III.

Duncan McArthur had the good fortune to establish such a character for energy, perseverance, and strict integrity, during the surveying expedition up the Scioto, that he was recommended as a man well qualified for the services of a spy or ranger, and he was accordingly employed. He and Samuel Davis, with two others, were directed to range the country from Limestone to the mouth of Big Sandy river, which is the extreme eastern boundary of the state of Kentucky, and never was a trust confided to more faithful and competent sentinels. In this employment they remained until the severity of the winter procured rest to the settlers. An incident occurred in one of these tours of duty, worthy to be related.

When McArthur and Davis were together, going up the Ohio, they had with them a light canoe. One pushed it up the stream, while the other walked in advance to reconnoiter. They stopped for the night a short distance below the mouth of the Scioto river. Early next morning they crossed the Ohio, and went back across the bottom to the foot of the hill, where they knew of a fine deer lick. This lick is situated about two miles below the town of Portsmouth, and near the residence of Judge Collins. The morning was very calm, and a light fog hung over the bottom. When they got near the lick, McArthur halted, and Davis proceeded, stooping low among the bushes and weeds, to conceal himself. He moved on with the noiseless tread of the cat, till he was near the lick, when he straightened up to see if the ground was occupied. At that instant he heard the crack of a rifle, and a bullet whistled by his ear. As the morning was still and foggy, the smoke from the Indian's gun settled around him, so that he could not see whether the shot had taken effect or not. Davis raised his rifle, and as the Indian stepped out of the smoke to make observations, shot him dead. Davis immediately reloaded his rifle, and by about the time he had charged his gun, McArthur came running to him, knowing that the shots he had heard were in too quick succession to be fired by the same gun. Running at the top of his speed to the aid of his companion, just as he reached the spot where Davis stood, they heard a heavy sound of footsteps, and in an instant more a number of Indians made their appearance in the open ground near the lick. McArthur and Davis were standing in thick brush and high weeds, and being unperceived by the Indians, cautiously retreated to their canoe, crossed the Ohio, and were out of danger.

Early in the spring of 1794, spies were again employed to range through the country, along the frontier line of stations. On the line from Maysville to Big Sandy, were employed Duncan McArthur, Nathaniel Beasley (late a major-general of Ohio militia, and frequently a member of the general assembly from Brown county, Ohio, and at the time of his death, one of the canal commissioners of this state), Thomas Treacle, and Samuel McDowel. These spies were generally divided into two squads. While two of them were going up the Ohio, the others were coming down. In this way they were continually on the alert, to watch the motions of their unmerciful enemies. During this summer the attacks of the Indians were not so frequent, nor made by such large parties as in the preceding years, owing to the circumstance of General Wayne having invaded their country with an overwhelming force. This kept them in considerable check, but at the same time small parties made frequent inroads into the frontier settlements.

This summer, the government of the United States, for the first time, employed men at the public charge, to carry a mail from what was then termed the old settlement (Wheeling, in Virginia, was then called the most

western point of the old settlement), to Maysville, and
as far down the Ohio as Cincinnati. Previous to 1794,
when intelligence, either public or private, was sought to
be conveyed, those interested employed express carriers
at their individual expense. This rendered correspond-
ence, of every sort, between the isolated new settlements
and the old, very uncertain and insecure. The mail was
carried in what was called a packet-boat. This boat was
light, and could be rowed by six men up the stream at a
rapid rate. Propelling the packet-boat up the stream was
the most laborious and dangerous employment which can
be imagined. The Indians were unceasing in their efforts to destroy small parties of whites, as they were
passing up or down the river Ohio. There were then
but few places between Cincinnati and Wheeling, for the
packet-boat to rest at night in safety. But such were the
enterprise and daring of the backwoodsmen, either on
land or water, that they were ready to undertake any enterprise within the power of man to accomplish.

During this summer, as the packet-boat was on her
way up, near the mouth of the Scioto, a party of Indians
fired into the boat as it was passing near the shore, and
one man, John Stout, was killed, and two brothers by the
name of Colvin were severely wounded. The boat was
hurried by the remainder of the crew into the middle of
the stream, and then returned to Maysville. The four
"spies" were at Maysville, drawing their pay and ammunition, when the packet-boat returned. Notwithstanding the recent and bloody defeat sustained in the packet-
boat, a fresh crew was immediately procured, and the
four spies were directed by Colonel Henry Lee (who
had the superintendence and direction of them) to guard
the boat as far as the mouth of Big Sandy river. As the
spies were on their way up the river with the packet-
boat, they found concealed and sunk in the mouth of a
small creek, a short distance below the mouth of the

Scioto, a bark canoe, large enough to carry seven or eight men. In this canoe a party of Indians had crossed the Ohio, and were prowling about somewhere in the country. Samuel McDowel was sent back to give notice to the inhabitants, whilst the other three spies remained with the packet-boat till they saw it safe past the mouth of Big Sandy river.

At this place the spies parted from the boat, and commenced their return for Maysville. On their way up they had taken a light canoe. Two of them pushed the canoe, whilst the others advanced on foot to reconnoiter. On their return, the spies floated down the Ohio in their canoe, till they came nearly opposite the mouth of the Scioto river, where they landed, and McArthur went out into the hills in pursuit of game. Treacle and Beasley went about a mile lower down the river and landed their canoe, intending also to hunt till McArthur should come up with them. McArthur went to a deer lick, with the situation of which he was well acquainted ; made a blind behind which he concealed himself, and waited for game. He lay about an hour, when he discovered two Indians coming to the lick. The Indians were so near him before he saw them, that it was impossible for him to retreat without being discovered. As the boldest course appeared to him to be the safest, he determined to permit them to come as near to him as they would, shoot one of them, and try his strength with the other. Imagine his situation. Two Indians armed with rifles, tomahawks, and scalping-knives, approaching in these circumstances, must have caused his heart to beat pit-a-pat. He permitted the Indians, who were walking towards him in a stooping posture, to approach undisturbed. When they came near the lick, they halted in an open piece of ground, and straightened up to look into the lick for game. This halt enabled McArthur to take deliberate aim from a rest, at only fourteen steps distance. He fired, and an Indian fell. McArthur remained still a moment, thinking it possible that the other Indian would take to flight. In this he was mistaken. The Indian did not even dodge out of his track, when his companion sunk lifeless by his side.

As the Indian's gun was charged, McArthur concluded it would be rather a fearful job to rush upon him ; he therefore determined upon a retreat. He broke from his place of concealment, and ran with all his speed. He had run but a few steps, when he found himself tangled in the top of a fallen tree : this caused a momentary halt. At that instant the Indian fired, and the ball whistled sharply by him. As the Indian's gun, as well as his own, was now empty, he thought of turning round and giving him a fight upon equal terms. At this instant several other Indians came in sight, rushing with savage screams through the brush. He fled with his utmost speed, the Indians pursuing, and firing at him as he ran. One of their balls entered the bottom of his powder horn, and shivered the side of it next his body into pieces. The splinters of his shattered powder-horn were propelled with such force by the ball, that his side was considerably injured, and the blood flowed freely. The ball, in passing through the horn, had given him such a jar, that he thought for some time it had passed through his side. But this did not slacken his pace. The Indians pursued him some distance. McArthur, though not very fleet, was capable of enduring great fatigue, and he now had an occasion which demanded the best exertion of his strength. He gained upon his pursuers, and by the time he had crossed two or three ridges, he found himself free from pursuit, and turned his course to the river.

When he came to the bank of the Ohio, he discovered Beasley and Treacle in the canoe, paddling up the stream, in order to keep her hovering over the same spot, and to be more conspicuous should McArthur make his escape

7

from the Indians.   They had heard the firing, and the
yelling in pursuit, and had no doubt about the cause, and
had concluded it possible, from the length of time and
the direction of the noise, that McArthur might have effected his escape.   Nathaniel Beasley and Thomas
Treacle were not the kind of men to fly at the approach
of danger, and forsake a comrade.   McArthur saw the
canoe, and made a signal to them to come ashore.   They
did so, and McArthur was soon in the canoe, in the
middle of the stream, and out of danger.   Thus ended
this day's adventures of the spies and their packet-boat,
and this was the last attack made by the Indians upon a
boat in the Ohio river.

Till late in the fall of this year he was retained in
this arduous and dangerous employment.   At the
approach of the winter, and after the severe chastisement of the Indians by General Wayne's army, there
was a cessation of arms, and the spies were discharged.
McArthur's disposition was for constant action.   When
he was unemployed he was as restless (to use one of
the backwoods' comparisons) as a wild animal chained.
The winter of 1794 and '95 was just setting in.   He
could choose either to return to the salt lick and make
salt, or go to the woods and hunt and trap.   While he
was settling a plan for his winter operations, he fell in
with Mr. George Hardick, an experienced hunter and
trapper, who was never at ease but when he was ranging
through the solitary woods.   McArthur and Hardick
were kindred spirits, who never quailed at danger, or
wearied by labor.   They agreed to go in partnership for
a winter hunt.   They made a light canoe, ammunition
and beaver traps were procured, and our adventurers set
off from Manchester, down the Ohio to the mouth of
the Kentucky river, thence up the Kentucky river far
above the settlements.   Game of every description was
found in abundance.   Deer and buffalo were killed for

their tallow and hides. Beaver and otter were the principal game pursued, and were caught in considerable numbers. They went up the Kentucky river as far as they could find water to float their canoe. About the middle of January the river froze up, and they could neither move their canoe backward nor forward. Here they built a close hut, in which to secure the proceeds of their hunt from the depredations of wolves and other wild animals. They left their canoe, peltry, &c., packed their traps, ammunition, and blankets, on their backs, and proceeded up the main branch of the Kentucky river, as far as the beaver could find water in which to swim. In this way, these two backwoodsmen spent their winter in the midst of the spurs of the Cumberland mountains, more than one hundred miles from the habitations of civilized men. Although their hunting range was sometimes on one side and sometimes on the other of the old war-path, on which the Indians from the south went to visit and assist their friends north of the Ohio river, yet during the winter they saw no fresh sign of Indians.

As soon as the winter broke, and the ice and snow melted, they returned to their hut, loaded their canoe, and leisurely went down the river, stopping to trap wherever they saw signs of game. They continued down the Kentucky river to its mouth, thence up the Ohio to Cincinnati. Here they disposed of the proceeds of their hunt to some advantage. They then returned to Manchester. Look, reader, at the map of Kentucky, and trace the route of these men from Manchester in Ohio, to the mouth of the Kentucky river; thence up the Kentucky river to the Cumberland mountains, and you can form some faint idea of the toils and labors overcome, and of the perseverance of the old backwoodsmen, in pursuing any enterprise which once engaged their attention.

In the month of March, 1795, he again went on a

surveying tour with General Massie. This expedition
was subsequently called the "starving tour," for a description of which read the life of General Massie. On
this distressing expedition McArthur distinguished himself for his patience under the most severe privations.
Being strong and robust, he was capable of enduring
more toil than most men. His perseverance rendered
him valuable in such trying circumstances. From this
time forward his destiny was closely linked with that
of Gen. Massie.

During the summer Gen. Wayne made a treaty of
peace with the Indians, and the prospects of the white
settlers in the western country were more flattering than
at any former period in their history. The ground on
which every station was erected in the western country,
had been heretofore battle ground. While working their
corn-patches, sentinels were constantly required to guard
those at labor. Notwithstanding the utmost vigilance,
many were shot or tomahawked by the enemy. Their
steady perseverance had caused a day of brighter aus-
pices to break forth. The red man, notwithstanding "his
soul is great—his arm is strong—his battles full of fame,"
with all his bravery and stratagem, was compelled to
yield to his more civilized neighbor. A new epoch is
just dawning. The vast wilds of the west are now open
to emigration. The dense population east of the Alleghany mountains are standing on tip-toe, watching the
issue of this long and direful conflict of arms. At length
in the month of August, 1795, from Fort Greenville,
Gen. Wayne sends forth the glad tidings to the west,
that peace is made with the red man. No more sentinels
were necessary to guard the plowman at his labor. The
population east of the mountains, and also from Europe,
make a rush into the western wilderness, and a new
world arises. The states of Ohio, Indiana, Illinois, Mis-
souri, and Michigan, now sustaining their millions of

An Early Settler in the West.

inhabitants, were trophies won in a fifty years' war, by a few pioneers of western Pennsylvania, western Virginia, and Kentucky. The nation owes a debt of gratitude to the men, whose march was in the van in those trying times. Their memories should be held in veneration by the millions who now reap in peace and quiet the fruits of their toil and labor.

CHAPTER IV.

A LARGE district of country had been ceded by the Indians, at the treaty of Greenville. The backwoodsmen, who had spent a great part of their lives in the front of the war by which these lands were acquired, believed the country of right belonged to the conquerors. In consequence of this opinion, during the winter of 1795–96 they poured into the newly acquired territory by thousands; each endeavoring to select the most advantageous site for a farm, on which they could pass the evening of their days in peace and quiet. Parties of explorers would sometimes meet with others on the same errand, on some inviting tract of first-rate land; quarrels would ensue, about priority of discovery and improvement, which frequently ended in battles, and sometimes in the death of some of the parties. During this winter, McArthur made tomahawk improvements in many of the finest bottoms on the east side of the Scioto river. This pleasing dream of wealth was of short duration: the pioneers soon discovered they had no favors to expect, for conquering and defending the country. They were generally poor, did not understand farming for profit, and were entirely unacquainted with trade and traffic; and when peace came, they were far behind the new emigrants, who settled among them, in all the arts which distinguish civilized life. The old backwoodsmen were strangers to the various arts of making money: hunting, trapping, and war was their trade; and before they could change their habits and customs to the new order of things which a state of peace brought about, they found themselves elbowed out of the way by the more wealthy and dexterous emigrants.

Duncan McArthur, while engaged on the numberless surveying tours with General Massie, would sometimes settle the compass to the proper course, and sometimes would be permitted to run lines; in this way he became familiar with the face of the compass. Being then in the twenty-fourth year of his age, he went to school a few weeks, and studied arithmetic, till he mastered the rule of Three. He then exchanged his rifle, his beaver traps, and other hunting accouterments, for a surveyor's instruments, determined at least to learn the practical part of surveying. This was a new and hopeful era in his life.

Duncan McArthur studied surveying about as long as the illustrious Patrick Henry is represented to have studied law, and with the same intuitive success. Neither knew but little of the theory of their professions when they commenced their career, yet both excelled in their vocations. Mr. Henry was an unrivaled orator, and only a theoretic statesman, and from indolence was unversed in the details of legislation. General McArthur was no orator, but by his habits of close investigation and persevering industry, he was a competent surveyor, and a practical statesman, understanding the wants and the condition of the people, and pursuing that course in his public career, best calculated to promote their interests and happiness.

Duncan McArthur's ambition would have been completely gratified at this period of his life, could he have then acquired a competent estate in lands, free from in-

cumbrance, on which he could live in a state of independence. How little we know what would be our feelings and conduct under a change of circumstances.
Having now a surveyor's compass, he was prepared to
become an assistant surveyor to the first who would furnish him employment.

General Nathaniel Massie was a man of enterprise,
largely engaged in locating warrants and surveying lands.
An assistant surveyor of McArthur's energy and perseverance was, to General Massie, an invaluable acquisition. He soon became a competent and skilful surveyor.
At no period of his life did he possess a very sprightly
and active mind; but although his conceptions were
slow, what he once acquired he never lost. In whatever
business he engaged, he was distinguished for an untiring
diligence, and an energy that never yielded to difficulties.

In February, 1796, General McArthur was married to
Nancy, daughter of William and Effie McDonald, and
sister to the author of this narrative.

In the month of March, in this year, General Massie
was preparing and engaging a party to make a new settlement somewhere in the fertile valley of the Scioto
river. The inducements held out by Massie, to encourage emigrants to follow him into the wilderness, were an
in-lot and an out-lot in the new town, which he intended
to lay out, and one hundred acres of land for eighty
dollars. A numerous party, principally from Kentucky,
collected at Manchester. Some of them went by water
in canoes, taking with them plows, hoes, axes, &c., &c.
The residue of the party went by land, with their horses,
to meet those who went by water, at the mouth of Paint
creek. They met at that point; and the site on which
Chillicothe was erected, was selected for the new town.
The town was laid out into lots, and all went to work
with spirit. This was the first settlement made in the

western country in peace. It was a new era in their lives.

McArthur, now an assistant surveyor to General Massie, aided him in laying out the town of Chillicothe; and whilst thus engaged, Massie employed him for one year, for one in-lot and one out-lot in Chillicothe, and one hundred and fifty acres of land in the vicinity. This land soon became the residence of General McArthur; and to this small tract, others were soon added by industry and economy, and form the delightful residence of the general yet, so well known as " Fruit Hill."

The present appearance and beauty of this residence, is such as to command the admiration of all the lovers of beautiful scenery.

Much information was derived by McArthur from his skilful and experienced employer, and he derived all that an assistant surveyor could from a constant inspection and examination of Massie's plats and connections of this, then, new country. This year the contract of McArthur and Massie was fulfilled, to the mutual satisfaction of both parties.

McArthur having located himself in a cabin, on his land thus acquired, commenced the business of locating and surveying Virginia military warrants, on his own account. He was unable to progress with any extraordinary rapidity, in the first stages of his business, but only proceeded industriously and slowly, like most young men, in the business which he had selected for himself. Having, at this time, but a slight knowledge of books, and exhibiting in his manners the unpolished backwoodsman, it was not until after some slight experience and labor in his new vocation, obtained him a reputation for promptitude and unquestionable capacity in the discharge of the important duties of a locator of warrants in the Virginia Military District, that he acquired the confidence of holders of warrants, then con-

stantly visiting this region of country. But he soon
acquired a reputation equal to any in this business,
and combining with it the purchase and sale of warrants
and land himself, he soon began to reap the rewards of
industry and perseverance, in the acquisition of property,
and in establishing a decided character, as a man of
business, and most competent locator and surveyor.

In 1798, after Ross county was organized, he was appointed and commissioned a captain in the militia, by
Governor St. Clair.

McArthur continued his land business with his wonted
industry. Fortune favored his efforts, and with his ac-
quisitions of property, he acquired a popularity equal to
any of those, who had been favored with an early education and patronage. He was now largely engaged in
land speculations, and used all the means within his
power, to inform himself in the land laws of Virginia
and Kentucky. His entries and surveys were made so
special and correctly, that few, if any, of them could be
interrupted or interfered with. Notwithstanding his care
and precaution in this business, he had to cope with
many men of unsurpassed energy and unquestioned
capacity, and who, anxious, like himself, to promote
their interests by every laudable and legal means, have
had with him much litigation. Controversies relative to
land and land titles, have given him an immense deal of
trouble, vexation, and litigation. This has tended to
impair his good opinion of mankind, and somewhat al-
loyed his happiness, but his success was as signal and
general as he could have expected.

Having acquired more wealth than any of his fellow
citizens in the Scioto valley, he began to take an active
part in the politics of the country. Gen. Massie was
then one of the most popular men in Ross county. He
admired McArthur for his persevering industry, and close
application to business ; and was upon all occasions his

supporter and friend. In 1805, he was a candidate for
the House of Representatives in the General Assembly
of Ohio; and as all the old pioneers were his personal
friends and supporters, he was elected triumphantly, notwithstanding the violent opposition of many settlers of
talents and capacity about Chillicothe.

I have now sketched his character from his boyhood,
as a packer across the Alleghany mountains—a private
soldier—a salt boiler—a hunter and trapper—a spy on
the frontier—a chain-carrier—a surveyor—and now a
member of the legislature of Ohio. In every situation
in which he was placed, he endeavored to lead those
with whom he was associated. He was now placed in
a situation of a new kind, and which required acquisi-
tions of a different character from those he already possessed. To attain these, he devoted himself to study.
Not content to be a silent and passive member of the
legislature, he soon exhibited his capacity for his new
station and was heard with attention and respect, whenever any subject was discussed in which he felt a peculiar interest.

He became, unquestionably, the most popular man in
Ross county, and continued to represent this county in
the legislature, as often as his other avocations would
permit. He was exceedingly popular with the members
of the General Assembly, as is evidenced by his being
elected speaker, to preside over the deliberations of that
branch of the General Assembly of which he was a
member.

In 1806, he was elected Colonel of the first Regiment,
second brigade, second division of Ohio militia. This
division was then under the command of his old and tried
friend Gen. Nathaniel Massie.

When the United States had purchased Louisiana from
France, it was rumored that Spain would refuse to surrender the possession of the country to the United States,

agreeably to her compact with France. Under these circumstances, Congress authorized the President of the United States to raise a sufficient number of Volunteers, to take forcible possession of Louisiana, in case Spain should refuse peaceably to surrender the country. On this subject intense interest and excitement prevailed in the western country. It was there our trade must center. To be deprived of the advantage of this out-let for trade, the mouth of the Mississippi river, would it was supposed completely ruin the prospects of the western farmers. The state of Ohio was called upon to furnish her quota of men to be in readiness to march, to move on New Orleans, when required. When the call was made on the second division of the Ohio militia, the Scioto valley, although its population was sparse, furnished a full regiment of men. The company officers of the regiment assembled in Chillicothe, and unanimously elected Duncan McArthur to the command of the regiment. Happily for the country, these troops were not called into service. The extensive country of Louisiana was obtained, and peaceable possession given, through the wise and moderate measures of President Jefferson.

During the session of the General Assembly of 1807 –8, General Massie resigned his commission as Major General of militia, in the state of Ohio. His office being vacant, the General Assembly elected Duncan McArthur, who was commissioned Major General of the second division of Ohio militia, on the twentieth day of February A. D. 1808.

CHAPTER V.

In the spring of 1812, the difficulties which had been long increasing, between the United States and the English nation were drawing to a crisis. The British had so long, and so wantonly, vexed our commerce by restrictions, confiscations, and impressing our seamen, that they had completely exhausted the patience of the country. In consequence of the many vexations practised by that government upon our commerce and citizens, Congress authorized the President of the United States to enroll and organize a number of volunteers, to hold themselves in readiness for marching at the shortest notice. McArthur, now a major general of militia, issued orders for his division to assemble by regiments, to see how many men would enroll themselves to march in the defence of the country, and to redress the wrongs which our citizens had suffered. He attended in person every regimental muster in his division, employing every argument in his power, which might induce his fellow-citizens to take the field. A sufficient number enrolled themselves to form a regiment. They were immediately organized into companies. McArthur enrolled himself as a private in a company raised in Chillicothe, commanded by Captain William Keys.

As soon as the companies were organized, they had orders to march to Dayton, the place of general rendezvous for the volunteers of Ohio. Here they were organized into battalions and regiments. The company officers, agreeably to the laws of the state of Ohio, proceeded to elect their majors. Gen. James Denny of Circleville was elected to command the first battalion, and Mr. William Trimble of Highland county was elected to command the second battalion. The company officers and majors immediately went into an election for a colonel to com

mand the regiment; when on counting the ballots, Mc-
Arthur received the unanimous vote of the officers of
the regiment, and was accordingly commissioned Colonel
of the first regiment of Ohio volunteers, on the 7th of
May, 1812.

Two other regiments of volunteers were enrolled in
the state of Ohio, and rendezvoused at the same time
and place. The one was commanded by Col. Lewis
Cass, the other, by Col. James Findlay of Cincinnati.
To these volunteer regiments, was added the fourth regiment of United States infantry, commanded by Colonel
James Miller. These troops, when united, were placed
under the command of Brigadier General William Hull
of the United States army. Gen. Hull had been a soldier of some distinction in the war of the Revolution.
James Taylor of Newport, Kentucky, was appointed
Pay, and Quarter Master General.

Our country had been so long blessed with peace, that
organizing and equipping an army was new to the officers. The necessary camp equipage to prepare the army
for marching was slowly procured. This army of about
eighteen hundred men, were camped in the environs of
Dayton, till some time in June, before they were prepared to set forward on their march.

From Dayton to Manary's Block-house (now Belle-
fontaine) there was something like a wagon road for the
army to march on. This was then the most northwardly
settlement in the state of Ohio. From Manary's Block-
house to Detroit was one unbroken wilderness; a part
of the way without even a foot-path. The country is
remarkably level, intersected with swamps, marshes, and
rivers. No provisions had been previously laid up
by the government in advance of the army. They were
compelled to carry their subsistence and forage in wagons. The road was to be made through the thick
forests. Bridges were to be constructed over the marshy,

spongy ground, where none but the solitary red, or white, hunter, or the Indian trader with his Canadian ponies had ever passed. The energy and perseverance of the Ohio volunteers overcame all the difficulties placed by nature in their way.

Although war was not declared, the signs of the times were such, that the secretary of war sent an express rider after General Hull, with orders for him to hasten his march with all possible expedition to Detroit.

General Hull employed through the recommendation of General McArthur, the most efficient men for pilots. These guides were, first, Mr. Isaac Zane (brother to Col. Zane of Wheeling) who was then an old man. He had been taken prisoner by the Indians, when quite a youth; he had married an Indian woman, and raised a numerous family. He had lived near the head of Mad river, (where Zanesfield now stands,) about fifty years; and had been passing through the country to Detroit almost every year, either on hunting or trading expeditions. No man could be better acquainted with the localities and features of the country. A Mr. McPherson, an old Indian trader and a man of vigorous mind, who had been passing through the country, for upwards of twenty years, on similar business with Zane, was another; and Mr. Robert Armstrong, who had been taken prisoner by the Indians when a child, and raised by them, was also selected. He had married a daughter of Mr. Zane, and was acquainted with every spot of ground between Manary's block-house and Detroit. To these was added Mr. James L. Reed, an Indian trader for many years, and who, in his frequent travels to and fro, through the country, between Mad river and Detroit, was well acquainted with every marsh and swamp in the country. With these efficient men for pilots, the army commenced its march, with a numerous train of wagons. The making a new road through a wilderness country, inter-

ɔersed with rivers, marshes, and swamps, where few
civilized men had ever passed, was, in itself, an enterprise of considerable magnitude.

The army went forward, till it arrived at Manary's
block-house, then the outward settlement of Ohio. From
this point north, a road was to be constructed. Colonel
McArthur and his regiment went in advance, to make the
road. The arms, and other accouterments, belonging to
the regiment, were carried in wagons. The guides went
forward, and with tomahawks marked the way. Mc
Arthur divided his regiment by companies, and gave each
company a distance of the road to make, in proportion
to their numbers. Axes, grubbing-hoes, spades, and
shovels, were provided; and the regiment went to work
with spirit. McArthur, accustomed to hard labor and a
life in the woods from his youth, was perfectly at home
while constructing the road through the wilderness. He
showed the men, by his own example, that he was determined to do as much labor as was required of
any of them. No difficulties discouraged him. By his
example and encouragement, he excited such enthusiasm
in both officers and privates, that every man worked as
though the completion of the road depended on his single
arm. He excited emulation amongst the companies,
each endeavoring to do more than the others. With his
regiment he constructed a road from Manary's block-
house to Fort McArthur, a point on the Scioto river, in
two days; a distance of thirty miles. It is probable
that more labor was performed in those two days, than
ever was done in the same time by the same number of
men.

Colonel McArthur's regiment was relieved, and the
other regiments now in turn went in advance, to construct
the road. Notwithstanding there was rain almost every
day, there was no skulking or dodging: every regiment
used all the exertions that were in the power of man, to

8

forward the work. There was probably as much talent
and ambition in this little army, as was ever collected in
one mass of equal numbers. Animation, enterprise,
ambition, and emulation, concurred to enhance the progress of this determined band. Here was Colonel James
Miller, of the fourth regiment of United States infantry :
a man of as cool, intrepid courage, as ever drew a blade
to glitter in the sun. And Colonel Lewis Cass, who,
though naturally of a good humored and indolent temper,
would, when roused by emulation or danger, do all that
man could be expected to do. There was Colonel James
Findlay too, who, though usually dilatory, was now excited by patriotism and ambition, to use every effort to
outstrip the subject of this narrative. He had no superior in his energy and decision, when stimulated, as he
now was, by the call of his country, and competing
with such men as Cass and McArthur in his country's
service.

To show that it was not a mere flash of popularity,
which placed these gentlemen in the command of regiments, it is only necessary to point to their services in
their subsequent career. In the tremendous battle near
the Falls of Niagara, it was Colonel Miller who commanded the successful assault, with the point of the
bayonet, which took possession of the British artillery.
He was promoted to the rank of brigadier-general, and
as such, when the war closed, was retained in the peace
establishment of the army ; and subsequently appointed
governor of Arkansas territory.

Colonel Findlay was a citizen of Cincinnati, and had
long possessed the confidence of the government, as well
as of his fellow-citizens. When peace blessed our land
with her smiling presence, he was elected a member of
congress. He was an efficient member of that body,
always acting independently, without permitting himself
to be trammeled by the intrigues of party. A little more

than a year since, he was commanded by the Judge of
the universe, to render an account of his stewardship.
It is believed, by those who knew him well, that his
vouchers will be found genuine, and that no defalcations
will be found against him.

Colonel Cass was subsequently appointed a brigadier-
general in the United States army ; and when peace was
made, he was appointed governor of Michigan territory.
He recently filled the office of secretary of war, and now
is our minister plenipotentiary at France.

The two majors of Colonel McArthur's regiment,
were men who could be relied on in all situations.
Major Denny, of the first battalion, was a gentleman of
talents and unquestioned courage. He was frequently
elected a member of the legislature, clerk of the county
and supreme courts, and also a major-general of militia.
He has long since passed " the bourn whence no traveler returns." He was buried in the city of Philadelphia.

Major Trimble, of the second battalion, was a young
man of much promise. He was promoted to the rank
of colonel in the United States army ; and when the war
ended, he was retained on the peace establishment of the
army. He was subsequently elected a senator in the
congress of the United States, by the general assembly
of Ohio. His public career was of short duration. He
had received a severe wound in the battle of Fort Erie ;
from the effects of which he never recovered, and which
no doubt sent him prematurely to his grave.

Colonel McArthur appointed for the staff-officers of
his regiment, the following persons, viz. William
Henry Puthuff, Adjutant ; Richard Douglas, Quarter
Master.

Adjutant Puthuff was a man of talents and education,
and unquestioned bravery ; very energetic and punctilious
in the performance of his duty ; and in exacting the sub-
ordination of others. He has long since paid the debt

of nature ; and now lies buried on the banks of Lake Michigan.

The quarter-master was a man of eccentric genius and of singular humor. He has been a member of the Ohio legislature, and is now a practising lawyer of distinguished eminence.

The humble author of this narrative received the appointment of paymaster to the regiment. Of his character and actions it would be improper for him to speak. Suffice it to say, that he served in the army, in various situations, to the close of the war, free from censure. This circumstance is only referred to, to show how he came by a knowledge of the men and things of which he writes. Having endeavored to do his duty in the army, he is now attempting to record, for the gratification of posterity, the characters and actions of men, who risked their lives in defence of their country.

I will now return from this digression to the army. The army went forward without making a halt, till they arrived at the foot of the rapids of the Maumee. Here one day of repose was allowed the soldiers, to rest their weary limbs. The march was again resumed, with renewed vigor. On their march, between the Maumee and the river Raisin, an express rider from the secretary of war, came up with the army, with official intelligence, that congress had declared war. This official news put the army out of suspense. They now knew that they would soon be engaged in very different labor than in constructing roads. The army went on at a rapid pace, passed the river Raisin, and went on till they came to the river Huron. This river was so deep, that it could not be forded with the numerous train of wagons. It is nearly three hundred feet over, and it was necessary to construct a bridge. The bridge was erected in one day, and by night the army and baggage were safely across the river, and camped for the night on the north bank of the river Huron. The bridge was nearly a mile from lake Erie. Late in the evening of this day, the enemy's brig, Queen Charlotte, came sweeping up the lake, and hovered about the mouth of the river Huron, to make observations on the movements of our army. When daylight returned, the Queen Charlotte was not to be seen. The army resumed its march, and that evening, the fifth of July, arrived at Detroit, the place of their destination. Here a few days of repose was allowed the weary soldiers.

CHAPTER VI.

THE artillery, which lay in the fort and batteries in and around Detroit, were in the worst possible condition. The gun carriages were old and decayed, and in every respect unfit for immediate use. The artificers were set to work to repair the artillery carriages; every means in the power of man was exerted, to place the army in a situation to march upon Fort Malden, only eighteen miles distant. Repose and inaction did not suit the enterprising character of General Hull's field officers. The unavoidable delay in preparing the artillery for effective service, appeared like eternity to the fiery spirits under the command of General Hull. Among the most impatient and restless at this delay, was McArthur. He urged General Hull to cross the river Detroit with the army, and attack Fort Malden without delay; insisting that the present was the auspicious moment to carry the fort; that the garrison consisted only of a few regular troops and some Canadian militia; that, from unquestioned information, the walls of the fort were in a state of dilapidation, the pickets rotten, and that the Canadian militia were not disposed to risk much in its defence. General Hull thought the enterprise more hazardous than his field officers were willing to admit, and did not wish to invade Canada, and attack Malden, till his artillery was repaired ; he would then be prepared to batter down the walls, should the enemy refuse to surrender the place.

As soon as two or three of the gun carriages were repaired, the cannon were placed on them, and the field officers again urged General Hull to cross into Canada. They contended, that if the army would cross the river Detroit, and camp in Sandwich, that it would cut off the communication between Malden, and the settlements on lake St. Clair and the river Thames, and thus weaken the resources of the enemy. At length, General Hull, to get rid of the importunities of his field officers, issued orders for the army to prepare to invade the enemy's country. The morning of the 12th of July was fixed upon for the purpose. Boats were prepared, and rowed up the river with muffled oars, to opposite the lower end of Hog Island, about two miles above the city of Detroit. McArthur, during this busy night of preparation, had marched his regiment down the river to a place called Spring Wells, three miles below the city, and had floated down the river some old boats to the same place, and appeared to be making every demonstration of crossing the river Detroit at this place. This maneuver was only a feint, to draw the attention of the enemy to defend a point where no attack was meditated. There was considerable marching and counter-marching kept up till near day, when a few men were left at Spring Well, to keep up a noise, while McArthur silently drew off his regiment, and marched up in rear of Detroit, to opposite the lower end of Hog Island, where he joined the main body of the army. Here a sufficient number of boats were provided, in which to convey two regiments of troops at a time. To Colonels Cass and Miller was confided the honor of leading the van. The men composing the regiments were seated in the boats; and as soon as it was light enough to distinguish objects at a distance, General Hull gave the word to shove off with the boats for the Canada shore. The boats were crowded with soldiers, the oars were double manned, and moved off in a line, and kept their front well dressed: not a word was spoken by the soldiers in the boats, nor by those on land; every eye was strained towards the Canadian shore. The river is a mile broad at this place: it took a good while to row the heavy loaded boats across. The anxiety and intense feeling which pervaded that part of the army on shore, as well as the citizens of Detroit, who were viewing the scene, was painful in the highest degree. When they had got about half way across the river, two men in British uniform came riding up the river at full speed. The question of interest was, were they backed by soldiers, to attack our companions, when they would reach the shore. The boats went on in good order, keeping abreast of each other, and went ahead in the most profound silence. As they had neared the shore, the two British horsemen galloped down the river. The boats having kept their line well dressed, they nearly all made the shore at the same time. The moment the boats touched land, Colonels Cass and Miller were the first to leap on shore. Their men followed, and rushing up the bank of the river, formed in line without any resistance. Now was raised a tremendous shout. The boats returned with all possible expedition, and one regiment after another crossed the river in quick succession. In a few hours the main army was safely landed on the Canadian shore. The maneuver played by Mc-Arthur the previous night, about Spring Well, had drawn the attention of the enemy, to guard against an invasion from that quarter; and as there was but a small number of the enemy at the place, as soon as they knew our army had landed above them, they retreated to Malden.

The army marched down the river, opposite the city of Detroit, and less than a mile above the village of Sandwich; and commenced making a regular encampment. The baggage, tents, ammunition, and provisions, were brought across the river the same evening, and the army now appeared to be perfectly at home in the enemy's country. So much can ambitious, energetic spirits, accomplish in a short time, when their whole souls are fixed on any particular enterprise.

The army having safely landed without opposition, Upper Canada appeared to have fallen without a blow. The northern army, under the command of General Dearborn, it was understood, would simultaneously invade Canada from Black Rock, and so divide the force and attention of the British general, that he would be unable to send any efficient aid to his forces in the neighborhood of Malden. Our troops were too sanguine: they were entire strangers to the manner of carrying on war with a people, as full of resources as was the British nation. In General Hull's army, there were few who had ever smelled the smoke of enemies' powder; and the few who had seen any thing like war, were those frontier men who had been engaged in the old Indian wars. An Indian campaign was like a horse race—it was soon ended. As neither the Indians nor whites of that day had stores, or resources, except such as were carried with them in their armies, neither could remain long in the field. A battle must be immediately fought, or their armies must disband for want of subsistence.

As soon as the army were camped near Sandwich, there was then no material obstruction in the way to Malden; and Colonels McArthur and Cass urged an immediate attack on Malden, which was only eighteen miles distant. General Hull represented an attack on a fortified place, without artillery, as an act of rashness, for which he would not be responsible; that the army would be in danger of meeting a repulse, which might damp the ardor of the troops, and thus essentially injure the service.

General Hull had previously employed some confidential men, who were friendly to the United States and residents of Canada, to pass through the country around lake St. Clair, and up the river Thames, and down lake Erie as far as Long Point. From the report of these men, he had learned, that the enemy had considerable military stores collected on the Thames; and as Colonel McArthur appeared to be the most restive and uneasy in a state of inaction, General Hull concluded to find him some employment, and ordered him, with a detachment, to proceed up lake St. Clair and the river Thames, to seize, if possible, the stores which the enemy had collected at that place.

Being now in the enemy's country, some circumspection was to be used, that the object of the expedition should be crowned with success. The country through which his detachment had to pass, along lake St. Clair and up the Thames, was filled up with a dense population; and to effect his object secrecy and dispatch were indispensable in his movements. He left General Hull's camp a little after night set in, with Major Denny's battalion of infantry and a few horsemen, and made a rapid march up the river Detroit, and up lake St. Clair. At morning light he was more than twenty miles on his way. As delay would enable the enemy to conceal, or move the stores out of his reach, no time was lost on the march.

In passing up what is there called the king's highway, an incident occurred which caused a short halt. A deep, narrow stream runs into lake St. Clair, over which creek is constructed a good frame bridge, and near this bridge was an Indian trading establishment. Here were some British Indians, who, a few minutes before McArthur's detachment arrived at the place, had, by some means been apprised of his advance, and immediately got into their canoes, and pushed up the creek. As soon as McArthur was informed of their movement, he took with him some horsemen, and pursued the Indians up the creek, at full speed. The low ground along the creek was a prairie. This open ground afforded the Indians an opportunity of seeing their pursuers at a distance. When they discovered themselves pursued, they landed their canoes, and took to flight on foot, and made for the thick brush; and were soon out of danger from horsemen. Search was made for them, but all in vain. " The birds had flown." As they were about giving up the pursuit, they found, in the thick top of a fallen tree, concealed, an Indian woman and two papooses, the one about two years old, the other about four or five. These poor creatures were almost frightened to death: they were the most perfect representations of despair I ever witnessed. They were conveyed back to their canoes, and thence down the creek to the bridge: here they were set at liberty. This Indian woman appeared to be about twenty-five years of age, with a full formed and interesting person. She expected that herself and her little ones would be instantly put to death. When she found herself undeceived, and that she and her little papooses were treated with kindness, I never witnessed such a transformation in the countenance of a human being. From a fixed state of gloomy, sullen desperation, her countenance brightened with gratitude, and in an instant she was transformed into a lovely and interesting female. This little incident detained the detachment probably an hour.

The march was resumed with fresh vigor, and late in the evening they arrived at what was called the Dolson settlement on the river Thames. The detachment had marched one night and day without taking any repose. So rapid had been the march, that no tidings of their

approach had reached his majesty's loyal subjects on
the Thames. The detachment were considerably wearied by the hard march and want of sleep, and camped
this night around the house of a Mr. Dolson ; this Dolson was a man of wealth ; the moment he saw the detachment, he fled to the woods. After the camp was
formed, and sentinels stationed, Mrs. Dolson invited the
officers to take supper with her ; the invitation was cheerfully accepted. McArthur inquired for her husband, she
replied "that her husband was not very distant; but
that he did not feel himself quite safe at home, on the present evening, and had stepped out of the way." Mc-
Arthur assured her, that the Americans only made war
on soldiers with arms in their hands, that neither private
citizens nor private property would be disturbed ; that if
her husband was within reach he would like to see him
at the head of the table. Upon this assurance, and the
privilege of passing the watchful sentinels, Mrs. Dolson
sent a messenger, and in a little time Mr. Dolson came
in and presided at the table. The evening passed off in
as social glee, as if war had never been heard of.

By the dawn of day, McArthur had his detachment in
motion, and proceeded rapidly to Col. McGregor's mills,
the place of his destination. This Col. McGregor was
a man of large property, a member of the Canadian parliament. His mills and warehouses were on an extensive scale. In his warehouse was found upwards of
three hundred barrels of flour, branded " for his majesty's
service ;" there was also found a number of bales of
merchandize, marked for the " Indian department :"
several keel boats were lying near the mills to convey
the flour and merchandize to such places, as they might
be most needed.

McArthur took possession of the property, and passed
receipts to Col. McGregor for these stores, that Col.
McGregor should be able to show his majesty how they

had been disposed of; and then stowed them into the keel boats which were before prepared for that purpose. As soon as the boats were loaded, Major Denny was placed in charge of them, and proceeded down the Thames with the booty. As Col. McGregor was a member of the Canadian parliament, McArthur made a prisoner of him, but permitted him to go on parole. The few horsemen who accompanied the expedition were divided into two squads; one squad went in advance of the boats, to reconnoiter lest some ambuscade might be planned to intercept their return; the other squad remained in the rear of the boats lest they might be pursued and surprised; they moved on rapidly till they arrived in Lake St. Clair, at the mouth of the Thames. Here McArthur in person took command of the boats, and went down Lake St. Clair with them to Detroit; whilst Major Denny took charge of the horsemen and made a rapid move for General Hull's camp. No accident or loss happened during this excursion of upwards of sixty miles into the enemy's country. This expedition was performed in three days and nights; and shows the activity and perseverance of the commander of the detachment. The flour lent by his majesty on this occasion was a very seasonable supply, as the store in our army was not abundant.

Whilst Col. McArthur was on the expedition up the Thames, General Hull was using every effort in his power to cause the artillery to be prepared for effective use. Two large floating batteries were constructed, on which to carry the large thirty pounders, to drive the enemy's brig, the Queen Charlotte, from her anchorage above Malden, and to aid in battering down the walls of Malden.

On the same evening that Col. McArthur returned to the camp with his detachment, in his absence General Hull had ordered Col. Cass with his regiment down the

Gen. Cass.

river Detroit, to the neighborhood of Malden to make observations. Col. Cass had proceeded down nearly to the
mouth of the river Auxcanard, which is very deep and
narrow, over which was constructed a good frame bridge;
near the bridge lay a detachment of the enemy, for the
purpose of preventing our troops from crossing. By his
reconnoitering parties, Col. Cass was advised of the probable number and situation of the enemy at this place.
There was a ford on this river, about three miles above
the bridge; he concluded that if he could cross the
country and pass the river at this shallow ford unperceived, that he could come down the river on the Malden side, and take or destroy the party of the enemy,
who were guarding the bridge. His plan was well laid,
and as promptly executed, but without the success which
was anticipated. Military affairs sometimes appear to
be the sport of chance : a few minutes of time, sooner or
later in occupying a particular point decides favorably,
or frustrates the best laid plans. Col. Cass crossed the
river, and got within about half a mile of the enemy before
he was discovered. Some of their reconnoitering parties
had espied him, and gave the alarm. The enemy retreated rapidly, and Cass pursued, keeping up a
scattering and distant fire, which did but little injury.
The enemy retreated under the walls of Malden, and
Cass pursued them till he was within range of their
cannon ; he then retired, and returned to camp without
being pursued or disturbed on his march. In this skirmish several lives were lost on both sides.

The British commander believed that Col. Cass commanded the advance of Gen. Hull's army, and under this
impression, he began to prepare himself to endure a siege.
He concluded the retreat of Cass only a feint to draw out
the garrison ; under this belief he permitted a handful of
men to depart unmolested. Cass and McArthur returned to
camp about the same time. McArthur's success added to

the resources of the army ; Cass obtained a personal knowledge of the difficulties to be encountered on their future
march to Malden.

The artillery were at length in a state of preparation
for effective use, and the long-looked for time to make a
descent on Malden, appeared to be fast approaching.
Troops were kept constantly on the road between Sandwich and Malden ; several unimportant skirmishes took
place on and near this road. The enemy constantly kept a
guard at the Auxcanard bridge ; and any of our small parties
who had a relish for a fight, knew where they could be ac-
commodated. If they went to the bridge, they were sure
of meeting some of the red coats, or Tecumseh with his
Indians.   Here Col. Findlay had a bout, in which he
took and lost some lives.   Here, Captain Snelling of the
fourth infantry had some practice.   Here, McArthur had
a flurry with the Indians, in which he had several men
wounded and his horse shot in the top of the forehead ;
the horse reeled but was not materially injured.   Here,
too, the brave Major Denny had a severe brush with the
Indians, in which he lost seven or eight men killed, one
taken prisoner, and several wounded.   The prairies and
woods in the neighborhood of the bridge were the theater
of considerable maneuvers, where the raw soldiers were
drilled and practised to the sharp whistle of the enemy's
balls.

On the seventh of August, General Hull issued orders
for the troops to be in readiness to march for Malden the
next morning.   The artillerists had their guns prepared,
the heavy thirty-two pounders were placed on the floating batteries.   The infantry scoured and oiled their fire-
arms ; the horsemen sharpened and oiled their swords,
that they might be easily drawn from their scabbards.
Every officer and private appeared as anxious for the
combat, as ever bride or bridegroom were for the wedding
night.

The long-looked for morning came, the word for marching was given by the General, not upon Malden, but to retrace our steps to the American side of the river Detroit. Surprise and amazement shrouded every face in sullen gloom and disappointment! Was it caprice, or cowardice, or was it treason in the General, which so suddenly and unexpectedly changed the destination of the army? Mystery appeared to hang over the movement! No explanation for the retrograde movement of the army was given. Major Denny of McArthur's regiment, was left on the Canadian shore in charge of our old camp; and before night, the main army was stationed in the forts, and on the commons of the city of Detroit.

By this sudden, retrograde movement of the army, General Hull lost the army's confidence; a kind of gloomy suspicion of the General's patriotism was openly expressed, by officers and privates. No council of officers was called before this hasty retreat was made: the army was completely at fault, no reason having been assigned for this mysterious movement.

It is believed, when General Hull first invaded Canada, that if he had gone down (it was only eighteen miles distant) and paraded his army before Malden, that the garrison would have surrendered without an effort at defence. This might have been the case, but it might not. Had his troops been repulsed with loss of men, the world would have reprobated his rashness in attempting to take a fortified garrison without artillery. The delay necessary to repair the gun carriages was a misfortune for which he was not responsible. For this delay the then administrators of government were culpable; at least the secretary of war, who was acquainted with the views of the administration, should have caused the artillery, at the most exposed frontier post, to be in a state of such repair as to be fit for immediate use.

It is necessary now that the cause of General Hull's

9

retreat from Canada should be given. On the seventh
of August, he received some letters sent by express, by
General Hall and General P. B. Porter, who commanded the American troops on the Niagara frontier, informing him that a large British force from the neighborhood
of Niagara were preparing to move up Lake Erie to
Malden. In addition to this startling intelligence, as
previously stated, General Hull had employed some
Canadians, in whom he had the utmost confidence, to
travel through Canada, to observe the motions of the
enemy, and give him intelligence of their movements.
On the night preceding the contemplated attack on fort
Malden, a Mr. Watson, one of his confidential Canadian
spies, arrived in camp, and assured General Hull, that
the British General Brock was at fort Erie collecting all
his disposable force, and placing them on board ships and
boats destined for Malden. That as soon as he (Watson)
learned the destination of General Brock, he mounted
his horse, and came with the utmost speed to acquaint
General Hull with the reinforcements with which Malden would be strengthened. The letters from Generals
Hall and Porter, and the communication made by Mr.
Watson, all came upon General Hull simultaneously,
alarmed him, and were the cause of his retreat from
Canada. That the intelligence received by General Hull
was correct, is proved by the fact, that General Brock
arrived at Malden in a day or two after, with six hundred regular troops. To understand this movement of
the British army, we must turn our attention to the conduct of General Dearborn, who then commanded the
American armies on the northern frontier; that on the
Niagara, down Lake Ontario, and on the St. Lawrence.
General Sir George Prevost was the commander in chief
of the enemy's armies. The English government had
repealed their " orders in council," which " orders" were
one of the prominent causes of the war. On the repeal

of these "orders in council," General Prevost made application to General Dearborn for a cessation of arms, thinking it probable that a repeal of those vexatious "orders in council" would pave the way to a restoration of peace. General Dearborn, without reflecting on its consequence, in an unguarded moment, agreed to a cessation of arms on the whole length of his line of command, for forty days, commencing on the first day of August, 1812. As soon as a copy of the arrangement for this armistice reached the city of Washington, it was obvious that General Dearborn had been overreached by his antagonist. As General Hull's field of operation was not included in the armistice, the British General would now have an opportunity of concentrating all his forces, and overwhelm General Hull's army during the continuance of the armistice.

The secretary of war "promptly informed General Dearborn that the arrangement was disapprobated by the President of the United States, and peremptorily ordered to put an end to it as speedily as possible." The armistice was broken off on the twenty-ninth day of August, but not before the British General had effected the destruction of General Hull. Of all the military blunders during the late war, that produced the most fatal consequences. It was the primary cause of the capitulation of the garrison of Detroit; General Hull's surrender was the cause of preparing the way for those scenes of savage butcheries and miseries, that were perpetrated in Michigan and on the frontiers of Ohio, which clothed Kentucky and Ohio in mourning.

Had it not been for that fatal armistice, the American troops from the lower end of Lake Erie, would have invaded Canada at the same time that General Hull was preparing to attack Fort Malden, and thus would have kept the British General Brock in play on the Niagara frontier; and General Hull would doubtless have taken Malden; the Indians would then have been quiet, and the upper lakes, for a time at least, would scarcely have heard the alarms of war.

CHAPTER VII.

About the time General Brock was concentrating his forces at Malden, Captain Henry Brush, of Ohio, with a company of volunteers, consisting of about a hundred and fifty men, raised in the town of Chillicothe and its vicinity, arrived at the river Raisin, thirty-six miles south of Detroit, escorting a large supply of provision for our army. General Brock received intelligence of the approach of Captain Brush, and as this escort would necessarily have to pass Brownstown, which is opposite to Malden, and only four miles from thence, he determined to intercept Captain Brush's convoy. General Brock placed his Indians, and a few regular troops to give the Indians confidence, at Brownstown, to watch the motions of Captain Brush, and to cut off the communication from Ohio with Hull's army.

Captain Brush was a lawyer of distinguished eminence, a man of talents, and a vigilant officer. He was advised of the trap laid by the enemy, to intercept him on his way to the army; and sent an express rider through the woods to General Hull, to advise him of his critical situation. General Hull sent Major Vanhorn, with a battalion of troops, to meet Captain Brush, and to escort the convoy of provisions to Detroit. The British and Indians met Major Vanhorn's detachment at Brownstown, a battle ensued, and Vanhorn was defeated with considerable loss. This has been called the battle of Brownstown.

As provision was running short at Detroit, and as

Captain Brush had a considerable quantity with him, General Hull determined to make another effort to aid his advance. For this purpose, he sent Colonel Miller with the fourth regiment of United States infantry, and Major Vanhorn with his battalion of volunteers, to bring in Captain Brush's convoy of provision. When this detachment had marched to an old Indian town, called Maguagua, three miles above Brownstown, they were met by a numerous party of British and Indians. A severe and stubborn battle ensued: the enemy were defeated. Colonel Miller, with the energy and promptitude which distinguished him in numerous battles since, drove the red coats and yellow jackets from their coverts with the bayonet. The loss of the enemy in this obstinate affair was very considerable; nor was the victory cheaply gained. We had a number of men killed, and about eighty wounded: nearly one-fourth in all. Colonel Miller camped on the field of battle. He sent an express to General Hull, with the intelligence of his victory, and the loss he had sustained in the battle. The express from Colonel Miller arrived in Detroit some time before midnight. General Hull ordered Colonel McArthur to take two hundred of his regiment, and proceed forthwith to Colonel Miller's camp, and bring up the wounded to head quarters. Colonel McArthur procured some boats, in which he went down himself, and as many of his men as could procure horses went down by land. Some time after midnight, the detachment set off for Miller's camp. The night was dark and stormy, the rain fell in torrents, the thunder rolled in long vibrations along the broad river Detroit; but the poor soldier had no choice: he had voluntarily placed himself as the sentinel and guard of his country; he must endure the storms of the elements, as well as repel the storms of the enemy. The detachment arrived at Colonel Miller's camp some time after daylight, a distance of fifteen miles. About this

time it ceased raining. Arrangements were soon made
to place the wounded in the boats, in order for their removal to head quarters. Colonel McArthur sent two
companies in advance of the boats, to keep a look out,
lest the enemy should lay in ambush along the shore;
whilst he in person directed the movements of the boats,
to encourage the boatmen and soldiers to propel them up
the heavy current, with all possible dispatch. The
Gros Isle, which is eight miles long, is situated betwixt Colonel Miller's camp and Malden; the main
channel for large vessels is to the Malden side of the
island, Miller's camp is opposite the middle of the island,
and Malden nearly opposite the lower end. That part
of the river which runs between Miller's camp and the
island is about four hundred yards over. On this busy
day the British and Indians were seen running up and
down the island, watching the motions of our troops on
the main land. From the other side of the island, they
could communicate by signals to their friends in Malden
the movements of our troops.

McArthur was making all the head way he could with
his squadron of boats along the shore. The enemy's
brig Hunter, well manned, was discovered sailing up the
river with a fair breeze, to intercept our boats, as soon
as they should pass the upper point of the island. The
boats being crowded with the wounded, to attempt passing the enemy's ship, which was mounted with twelve
guns of six and nine pounders, would have been mad-
ness. The Hunter came round the point of the island,
within two hundred and fifty yards of the American
shore, and dropped anchor with her broadside facing the
shore. McArthur was now placed in an unexpected
dilemma; to pass the enemy's ship in safety was impossible; he had no wagons or other carriages in which
to convey the wounded to Detroit; he landed his boats
and sent an express to Colonel Miller with the intelli-

gence of his critical situation.   Col. Miller had three
wagons and two carts with his detachment, which were
sent to McArthur, and into these, the wounded were
literally stowed away, and the escort commenced its
march. When they came opposite to where the enemy's
ship rode at anchor, the road passed immediately on the
bank of the river, in full view of the enemy. A marshy
quagmire from the land side reached nearly to the river
edge, so that it was impossible to go with the wagons
through the marsh, and no other alternative presented itself than to drive the teams at full speed past the ship.
The distance on the road, on which the wagons would
be exposed to the enemy's broadside, was a little over a
hundred yards, after that distance, the wagons would be
covered by thick woods. When the first team was
driven near this exposed piece of road, the driver halted,
and refused to drive the team where he knew he would
be exposed to the fire of the enemy's broadside. A Mr.
Robert Smith, from the neighborhood of Chillicothe,
came up, and swore he would drive the team through,
if the enemy should send at him a storm of thunder and
lightning. He mounted the saddle-horse, and with his
whip fretted the team, and then at full speed set off to
pass the enemy. As soon as Smith was in the open
ground, as was expected, the enemy fired a broadside at
the wagon. The wind was blowing a moderate gale,
this caused the ship to rock with the waves, so that their
aim was uncertain. The wagons and carts were all passed at full speed, at every one of which was fired a
broadside, from which no injury was received. This
rapid drive of the wagons and carts, there is no doubt,
was the ultimate cause of the death of several of the
wounded. When the teams were running at full speed,
and when the wagon wheels would come in contact with
a stump, a root, or a stone, the jar would throw the
wounded soldiers, in heaps upon each other ; in this way

the bandages would come loose, and the broken bones be torn from their places, and their wounds bleed afresh ; by the time the carriages had passed, the road was made slippery with the blood of the poor wounded soldiers. After passing this place, Colonel McArthur proceeded without meeting any further difficulties till he arrived at Detroit, where the wounded where placed in hospitals under the care of the surgeons.   The next day, Colonel Miller returned to head quarters without having effected the object of his expedition, which was to meet Captain Brush's detachment, and escort the military stores to head quarters.

Dangers were now thickening around Gen. Hull and his troops, and to add to his other perplexities provisions were growing short with the army.   It was understood that Captain Brush, with his detachment and military stores, still remained at the river Raisin, only thirty-six miles distant on the direct road.   Gen. Hull determined to make another effort to bring forward Captain Brush and the stores he had with him.   For this purpose, he detached Colonels McArthur and Cass with five hundred men, with instructions to proceed in a southwest direction, on a path which leads from Detroit to Fort Wayne, so far that an east course would make the settlement of the river Raisin : by taking this circuitous direction they would shun the dangerous, though direct, road passing through Brown's Town ; but the distance to the river Raisin, where Captain Brush lay would be greatly increased.   Guides who were well acquainted with the country were procured to pilot the march of the detachment, which on Friday the 14th of August set off on this secret expedition.   As the detachment were on foot, they went forward without baggage or provision, Gen. Hull having assured them that he would send provisions on pack-horses after them.   The provisions were sent, but the packers lost their way, and did not find the detachment. McArthur went on till Saturday afternoon, the 15th of August, when he was overtaken by an express rider from head quarters, with instructions to return to Detroit with all possible expedition. He was informed that Gen. Brock had come up from Malden, and camped in the vicinity of Sandwich, immediately opposite to Detroit, and had demanded the surrender of the American army. This news was unexpected, painful and alarming. McArthur with that promptness which marked his character through life, commenced retracing his steps for Detroit. This was in the evening of Saturday, he was now more than thirty miles from head quarters, his detachment had been two days without subsistence. The path on which they had to march was narrow, muddy, and full of logs and brush ; the soldiers were nearly exhausted by hunger and fatigue. The startling intelligence that Detroit, the head quarters of the army, was in danger of falling into the hands of the enemy in their absence added spurs to their march, they went on without a murmur as long as they could see the path ; at length they were halted, and supperless lay down to rest their weary limbs. Here they rested till the moon rose, which was some time before day-light, when they resumed their toilsome and feeble march. This was Sunday morning, August the 16th, and the third day they were without subsistence. About sunrise they had got within ten miles of Detroit ; they began to hear the roar of cannon ; the sound of the artillery was distinctly heard rolling up the river Rouge ; there was no doubt but that the two armies were engaged in deadly strife. Our faithful soldiers pressed steadily forward till they came within about four miles of Detroit. The fire of artillery had ceased for some time. Here they discovered a Canadian Frenchman running through a prairie. Col. McArthur sent some horsemen in pursuit, who overtook and brought in the fugitive. This man was a

Canadian who had joined our army, and who was now fleeing to bush to save his neck from the halter. He informed Col. McArthur, that Gen. Hull had surrendered the town, fort, and army to the enemy: that just as he had left the city, the English were marching into the fort; that when he saw this, he knew that it was time for him to take to the woods to save his life. McArthur did not know whether to place confidence in the Frenchman's story or not. He continued his march on what was called the back road, and dispatched some horsemen to go in the rear of Detroit to make observations. These men returned with the assurance that the British colors were waving over the fort. Col. McArthur and his detachment were now placed in a most critical situation; the enemy in front and famine in the rear. This was the third day they had been without subsistence, and all the time engaged in forced marches; such are the distresses, hardships, and privations common in a sol dier's life. Not a murmur nor complaint was uttered during this painful and perplexing scene. Here were five hundred of the choice spirits from the Scioto and Muskingum valleys, commanded by their favorite officers. McArthur now ordered a retreat. After they had marched about two miles, a large ox was discovered feeding by the road side. Notwithstanding the critical and perplexing situation of the detachment, a halt was made to satisfy our pinching hunger. The ox was considered a " God-send," he was shot, and fires were prepared in a shorter time than ever before witnessed. The ox was slaughtered in less time than any professed butchers could have done the deed.

Whilst they were roasting their meat, two men on horseback, dressed in British uniform, and two Indians, were discovered with a white flag approaching us. The white men were Major Chambers and Captain Elliot, both of the British army, accompanied by two Indian chiefs ; they carried with them the articles of capitulation of the American army by Gen. Hull. The bearers of the flag were placed under guard ; Col. McArthur called all the commissioned officers together to consult about the propriety of embracing, or rejecting the proffered terms of the capitulation. After the most mature deliberation, it was concluded, that the chance of effecting our retreat to Fort Wayne, which was the nearest place that supplies could be obtained, was too desperate to be effected by men already nearly exhausted with fatigue and famine : the proffered terms of the capitulation were acceded to, and the detachment forthwith marched into the city of Detroit, grounded their arms, and were prisoners of war. We were treated with kindness by the enemy. The terms of the capitulation were scrupulously complied with by the British general. The regular troops, with Gen. Hull at their head, were sent to Quebec. The volunteers and militia were soon on their way to their respective homes ; where they safely arrived among their friends and relatives without any thing occurring worth relating.

Thus was closed the disastrous expedition under the command of General Hull. I am aware that it is fashionable to call General Hull a traitor ; and perhaps I may risk my character for patriotism, for doubting the allegation. Gen. Hull was surrounded with difficulties, which were not at the time sufficiently estimated. A wilderness of nearly two hundred miles in his rear ; add to this, the enemy had the undisputed command of the lakes ; they could convey their troops and military supplies by water to any point on which they wished to act, their men could step out of their ships fresh for action. This gave the British General a decided advantage. Numerous were the difficulties which General Hull had to encounter during the last eight days previous to the capitulation. The first, in importance, was the fatal armistice, by

which General Dearborn was overreached by Sir George
Prevost, the British commander; which afforded the
enemy an opportunity of concentrating all their troops
on the lower lake, as well as on lake Erie, to act against
General Hull. About this time, Captain Henry Brush
arrived at the river Raisin, with about one hundred and
fifty men, and a considerable quantity of military stores.
The river Raisin is about thirty-six miles south of Detroit; and fort Malden, the head-quarters of the enemy,
about half way betwixt Detroit and the river Raisin: of
course, Captain Brush, to go to Detroit, would have to
pass near Malden. Between the eighth and sixteenth of
August, two battles were fought, with a view of aiding
Captain Brush forward. The first at Brownstown,
where Major Vanhorn was defeated. The second at
Maguagou, where Colonel Miller defeated the enemy,
but with the loss of nearly one fourth of his men killed
and wounded. Such was his loss of men, that he was
compelled to return to head-quarters without effecting the
object of the expedition. General Hull, by express carriers, who passed through the woods, kept up a corre-
spondence with Captain Brush. As Brush commanded
a volunteer company of the *elite* citizens of Chillicothe
and its vicinity, Colonel McArthur, being their neighbor,
felt more than the usual interest to get them forward;
and as two previous expeditions had failed to effect that
object, Colonels McArthur and Cass, with five hundred
men, were detached to escort Captain Brush and the
military stores from the river Raisin. It will be recollected, that General Hull's army consisted of only
eighteen hundred men, exclusive of the citizens of Detroit. He had lost many of these in battle, more were
disabled by wounds, and more still by disease: McArthur and Cass absent, with five hundred effective men,
when the British general assailed him. Under all these
untoward circumstances, something like despondency

might show itself in a mind more vigorous than General Hull possessed, without any traitorous design. Had General Hull been advised that Colonels McArthur and Cass were within five or six miles when he capitulated, he should have been shot; but this was impossible for him to know.

How much of what appears to be accident, has a powerful influence in fixing the character and destiny of man. Had Colonels McArthur and Cass arrived at Detroit only three short hours sooner, no capitulation would have taken place; a battle would have been fought, and, in all probability, General Hull's head would have been covered with laurels of victory.

It was thought strange at the time, that the British general permitted Captain Brush to linger quietly for eight or ten days, within eighteen miles of Malden, when he could have sailed in two hours within a mile of Brush's camp, and thus with an overwhelming force have crushed him at a blow. General Brock displayed considerable generalship in not crushing Captain Brush, nor frightening him off. Captain Brush's long presence at the river Raisin, kept General Hull continually maneuvering to relieve him. General Brock kept a strong force at Brownstown, through which place he knew Brush must pass to go to Detroit. Had General Brock crushed Brush, or driven him off, Colonels McArthur and Cass, with their five hundred men would have been in Detroit at General Brock's approach, and would, I have no doubt, have defeated him. Such is the uncertainty of war, that a few hours sooner or later in occupying a particular point, changes the destiny of an army, and the character of its commander. The gross negligence and imbecility of the war department, in neglecting to have the artillery in repair at the most exposed frontier post, was culpable in the highest degree. Had the artillery been fit for use when the army arrived at Detroit, there is not a doubt General Hull would have taken Malden. But could he have retained its possession, with his small force divided for the protection of Detroit as well as Malden, had he possessed the cautious intrepidity of General Brown, or the fiery, impetuous spirit of General Jackson? every military man will answer " No." The enemy having the undisputed control of the lakes, this combined with the advantage of the armistice, would have afforded the British general an opportunity of concentrating his forces, without resistance from any other quarter, to act against either post, and so have beaten him in detail. General Hull's proper course was, to have retreated to Ohio. True, he would have been censured as a pusillanimous wretch; but he would have saved his army, and time, which unfolds dark things, would have retrieved his character. He had not sufficient courage to endure the ignominy attached to a retreat, nor the firmness to meet the enemy in the field under disadvantageous circumstances. He stood wavering and irresolute, till he lost the confidence of his soldiers: while dangers were crowding around him, he lost the proper time for action, and thus fell a sacrifice to his irresolution.

CHAPTER VIII.

GENERAL McArthur returned to his residence on Fruit Hill, near Chillicothe. He was now a prisoner of war on parole, not to serve in the army against the enemy, till regularly exchanged. It did not comport with his ambitious, enterprising genius, to be an idle spectator in such stirring times, when the very existence of his country's civil institutions was at stake. Although the expedition under the command of General Hull had been most disastrous, none of the disgrace was attached to him. His courage, and active perseverance in every situation in which he had been placed during the expedition, increased his popularity with the army, with the administration, and with his fellow citizens generally.

Although he could not serve in the army, he was eligible to serve his country in a civil capacity. In the fall of this year (1812), the democratic or war party brought him out a candidate for a seat in the House of Representatives of Congress ; and he was elected by an overwhelming majority. This was direct evidence, that although he was second in command on the unfortunate expedition with General Hull, none of the stigma of that disastrous affair was attached to him.

The session of 1812–13, Congress passed a law to employ a large additional number of regular troops ; and although McArthur was still a prisoner of war, not being exchanged, the President of the United States nominated him Colonel to the twenty-sixth Regiment of United States Infantry, and the Senate confirmed the appointment. On the 20th day of February, 1813, his commission was dated, and immediately forwarded to him. He accepted the appointment. He was authorised by the President of the United States, to appoint the company officers of his regiment. The platoon officers were soon appointed ; and immediately engaged with enthusiasm in the enlistment of soldiers for the war. He was now active in stimulating the military feelings of the citizens of the country. By his energy and perseverance, the recruiting business went forward as well as could be expected, and the ranks of his regiment were fast filling.

Although the regimental officers were appointed and commissioned, for the large addition made to the regular army of the United States, no general officers were yet appointed. On the 23d day of March, 1813, the President of the United States, by and with the advice and consent of the Senate, appointed and commissioned him a brigadier-general in the regular army. His prospects were now flattering. As a politician, he was the most popular man in the Scioto valley. Military promotions were crowding upon him; and if ambition could be satisfied, it would be supposed that McArthur, in his rapid rise to distinction, would now be happy. This was not the case. All the honors conferred upon him, he conceived only foretastes of what was laid up in store for him. When he read history, he discovered that many others, before they arrived at his age, had climbed much higher on the ladder of fame; and he could not rest satisfied with a character which only placed him in mediocrity. When Bonaparte had conquered half the world, and was acknowledged dictator to half Europe, he was as far from being satisfied as when he was an humble lieutenant of artillery. So true is it, that "man never is, but always to be, blest."

In April, 1813, General McArthur was officially informed by the war department, that the prisoners captured at the surrender of Detroit by General Hull, were exchanged. He was again free to act in the army. He then resigned his seat in the House of Representatives of the Congress of the United States; preferring the honors and dangers, and thrilling excitements of the "tented field," to the dull round of tautology in civil life. General Harrison then commanded the north-western army; and to his head-quarters McArthur repaired, with as much glee as ever young man or maiden went to a splendid ball, to riot in the pleasures of the lively dance.

The fall of Detroit into the enemy's possession, afforded them the means of controlling the movements of the north-western Indians. This advantage, together with the hitherto uncontrolled navigation of lake Erie, afforded the enemy an easy and speedy means of concenrating their whole force at any point, where they might think proper to invade our frontier. General Harrison had now a critical and responsible duty to perform. The enemy having the command of the lakes, could move from place to place without risk or danger; and if any of our advanced posts were weakly guarded, they could attack them, and fly to their shipping before their audacity could be punished. In this predatory warfare, the enemy kept our frontier settlements, from Cleveland to fort Meigs on the Maumee bay, in continual alarm; as it was impossible for General Harrison to keep a strong force at every exposed post.

About the time the enemy were preparing to make the attack on fort Stevenson, at Lower Sandusky, where the brave Major Croghan commanded, General McArthur was at Chillicothe, arranging some money matters for the supply of the army. General Harrison sent an express to General McArthur, with orders to hurry on to the scene of action, and bring with him all the militia he could; as the enemy, both white and red, were collecting in force, and were hovering on the coast of lake Erie, and were preparing to strike a fatal blow at some of the exposed posts. McArthur had not resigned his office of major-general of Ohio militia; and as time would be lost in making a regular draft on the militia, he ordered the second division of militia to march in mass. This march of the militia was named the "general call." As soon as Governor Meigs was advised of the call made by General McArthur, he went forward and assumed in person the command of the militia now under arms. General McArthur went forward to the scene of action, and the militia followed in thousands. So promptly were his orders obeyed, that in a few days the Sandusky plains were covered with nearly eight thousand men, mostly from the Scioto valley. This rush of militia to defend the exposed frontier of our country, bore honorable

10

testimony that the patriotism of the citizens of the Scioto valley did not consist of noisy professions, but of practical service in defense of their country. This general turn-out of the militia, proves that General Massie, and the few pioneers who followed him into the wilderness, and assisted him in making the first settlements in the fertile valley of the Scioto river, had infused their own daring and enterprising spirit into the mass of the community. Among these eight thousand militia, were found in the ranks, as private soldiers, judges, merchants, lawyers, preachers, doctors, mechanics, farmers, and laborers of every description; all anxious to repulse the ruthless invaders of our soil. Indeed, the Scioto country was so stripped of its male population on this occasion, that the women, in their absence, were compelled to carry their grain to mill, or let their children suffer for want. The wife of the author of this narrative went to mill several times, sitting on her bag of wheat, during his absence; and he trusts she would do it again, if the same exigency should take place.

At the time this host of militia arrived in the Sandusky plains, General Harrison's head-quarters was at fort Seneca, nine miles from fort Stevenson. The brave Major Croghan, of Kentucky, was entrusted with the command of the latter fort, when the British general, with his mongrel host, made a violent attack on the place. The enemy were resisted by some of the best game blood of the western pioneers; and although the enemy made repeated and most desperate assaults on the place, they were repulsed at every onset, with considerable loss in killed, wounded, and many prisoners. The enemy, after receiving this severe drubbing, hauled off to their den in fort Malden.

About the same time, Governor Meigs arrived at Upper Sandusky with his thousands, and formed what was called the " grand camp of Ohio militia." During the time of these transactions, Commodore Perry, and his artificers and crews, were using every effort to prepare a fleet of ships, to contend with the enemy for the mastery on the lakes. The Kentucky volunteers, consisting of four thousand men, under the command of the venerated Governor Shelby, were shortly expected on the coast of lake Erie. General McArthur was detailed to assume the command and defense of fort Meigs. General Harrison directed Governor Meigs, to discharge all his men but two thousand. Commodore Perry at length was on the lake with his ships and crews, seeking the enemy's fleet. Governor Shelby was on his march with his four thousand volunteers, all was bustle and preparation for the invasion of Canada. These were stirring times : Kentucky and Ohio's best blood was in motion. General Harrison had now more force under his control, than was deemed necessary to accomplish the object of the expedition. Governor Meigs was directed to discharge the remaining two thousand Ohio troops under his command. This order gave great offence to the officers of Ohio militia, as they were anxious to be employed on the expedition against Canada. On the morning of the day on which they were discharged, the officers held a grand caucus, in which they passed some resolutions, disapprobating the conduct of General Harrison. They were now in ill humor, and remembered that they had suffered numerous grievances at his hands. General Harrison had given orders to the commissaries of provision, first to issue such flour as was "in a damageable state." This order was construed to mean, that General Harrison had ordered the Ohio troops to be fed on damaged flour. The true cause of this ill humor among the Ohio officers, was chagrin on account of being disappointed, in not being employed on the meditated expedition against Upper Canada. They were wrathy that the Kentuckians were to have the honor of breaking up the

Malden hornet's nest. They blamed General Harrison
for partiality in favor of the land that breeds " half horse,
half alligator, tipped off with the snapping turtle."

Commodore Perry, with his fleet, touched at the Sandusky bay; General Harrison lent him all the aid in his
power; and furnished him with as many men, to man
his ships, as could find room for action. It was now
evident, that could we force the command of the lakes, a
host would rush upon the Canada shore, that would be
irresistible. On the 10th of September, Commodore
Perry met the British fleet: a desperate conflict ensued,
but victory crowned " the star-spangled banner." The
enemy's fleet were defeated, and all captured. " This
victory removed the principal barrier to the conquest of
Malden, and the recovery of the Michigan territory, and
was the signal for active offensive operations," to recover
what had been lost under General Hull.

Commodore Perry's splendid victory gave a fresh
impetus to the army. " Immediately all was bustle and
preparation. The General began to concentrate his
forces at the mouth of the Portage river. Gov. Shelby
was on his march to join him with 4000 volunteers from
Kentucky. General McArthur had arrived at Fort
Meigs. Gen. Cass had also reached Upper Sandusky.
Col. Hill with a regiment of Pennsylvania volunteers
was advancing from Erie. In short about 7000 men
were in motion for the long-delayed invasion of Canada.
The greatest activity was visible in camp. Boats were
collected; beef jerked; bread baked, and the superfluous
baggage secured in block houses.

" On the 17th September, Gov. Shelby at the head of
4000 volunteers from Kentucky arrived at the mouth of
Portage. This formidable corps were all mounted;
but it was deemed best for them to act as infantry. In
order to secure their horses against escape, it was only
necessary to build a substantial log fence from Sandusky

(Face 134.)

Perry's Victory.

bay to Portage river, about two miles distant from each other ; this done, the horses were provided with a luxuriant natural pasture of nearly 100,000 acres. The number of horses left on the peninsula, during the absence of the army in Canada, was upwards of 5000, for the most part, of the first size and condition !

" On the 20th, Gen. McArthur's brigade, from Fort Meigs, joined the main body at Portage, after a fatiguing march of three days down the lake coast, and through a part of the immense prairie that skirts the southern shore of Lake Erie from Portage river to within a few miles of Brownstown. In this toilsome march, the guides often lost the point of direction as they were struggling with the thick and lofty grass that impeded their progress. Frequently it became necessary, to hoist a soldier until his feet rested upon the shoulders of another, before he could get a view above the top of the grass to ascertain their course.

" Col. Johnson's regiment remained at Fort Meigs, but had orders to approach Detroit by land. Such of Col. Hill's Pennsylvania detached militia as chose not to cross into Canada, were ordered to guard the British prisoners, taken by Com. Perry, to Chillicothe. The different posts on the American side of the lake were left in charge of the Ohio militia. Fort Meigs was reduced in its picketing from eight acres to one. About five hundred Kentucky volunteers remained on the peninsula to guard the horses and stores.

" Every thing being now ready, the embarkation of the troops commenced at the dawn of day, on the 21st. For the want of a sufficient number of boats not more than one third of the army could embark at once. There is a range of islands extending from the head of the peninsula, to Malden. These islands render the navigation safe, and afforded the army convenient depots for baggage and stores, as well as halting places. Put-in-bay

island, sixteen miles from Portage, was selected by the
general as the first point of rendezvous; the first stage
in his passage across the lake. The weather was favorable. As soon the first division of boats reached the
island, men were immediately detached to take back the
boats for a fresh load. Such was the eagerness of the
men to accelerate the embarkation of the whole army,
that they, in most cases, anticipated this regulation by
volunteering their services to return with the boats.
Every one courted fatigue. The fleet of Commodore
Perry was busily engaged in transporting the baggage of
the army.

"In the course of the 22d, the whole army had gained
the island, and encamped on the margin of the bay,
which forms nearly a semicircle. The Lawrence and
the six prize ships, captured from the enemy, were at
anchor in the center of the bay, and in full view. With
what delight did the troops contemplate this interesting
spectacle! The curiosity of the troops was amply in-
dulged; every one was permitted to go on board the
prizes to view the effect of the battle. The men were
highly pleased with this indulgence of the General and
the Commodore. The scene was calculated to inflame
their military ardor which was visible in every countenance.

"The army was detained in Put-in-bay during the 23d
and 24th by unfavorable winds. On the 24th, a soldier
of the regular forces was shot for desertion. He had deserted three times; had been twice before condemned to
suffer death, and as often pardoned; he met his fate
with stoical indifference, but it made a very sensible impression on the troops. Two platoons fired on him at
the distance of five paces, and perforated his body like a
sieve.

"On the 25th, the army again embarked partly in
boats and partly on board the fleet, to take a nearer

position to the Canadian shore. The flotilla arrived a little before sunset, at a small island called the *Eastern Sister,* eighteen miles from Malden and seven from the coast. This island does not contain more than three acres, and the men had scarcely room to sit down.

"On the 26th, the wind blew fresh, it became necessary to haul up the boats, to prevent their staving. The General and Commodore in the Ariel, made a reconnoissance of the enemy's coast and approached within a short distance of Malden. Capt. *Johnney** was dispatched to apprise Col. Johnson of our progress. Gen. Cass, Col. Ball, and Capt. McClelland were busy in arranging and numbering the boats. At sunset the lake had risen several feet; indeed, such was the violence of the surf that many entertained serious fears that the greater part of the island would be inundated before morning. However, the wind subsided at twelve and relieved our apprehensions.

"On the 27th, at nine in the morning, the army made its final embarkation. The day was fine, and a propitious breeze made our passage a pleasing pastime. It was a sublime and delightful spectacle to behold sixteen ships of war and one hundred boats filled with men, borne rapidly and majestically to the long-sought shores of the enemy. The recollection of this day can never be effaced from my memory. There was something truly grand and animating in the looks of the men. There was an air of confidence in every countenance. The troops panted for an opportunity to rival their naval brethren in feats of courage and skill, they seemed to envy the good fortune of our brave tars. They were ignorant of the flight of the enemy, and confidently expected a fight; indeed the belief was current among the troops that the enemy

---

* A large Shawnee Indian chief; the same that defeated the Edgingtons. See Massie's Life, page 40.

were in great force ; for it was believed that Dixon's Indians as well as Tecumseh's were at Malden.

"We landed in perfect order of battle, at 4 P. M.,
three miles below Malden. The Kentucky volunteers
formed the right wing. Ball's legion and the friendly
Indians the center ; the regulars on the left. The troops
were almost instantly in line and shortly commenced
their march, *en echellons* for Malden. The troops had
been drilled to marching in and out of the boats and to
forming on the beach. Every man knew his place ; and
so well were they masters of this very necessary piece
of service, that a company would march into a boat, de-
bark and form on the beach in less than one minute, and
that too without the least confusion.

"As we approached Malden, instead of the red coats
and war whoop of the Indians, a group of well-dressed
ladies advanced to meet us, and to implore mercy and
protection. They were met by Governor Shelby and
Col. Ball who soon quieted their fears by assuring them
that we came not to make war upon women and children
but to protect them. The army entered Malden by
several parallel streets, and we marched through the
town to the thunder of " *Yankee Doodle.*" The ruins
of the fort and the naval buildings were still smoking.
All the loyal inhabitants followed the British army in its
retreat. The fort is surrounded by a deep ditch and two
rows of heavy pickets. What cannon and small arms
they were unable to carry away were sunk in the river.
The enemy in their haste had left an eighteen pounder
in this battery. Three miles above the fort is an Indian
village which we found deserted, and so suddenly, that
many essential articles of Indian furniture, such as brass
kettles, were left in the houses. Here we procured a
plentiful supply of green corn, potatoes, &c. This village was not burnt.

"In the evening after our arrival at Malden, Col. Ball

dispatched an officer and twenty men to prevent the enemy's destroying the bridge across the Aux Canards. The enemy were found on the bridge, having just set fire to it. Our party fired on them ; they dispersed and the bridge was saved.

"On the 28th we passed, the Aux Canards, and encamped two miles beyond the river in a neat French settlement. A small party of British horse showed themselves at the bridge and then scampered off.

"The next day we reached Sandwich at two o'clock in the afternoon.* At the same time the fleet came up the river to Detroit. The General made dispositions for passing the river. Governor Shelby's corps remained at Sandwich, while Ball's legion and the brigade of Gen. McArthur passed over to Detroit. The Indians appeared in groups, on the bank of the river below Detroit; a few shots from the gun boats caused them to disperse. The Indians did not leave Detroit till the boats containing the troops were half way across the river. Just before we landed on the American side the inhabitants hoisted the United States' flag amid the acclamations of thousands. The army were received by the inhabitants with demonstrations of unfeigned joy. They had suffered all that *civilized* and savage tyranny could inflict save death. The Indians had lived at free quarters for several months. It was therefore natural for them to hail us as deliverers. The enemy had set fire to the

---

* Two miles below Sandwich, one of Governor Shelby's volunteers in the flank guard discovered an Indian at the distance of two hundred yards, in the act of leveling his rifle at our men ; he instantly left the ranks, made for the Indian and received his fire ; the Indian retreated, but was closely pursued by the volunteer, who soon gained on his foe ; he fired and brought him to the ground; but the Indian had previously reloaded his piece, and in his turn fired on the volunteer, who received the contents in his leg ; he was at this time half a mile from his comrades, but did not retreat till he had dispatched the wounded Indian, and secured his scalp, which he bore in triumph to his company.

buildings within the fort, but the walls and picketing remained entire. The public store, a long brick building near the wharf was injured only in the roof, which our men soon repaired. In the course of the night there was an alarm in camp, the fires were extinguished, and the men ordered to lie on their arms.

" On the 30th Col. Johnson's regiment arrived from Fort Meigs : they immediately commenced the passage of the river in boats;* Gen. McArthur with the greater part of the regular troops was charged with the defence of Detroit. It was the general opinion of the inhabitants that there were a thousand Indian warriors, under Marpot and Split Log, lurking in the woods between the river Rouge and Huron of lake St. Clair. The friendly Indians took several prisoners in the immediate vicinity of Detroit, in less than two hours after we landed.

CHAPTER IX.

" On the 2d of October every arrangement was completed for pursuing the retreating British army up the Thames. The force selected for this service were the mounted regiment of Col. Johnson, three companies of Col. Ball's legion and the principal part of Gov. Shelby's volunteers.

" From Sandwich to the Moravian towns is eighty-

---

* The entrance of the mounted regiment into Detroit presented a fine military spectacle. At 2 P. M. the advance of the column began to emerge from Belle Fontaine, and were visible at the distance of two miles from the town. The width and shortness of the road gave the military and citizens a full view of its approach. Both sides of the street for a considerable distance were lined with spectators. Suddenly our ears caught the thunder of 1100 horse in full motion. The whole regiment was rapidly approaching; and in a moment it was in the midst of us upon full speed and in admirable order.

four miles. We found the roads for the most part good.
The country is perfectly level. The advance of the
troops was rapid ; so much so, that we reached the river
Riscum, twenty-five miles from Sandwich, in the evening. The enemy had neglected to destroy the bridge.
Early in the morning of the 3d, the General proceeded
with Johnson's regiment, to prevent the destruction of
the bridges over the different streams that fall into Lake
St. Clair and the Thames. These streams are deep and
muddy and are unfordable for a considerable distance into the country. A lieutenant of dragoons and thirteen privates, who had been sent back by General Proctor to
destroy the bridges, were made prisoners near the mouth
of the Thames : from whom the General learned that
the enemy had no certain information of our advance.

 " The baggage of the army was brought from Detroit
in boats, protected by a part of Commodore Perry's
squadron. In the evening the army arrived at Drake's
farm, eight miles from the mouth of the Thames and encamped. This river is a fine deep stream, navigable
for vessels of considerable burden, after the passage of
the bar at its mouth, over which there is generally seven
feet water. The gun boats could ascend as far as Dalson's, below which the country is one continued prairie,
and at once favorable for cavalry movements and for the
co-operation of the gun boats. Above Dalson's the aspect of the country changes ; the river, though still deep,
is not more than seventy yards wide, and its banks high
and woody.

 " At Chatham, four miles from Dalson's and sixteen
from Lake St. Clair, is a small deep creek, where we
found the bridge taken up and the enemy disposed to
dispute our passage, and upon the arrival of the advanced guard, commenced a heavy fire from the opposite
bank as well as a flank fire from the right bank of the
river. The army halted and formed in order of battle.

The bridge was repaired under the cover of a fire from two six pounders. The Indians did not relish the fire of our cannon, and retired. Colonel Johnson being on the right, had seized the remains of a bridge at Mc-Gregor's mills, under a heavy fire from the Indians. He lost on this occasion, two killed and four wounded. The enemy set fire to a house near the bridge, containing a considerable quantity of muskets; the flames were extinguished and the arms saved. At the first farm above the bridge, we found one of the enemy's vessels on fire, loaded with arms and ordnance stores. Four miles higher up, the army took a position for the night; here we found two other vessels and a large distillery filled with ordnance and other stores to an immense amount, in flames. Two twenty-four pounders, with their carriages, were taken, and a large quantity of ball and shells of various sizes.

"The army was put in motion early on the morning of the 5th. The general accompanied Colonel Johnson; Governor Shelby followed with the infantry. This morning were captured two gun-boats and several bateaux, loaded with provisions and ammunition. At nine we had reached Arnold's mills, where there is a fording place, and the only one for a considerable distance. Here the army crossed to the right bank; the mounted regiment fording, and the infantry in the captured boats. The passage, though retarded for want of a sufficient number of boats, was completed by twelve.

"Eight miles above the ford, we passed the ground where the British force had encamped the night before. The general directed the advance of Colonel Johnson's regiment to accelerate their march, for the purpose of ascertaining the distance of the enemy. The officer commanding it, shortly after sent word back, that his progress was stopped by the enemy, who were formed across his line of march. One of the enemy's wagon-

TECUMSEH.

ers was taken prisoner, from whom the general obtained
much useful information.

BATTLE OF THE THAMES.

" The army was now within three miles of the Moravian town, and within one of the enemy. The road passes
through an open beach and maple forest, generally within
a few rods of the river. The enemy had made choice
of a judicious position, two miles below the Moravian
village. Two narrow but deep morasses run parallel
with the river for a considerable extent. The first, at the
distance of three hundred yards; the second, about a
quarter of a mile. The British, interspersed with a few
Indians, occupied the ground, in two lines forty paces
apart, from the river to the first swamp. Six brass and
two iron carriage guns were planted in different parts of
this short line. The Indian line of battle commenced at
the first swamp, and ran to the second, extending down
its margin about a quarter of a mile, forming an imper-
fect hollow square. The Indian force disposed in this
order, amounted to from twelve to fifteen hundred warriors, under the command of Tesumseh, Walk-in-the-
Water, and other daring chiefs. The British regulars and
Indians in the first line, amounted to about seven hundred. Such was the position, the order of battle, and
the numbers of the enemy. A deep river on the left, an
almost impenetrable swamp on the right.

" The troops at the disposal of General Harrison
might amount to three thousand men; yet from the natural strength of the enemy's position, and the peculiar
nature of the ground, not the half of this force could display to advantage. To turn the enemy in flank was im-
practicable. There was therefore no alternative, but to
attack in front, and that without cannon. To advance to
the combat on foot in regular order, was to render a serious loss of lives certain, and success doubtful. The

11

decisive mind of Harrison did not permit him to hesitate.
A plan of attack, at once bold and original, was instantly
conceived; which was to overwhelm the enemy with
consternation, and paralize his energies, by an unexpected and irresistible shock.

" For this purpose the mounted regiment, which from
the active nature of the service it had previously performed, might be termed the veterans of the army, was
drawn up in close column in advance, with orders to
charge and break through the British line. Colonel
Johnson had, however, a discretion either to attack the
British with his whole force, or with one battalion, reserving the other for the attack of the Indian line.

" The Kentucky volunteers, under Major General
Henry, formed close in the rear of Johnson's regiment,
in three lines extending from the river to the first swamp.
General Desha's division covered the rear of the left battalion of Johnson's regiment. In the rear of Henry's
division, Colonel Simral was placed with a reserve of five
hundred Kentucky volunteers. Governor Shelby was at
the *crotchet* formed by the intersection of Generals
Henry and Desha's divisions. General Cass and Commodore Perry volunteered as aids to General Harrison,
who placed himself at the head of the front line of infantry, to direct the movements of the mounted men and
to give them the necessary support. Such was the general order of battle. Now for the disposition of the
mounted regiment.

" Colonel Johnson perceiving that there was not sufficient room for his whole regiment, increased by fresh
volunteers to eleven hundred men, to act advantageously
against the British line only, determined to make a simultaneous charge upon the red and white enemy. Accordingly, he divided the regiment equally; gave the
command of the first battalion, and the honor of charging
the British line, to his brother, Lieutenant Colonel James

Johnson; leading the other battalion in person against the Indians. The advance guard of the regiment, consisting of a hundred and fifty men, under Major Suggett, were dismounted and placed in a line parallel with the enemy, in front of the first battalion. This line had the double advantage of distracting the attention of the enemy, and of keeping up a fire and maintaining the ground if the horses should recoil at the British fire (which was the case). The line was weak, but was supported by four charging columns of double files, with intervals of not more than sixty paces.

"Colonel Johnson also dismounted a hundred and twenty men under Captain Stricker, and extended them from the first to the second swamp, parallel with the Indian line and in front of the second battalion, which he formed in two charging columns, with an interval of four hundred yards; Colonel Johnson led the right column in person; Major Thomson the left.

"The dispositions for the attack were completed. The American army had arrived within a short distance of the enemy. It was now four o'clock in the afternoon; both armies were ready for the work of death. An awful silence succeeds. Soon, however, it is broken by the sound of the regimental trumpet, the signal for the commencement of the action.

"In an instant eleven hundred horse are in motion, at full speed; a fire of tremendous *sound*, at least, from the British line, checked for a moment the progress of the first battalion; but its gallant leader soon gives it an increased and irresistible momentum. The last fire of the enemy, although delivered at pistol-shot distance, had no other effect than to confirm the victory. The charging columns broke through the British ranks, wheeled and formed in their rear. Never was terror more strongly depicted on the countenances of men; with their pieces unloaded, their bayonets unfixed, broken, huddled in confusion or trampled under the horses' feet, and surrounded beyond the possibility of escape, officers and men were seen throwing down their arms, and, with uplifted hands, exclaiming ' quarter.'

"So unexpected was the shock, that they were totally unprepared to meet it; the whole was the work of a minute. Their artillery, which from its number and position ought to have been an efficient defense, was perfectly harmless to the assailants. There was something terrible in the sudden appearance of several hundred horsemen, clad in a motley garb, screaming like a band of furies, and approaching at full gallop through the woods! Besides, an opinion prevailed among the British troops, that the Kentuckians, vindictive of the massacres of the rivers Raisin and Miami, were resolved on giving no quarter. It is, therefore, not surprising, that terror and despair paralized their exertions. Six hundred British regulars were the fruits of this charge.

"On the left, between the two swamps, the contest was more serious. Colonel Johnson most gallantly led the head of his column into the hottest of the enemy's fire, and was personally opposed to Tecumseh. At this point a condensed mass of savages had collected. Yet, regardless of danger, he rushed into the midst of them; and as he broke through their line, so thick were the Indians, that several might have reached him with their rifles. He rode a white horse, and was known to be an officer of distinction. A shower of balls was discharged at him; some took effect; his horse, his saddle, his clothes, his person, were pierced with bullets. His men, as they advanced to his support, were successively killed, wounded, or dismounted. The combatants were now closed upon the whole line, and a desperate conflict ensued. Many of the Indians disdained a shelter, and fought openly; others lay concealed behind logs, trees, or bushes. More prudent than their white allies, they reserved their fire until our men were within ten or fifteen yards of them. Colonel Johnson, after receiving four wounds, perceived the daring Tecumseh commanding and attempting to rally his savage force, when he instantly put his horse towards him, and was shot by Tecumseh in the hand as he approached him. Tecumseh advanced with a drawn weapon, a sword or tomahawk, at which instant the colonel, having reserved his fire, shot his ferocious antagonist dead at his feet, and that too at the moment he was almost fainting with the loss of blood, and the anguish of five wounds. Yet he afterwards rode his bleeding horse several rods to the rear of the line, where he was helped from his horse, which immediately died.

" The death of Tecumseh was to the Indians an irreparable loss. They immediately gave way; but continued obstinately to dispute the ground for a considerable distance. Frequently the same tree would be occupied by the parties, but on opposite sides. The battle lasted about one hour and a half, not at one point, but from its commencement, where Tecumseh fell, to the extreme left, where the Indians attempted to flank Major Thomson's line, but were prevented by the timely reinforcement from the reserve under Colonel Simral, whose fire soon became too warm for the enemy.

" Of the mounted regiment twenty-five were killed or mortally wounded. About fifty were besides wounded, most of them slightly. Of Governor Shelby's corps, two were killed and six or seven wounded. About fifty horses were killed or disabled.

" Having considerable personal knowledge of the officers and men composing the mounted regiment, the writer cannot dismiss the subject without giving the reader some additional particulars of the character and services of this distinguished corps. It was raised in Kentucky in the spring of 1813. It was soon filled, although the busy season of the year was unfavorable for obtaining volunteers. It entered the service about eight hundred strong, but was increased to thirteen hundred from arrangements proper on such occasions. On the 5th of October, it amounted to a thousand men in round numbers; a part having been before dismounted by order of General Harrison.

" Its first service was an expedition to the banks of the St. Joseph of lake Michigan. This excursion covered the Ohio frontier, and prevented a large party of British Indians, collected at Chicago, from marching to besiege Fort Wayne. The inhabitants of the Ohio frontier felt perfectly secure when this regiment was protecting them. The greater part of the officers and privates were pious men, and when off duty, were often heard singing religious airs, or engaged in serious and instructive discourse. Indeed it resembled in this respect a religious congregation. Discipline and obedience was cheerfully observed. There was not an instance of desertion, and only two died of sickness till after the battle of the Moravian town. It is almost superfluous to speak of the courage of this corps, since it is now so well known. Yet there are some who deserve particular notice.

" Let us first speak of the gallant dead. Col. William Whitley a man of seventy years of age, a soldier of the revolution, and possessing an ardent patriotism, had fought the Indians in twenty battles and skirmishes, without injury. Having a particular esteem for Col. Johnson, he volunteered as a private in Capt. Davidson's company, although in easy circumstances. His love of country was an example to all around him, and would make common individuals ashamed at not being able to feel as he felt. When speaking of the war and his country's rights, he would say, " if I am killed the enemy will only deprive me of a few days." Col. J. had selected from fifteen to twenty individuals to assist him

in breaking the Indian line. The command of this forlorn hope was given to Col. Whitley. This select company was placed immediately in the rear of Col. Johnson and a few paces in advance of the charging column.
A moment before the action commenced, Col. Johnson
turned to Col. Whitley and observed : " Your presence
animates me, it will insure victory to our brave Kentuckians." With an aspect of uncommon firmness he
turned to his men and said, " Boys, we have been selected to second our Colonel in the charge, act well your
part ; recollect the watch-word : *victory or death.*" He
led on his Spartan band. The battle commenced ; he
fell without a groan the first fire, but his example was
not lost.

" With the solitary exception of Samuel Theobalds,
who alone remained on horseback with Col. Johnson,
the whole of Col. Whitley's command were dismounted
in ten minutes, by death or wounds, or horses shot under them ! Theobalds, by order of Col. Johnson, never
discharged his piece, keeping it in reserve for a case of
necessity, if it should occur.

" Lieut. Logan was mortally wounded. He lived in
honor and died gloriously, regretting his death only be-
cause he left a wife and several children to mourn his
fate. A young printer of the name of Mansfield, was
also mortally wounded. Joel Johnson and others were
anxious to put him in a place of security, as the battle
still raged. But he would not consent to be removed,
saying, " I shall die in a few minutes, return to the
charge and gain the victory that I may die in peace."

" The mounted regiment was greatly indebted for its
extraordinary discipline to the indefatigable exertions of
Lieut. Col. James Johnson, brother to the Colonel, who
has always been remarkable for military discipline. He
is about thirty-eight years of age : has been in several
expeditions, even while a boy, against the Indians living

on the Wabash, and has served in many civil situations in Kentucky, which has given him celebrity and standing. He was first a magistrate, then sheriff of Scott county, and afterwards senator in the legislature of Kentucky. He had two promising sons in the action; the eldest named Edward a few months above fifteen, and William, fourteen years of age. Such was the ardor of these young Spartans, that the officers had frequently to restrain their eagerness; they were both mounted and often among the first in pursuit. The youngest is now (1815) a cadet at West Point.

"Major Duval Payne, of the 1st battalion, inspired confidence wherever he appeared. He is now about fifty years of age. In 1792, he distinguished himself in a personal renconter with an Indian in an expedition against them; he succeeded in disarming his savage foe of his gun, tomahawk, and scalping knife, after having thrown the Indian several times, who as often extricated himself by rising with his antagonist!

"Major Thompson commanded the charging column on the extreme left. He dismounted his command; faced to the left and extended his line parallel with the second swamp, in order effectually to oppose the flank line of the Indians, previously formed. His line were instantly engaged and sustained their share of the action. He is apparently between thirty-five and forty years of age, Justice of the Peace, Colonel of a militia regiment, and Senator in the Kentucky Legislature; sensible and mild, but daring and undismayed in the hour of peril.

"Captain Jacob Stricker, who commanded the dismounted line in front of the second battalion, was not inferior to Tecumseh in his fame among the old Indian fighting men of Kentucky; a man remarkably taciturn and reserved, except in battle, when his character instantly changes. Always in front of his men his example was surprising. and his well-known voice was heard in

every direction. He is fifty years of age, and his attachment to Col. Johnson carried him into the field at a
time when he had given up all expectation of adding to
his well-earned fame.

  " Capt. James Davidson was wounded and fell from
his horse, and in attempting to give command fainted with
the loss of blood ; but this did not discompose his men ;
his subaltern officers knew their duty ; and while their
brave captain lay bleeding upon the ground, led their
company furiously to the charge.

  " Capt. James Coleman and men did not less distinguish themselves. After Col. Johnson was severely
wounded, he ordered these companies to dismount and
strengthen the line of battle, under Stricker ; animated by
the voice of Capt. Coleman, the most determined courage
was displayed.

  " Major Thomson's column was composed of Captains
Rice and Comb's companies. Capt. Rice was without
his superior in bravery or discretion. He was not less
distinguished than Stricker for his early and gallant conduct in numerous battles with the Indians.

  " Capt. Combs, a man of thirty-five, had fought under
General Wayne, as a private volunteer, and whose looks
and remarkable large whiskers struck the spectator with
strong impressions of his firmness and bravery.

  " Captains McCobe, Ellison, Matson, and Hamilton
of the 1st battalion deserve great praise for their intrepidity. They are all men of intelligence and reputation.
Each led a charging column through the British lines.
Capt. Ellison received several rifle balls in his clothes
and saddle. In breaking through the British ranks, a
soldier of the 41st attempted to fix his bayonet. At one
stroke of his sabre, Capt. E. severed his head and brought
him to the ground : a second made a show of resistance
and shared the same fate. Shortly afterwards the Capt.
led his company against the Indians. It was then that

his temerity had nearly cost him his life ; an Indian seized the bridle of his horse, and attempted a blow with the tomahawk ; but the sabre again prevented and the Indian lost his scalp.

" John Berry had his hand shot to pieces, but refused to retire ; he loaded his gun twice and fired, and the third time was prevented from the blood which filled the pan of his gun.

" Major James Suggett who commanded the dismounted line in front of the 1st battalion, and at other times the advanced guard, was a baptist preacher, about thirty-five years old, of stentorian lungs, considerable oratory, and remarkable for his personal courage from infancy. Associated with him were Captains Church, Berry, and Reding, men of distinguished valor and discretion, and whose men were equal to the most trying occasions.

" The forlorn hope were truly a *Spartan band*. Samuel Theobalds and Joseph Taylor, the first a lawyer, were both young men of promise. Benjamin Chambers, a member of the Kentucky legislature, a young man self-taught and of a strong mind. Eli Short, assistant dep. Quarter-master, Garret Wall, Forage-master, Robert Payne, William Webb, all equally determined, formed a part of this little corps, and survived the terrible ordeal.

" The greater part of Governor Shelby's corps had not an opportunity of participating in the action. This circumstance was very much regretted by them. Those that met the enemy on the left flank distinguished themselves. From Sandwich to the Moravian town the greater part marched on foot, and with a rapidity that was almost incredible. But their noble Governor was at their head.

" The Indians fought bravely and sustained a serious loss. Sixty-five warriors were left dead on the battle ground. Their loss was a hundred and twenty-five killed, besides wounded. Six Americans and twenty-two

Indians fell within twenty yards where Tecumseh was killed, and the trails of blood almost covered the ground.

" Among the trophies of this day were six brass field pieces, captured from the British at Bennington and Saratoga, surrendered at Detroit by Hull, and again recovered. May cowardice never again be entrusted with their defence. About five thousand stands of arms were also taken between the mouth of the Thames and the Moravian town.

" The day after the battle, a part of the army took possession of the Moravian town, which was deserted, but where was found most kinds of vegetables in abundance, which were very acceptable to men who had subsisted several days on fresh beef without bread or salt. Extensive corn-fields afforded an excellent range for the horses. So panic-struck were the Indian women at the advance of the troops to the town, that some of them actually threw their young children into the Thames, to prevent their being massacred by the Americans !* The flight of the Indians from the town was so sudden, that their kettles were yet boiling over their fires. The town was destroyed by the troops previous to their leaving it. Among the reasons assigned to justify the measure, it was alleged that these Indians had been among the foremost in massacring our men at the river Raisin, and that the town, if it were spared, would afford a convenient shelter for the British allies during the winter, and from which they could easily pass into the Michigan territory, to plunder and murder the inhabitants.

" General Proctor abandoned his army at the very moment Johnson's bugle sounded the charge. An escort of forty dragoons and a few cowardly Indians accom-

---

* I had this fact from an American gentleman, who was at Oxford, when Proctor and the Indians passed through there on their way to Burlington heights. The squaws were then bewailing the loss of their children.

panied him. A few of Governor Shelby's men, who had procured horses, pursued him; and at one time were within a hundred yards of him, but were too few in number to attack his guard. His flight was rapid, for in twenty-four hours he was more than sixty miles from the scene of danger. His carriage, wife, sword, and papers, fell into the hands of his pursuers. The carriage of Colonel Elliot was also taken.

" Three wagons loaded with specie escaped. A depot of three hundred barrels of flour was at Oxford. General Harrison having no orders to advance to Burlington heights by the way of Grand river, ordered the army to commence its march back to Detroit.

" At the skirmish near the mouth of the Thames, an Indian squaw was mortally wounded : she was left to shift for herself. Her little girl, six years old, remained with her. On the return of the army from the Moravian town, they were found in the woods, at the distance of half a mile from where she was wounded : to appearance she had been dead three days. The girl was still living. When our men approached the spot, she instantly raised her hands, and distinctly articulated " *dont !*" She was taken to Detroit, where her fate and sprightliness excited universal interest. An officer of Governor Shelby's corps took her to Kentucky, with the humane and honorable intention of adopting her in his family, and of giving her an education.

" While General Harrison was pursuing Proctor up the Thames, the Ottawas, Chippewas, Pottowatamies, Miamies, and Kikapoos, proposed to General McArthur, a suspension of hostilities, and agreed to " take hold of the same tomahawk with the Americans, and strike all who are, or may be enemies of the United States, whether British or Indians." They brought in their women and children, and offered them as hostages for their good behavior.

Face 155.   Walk-in-the-water.

" The army returned to Detroit. Captain Elliot, of
the Niagara, volunteered his services to command a naval
expedition against Michilimackinac and fort St. Joseph ;
but the weather proving unfavorable for a number of days,
the season became too far advanced to risk the squadron
on lake Huron, till spring.

" Lieutenant Le Breton arrived at Detroit on the 15th
bearing a flag, and a letter from General Proctor to General Harrison. This letter requested humane treatment
to the prisoners, and a restoration of certain property and
papers taken on the 5th. As the letter was addressed to
the general, " at Moravian towns," he saw no reason for
Le Breton's journey to Detroit, and ordered him to join
General Proctor by the way of Buffalo and fort George.

" After the return of the commander-in-chief to Detroit, Walk-in-the-water, who had been in the battle of
the Thames, came in to implore peace. When he crossed
from Sandwich, the white flag which he bore in his hand
had attracted a great crowd to the wharf, all anxious to
get a near view of the distinguished chief. I was struck
with admiration at the firmness and apparent nonchalance
with which he ascended the bank, and passed through
the ranks of the Kentucky volunteers, whom he had so
gallantly opposed in battle but a few days before. I
never saw more real dignity of carriage, or a more striking firmness of countenance. Yet his situation was calculated to depress his spirits and produce humility. His
town was in the power of the Americans ; the British
were all taken ; the Indians had just suffered a signal defeat ; almost all the other chiefs had submitted ; he was
without the means of living or resistance : still, his manner was that of a conqueror.

" A few days after Proctor's defeat, the town was so
full of famished savages, that the issue of rations to them
did not keep pace with their hunger. I have seen the
women and children searching the ground for bones and

rinds of pork, which had been thrown away by the soldiers; meat, in a high state of putrefaction, which had
been thrown into the river, was carefully picked up and
devoured: the feet, heads, and entrails of the cattle
slaughtered by the public butchers, were collected and
sent off to the neighboring villages. I have counted
twenty horses in a drove, fancifully decorated with the
offals of the slaughter yard.

" Governor Shelby's corps and the twelve month's
volunteers, were all honorably discharged. Traveling became safe, and business at Detroit began to resume its
wonted course, but the *price current* of the territory was
exorbitant for every thing to eat, drink, or wear.
Whisky sold at four dollars a gallon, beef at twenty-
four cents a pound, cheese sixty cents a pound, butter
seventy-five; potatoes two dollars a bushel. The
army was well supplied with rations, as were also about
three hundred of the inhabitants of Michigan, and about
two thousand Indians, men, women, and children, who
had no other means of subsistence. Adventurers soon
came on with a sufficient supply of dry goods.

" On the 23d of October, General Harrison, with all
his disposable regular troops, embarked on board the fleet,
and sailed for Buffalo, in obedience to the orders from
the secretary of war. Previous to his departure, he appointed General Cass provisional governor of the Michigan territory; the civil ordinances, as they stood at Hull's
surrender, were proclaimed in force. General Cass was
left with about one thousand men, not more than seven
hundred of whom were effective. The men were industriously employed in preparing winter quarters at the
fort. The Scorpion and Ohio schooners were engaged
in transporting the supplies from Erie and Cleveland, for
the troops during winter. Troops were stationed at
Malden and Sandwich. The campaign closed."*

* Brown's History of the Late War. 1815.

CHAPTER X.

THE winter 1813–14 was sedulously employed by Generals Harrison and McArthur, in providing ways and means to move an army of Ohio and Kentucky troops down lake Erie; that when they should join our northern army, they would form such an overwhelming force as would be able to break down all the enemy's strong holds, from fort Malden to Quebec.

The number of volunteers and militia called into service by General Harrison, had created a debt of large amount. The then secretary of war complained loudly of the expensive manner in which the war was conducted by the north-western army. General Harrison admitted that he had employed considerable numbers of volunteers and militia; that numbers were requisite to render success certain; that he had succeeded in every object the government expected; that by his success he had afforded peace and security to more than one thousand miles of exposed frontier, on the lakes, on the rivers Wabash and Mississippi. The secretary of war determined not to be satisfied, kept up such a continual grumbling about the expenses of the war, that General Harrison felt sore at his continual complaining, and in disgust resigned the command of the army.

General McArthur being the senior brigadier-general, the command of the north-western army devolved upon him; and with that command his responsibility increased. As this was the first time he was placed in a situation to be in chief command, he must have been proud of his exalted stand among his fellow men. He was popular with the army and with the administration; and was determined that no exertions on his part should

12

be wanting to retain that popularity, which cost him so much labor and frequent risk of life to secure. As he was large, strong, and healthy, and inured to toil and privations from his youth, the inconvenience of hard living, and exposure to the elements, did not depress his spirits. He was found at every post where his presence was necessary, enforcing discipline in the army, and stimulating his fellow-citizens to engage in the war with spirit.

General McArthur had, previous to the war, built an elegant stone mansion on his farm on Fruit hill. From his house is the most delightful prospect: the town of Chillicothe is as plain to the view as a map: from his door can be traced the serpentine windings of the Scioto river, by the range of white sycamore trees which over-hang the margin of the stream: farms, without number, present themselves to the eye, as far as vision can reach: the hills on each side of the Scioto river, rising to con-siderable heights, some gradually sloping off, whilst others shoot up in sugar-loaf peaks, whose summits at a distance appear to touch the blue sky: a more delightful prospect can scarcely be imagined. If an elevated situa-tion, with a variety of beautiful scenery, has any effect in inspiring the poet's muse with rapturous, melodious strains, here would be the spot for inspiration. Such was his place of retreat from the toils and cares of labor, or from the storms of war. "Riches take to themselves wings and fly away;" all our care and prudence cannot guard and secure us against the vicissitudes of life. About ten o'clock of the morning of the 15th of April, 1814, his splendid mansion was discovered to be on fire. The laborers on the farm were all out at work; none were about the house but females. The fire first broke out in the upper story: the citizens of the town of Chil-licothe, only two miles distant, could distinctly see the fire and dense smoke, and with praiseworthy activity hastened to the scene of action; some on horseback, others in carriages, and many on foot. The progress of the fire was slow, owing to the circumstance of all the partition walls being of stone; and the fire proceeded from room to room, by the burning and falling in of the roof. This afforded time to save all his papers, and all the furniture, except such as was in the upper rooms where the fire commenced. It was supposed that the fire was accidentally communicated. In one of the upper rooms, a chest had been laid in the fire-place, and a considerable quantity of cotton clothing had been piled on the chest. A heavy bunch of soot may have taken fire, and rolled down the flue of the chimney on the cotton clothing, and caused the conflagration. This pecuniary loss, though great, did not in the least check his exertions in the army.

As the enemy had retired discomfited from the upper end of lake Erie, and the Indians were suing for peace, most of the regular troops under his command were ordered by the secretary of war to be transferred to the army on the Niagara frontier. McArthur had a number of small forts to garrison along the frontier; whilst he kept his main force at Detroit and Malden, to overawe the Canadians, and the scattering Indians still in the British interest. The summer of 1814 was passing away, on the north-western frontier, without affording his enterprising genius an opportunity of striking a blow at the enemy. The dull monotony of going from post to post along our extended frontier, was not the kind of service which was agreeable to his active and energetic mind. He began to think of making an excursion through Upper Canada, to pass through the enemy's country, till he should join the army of General Brown, near the falls of Niagara. On the propriety of his intended expedition, he consulted his old commander, General Harrison, and likewise General Cass. They approved of his plan.

The continual growling of the secretary of war, deterred him from employing such a force as he wished. He called on the governor of Kentucky for a few hundred mounted volunteers ; a call which was promptly complied with by the brave and generous Kentuckians ; to whom were joined a few mounted volunteers from Ohio ; and the detachment set off on the expedition. The following is his own detailed report of his expedition through Upper Canada.

> " *Head Quarters*, 8*th M. District*,
> *Detroit*, 18 *Nov.* 1814.

' SIR :—I have the satisfaction to report to you the safe return of the mounted troops to this place on the 17th inst.

" In a former communication, I had the honor to inform you, that the mounted volunteers were marched in this direction in consequence of the regular troops having been withdrawn, and the apprehensions that were entertained for the safety of this Territory, of which I was advised by his Excellency Governor Cass.

" The militia detached from Kentucky and Ohio having arrived, they were assigned for the more immediate protection of this place ; it was then deemed expedient from the ardor and species of the force, that the mounted volunteers should be actively employed in the territory of the enemy, with a view to destroy their resources, and ultimately paralize any efforts which might be made against this place during the winter.

" The valuable mills at the head of Lake Ontario, and in the vicinity of Grand river furnished large supplies to the army in the peninsula, their destruction was desirable ; to that effect the mounted troops, consisting of six hundred volunteers, fifty U. States Rangers, and seventy Indians were put in motion on the 22d of October to pursue the route along the western shore of Lake St. Clair, and pass into the enemy's territory near the mouth of that river.

"The real object of the expedition was masked by the general impression, that it was destined against the Indian towns at Saguia. To favor that idea, boats were prepared for the reception of artillery, to be conveyed through lake St. Clair, up that river into lake Huron, and to co-operate with the mounted troops in the attack. The boats were, however, employed in the transportation of the troops and horses across the river St. Clair and Bear creek, which empties into Beldoon river. This movement was absolutely necessary to secure that secrecy to the expedition, which could alone render it successful. All military movements in this direction, are rapidly communicated to the enemy from Sandwich and this place : it was therefore deemed improper to pass the troops across this river, but to proceed over the river St. Clair, down to the Scotch settlement on the Beldoon, up Bear creek about thirty miles, and across to the Moravian towns, a few miles above the lower settlement on the Thames, where the detachment arrived on the 30th of October.

"We were very fortunate at this place, in taking a sergeant in the British service, who was proceeding to Burlington, with the information that the detachment had passed into the enemy's territory. The capture of this sergeant, at the commencement of the "long woods" between the Moravian towns and Delaware, enabled us to reach the latter place undiscovered. On our approach, the rangers were detached to move across the Thames below the settlement, pass in the rear of it, and guard the different roads leading into the interior, whilst the troops were engaged in swimming their horses, and transporting their baggage on rafts.

"We were thus enabled to arrive at the town of Oxford, one hundred and fifty miles distant from Detroit, before the inhabitants knew that a force was approaching. They were promised protection to their persons and property, upon condition that they remained peaceably at their respective houses ; otherwise, they were assured that their property should be destroyed. However, notwithstanding this injunction, and the sacred obligations of a previous parole, two of the inhabitants escaped to Burford with the intelligence of our arrival. Their property, consisting of two dwelling houses, two barns, and one shop, were instantly consumed.

" On the succeeding day, the 5th instant, the detachment proceeded to Burford, where we were informed that the militia had been embodied about ten days previously to our arrival, in consequence of reports received from Sandwich, that our expedition was expected to move from Detroit against Burlington. A few hours before our arrival, the enemy retreated from Burford to Malcolm's mills, ten miles distant, on the road leading from Dover to Burlington, when they were joined by the militia from Long Point. It was my intention to cross Grand river as soon as possible, without regarding the militia collected at Malcolm's mills, and attack Burlington. To my great mortification, on our arrival at the river, we found it high and rapid from the late excessive rains, and learned that General Brown had recrossed the Niagara, leaving only a strong garrison in fort Erie. No means were presented of even passing the river on rafts, and had it been effected, upon our return, the militia, contemptible as they were, might have been encouraged to attack when a rapid river divided us. Major Muir, with about fifty Indians and fifty militia, was preparing to contest the passage : a battery was also erecting, as was understood, for three pieces of artillery, distant twelve miles on the road from Burlington.

" These considerations presented serious objections to any attempts to pass the river. It was also due to the past sufferings, and the future safety of the gallant detachment under my command, that a direction should be given to its movements, calculated to afford compensation for the former and secure the latter. It was therefore determined upon, to attack and defeat or disperse the militia at Malcolm's mills, move down the Long Point road through the Grand river settlement, destroy the valuable mills in that quarter, and then return to our territory, either by a movement across Grand river at the mouth to fort Erie, or along Talbott's street to the Thames. To that effect, a detachment was directed to remain and engage the attention of the enemy, whilst the principal force should be withdrawn and marched to Malcolm's mills. We found the enemy consisting of four or five hundred militia and a few Indians, fortified on commanding ground, beyond a creek deep and difficult of passage, except at a bridge immediately in front of their works, which had been destroyed. Arrangements were made for a joint attack on the front and rear. The Ohio troops, with the advance guard and Indians, were accordingly thrown across the creek under cover of a thick wood, to approach the enemy in rear, whilst the Kentucky troops were to attack in front, as soon as the attention of the enemy was engaged by the attack in the rear.

" The enemy would have been completely surprised and captured, had not an unfortunate yell by our Indians announced the approach of the detachment destined to attack their rear. They were, however, defeated and dispersed, with the loss in the skirmishes on that day, of one captain and seventeen privates killed, nine privates wounded, and three captains, five subalterns, and one hundred and three privates made prisoners; whilst our loss was only one killed and six wounded. Early on the 7th instant the enemy was pursued on the road to Dover, many made prisoners, and five valuable mills destroyed.

" Apprehensive that the troops could not be supplied on the route to fort Erie, and that difficulties would occur in the passage of Grand river, together with the uncertainty which existed as to the position of our army below, I was induced, on the 8th instant, to commence my return to this place, by the way of Talbott street and the Thames ; which was happily effected on the 17th instant.

" In this excursion, the resources of the enemy have been essentially impaired, and the destruction of the valuable mills in the vicinity of Grand river, employed in the support of the army in the peninsula, together with the consumption of the forage, and provisions necessary for the troops, has added to the barrier, heretofore interposed by an extensive and swampy frontier against any attempts which may be made this winter in the direction of Detroit.

" With the exception of nine thousand rations, and eight hundred bushels of forage, the detachment subsisted entirely on the enemy. Of private property, no more was destroyed than was absolutely necessary for the support of the troops, for which regular payments or receipts were given. It is, however, much to be regretted, that there were some partial abuses produced by the unfortunate example presented by the Indians, whose customs in war impel them to plunder after victory ; but for this blemish there was some excuse, in their correct and gallant conduct before and during the battle. It is also gratifying to know, that they were forgetful of the *atrocious deeds committed* by the Indians in the service of the enemy : neither the *innocent* or *disarmed* have been massacred or molested.

" The honorable deportment of the chiefs Lewis Wolfe and Civil John, was truly animating to all the troops.

" It was essential to the progress of the expedition, that the horses of individuals should be taken to supply

Civil John.

the place of those that were disabled and lost on the
march : in all cases receipts were given. The Michigan
militia were invited to accompany us on the expedition :
not more than twenty accepted it. Of those, six deserted
near Delaware, and the remainder were permitted to return on the next day. Lieutenant Ruland, of Captain
Audrain's company of rangers from Detroit, was distinguished for zeal and intrepidity.

" The patriotic volunteers under my command have
just claims on the gratitude of their country, when it is
recollected that they tendered their services with no
other assurances than the approbation which always at-
tends disinterested sacrifices; that they have performed
much severe service duly, at an inclement season, through
an extensive and swampy district, frequently intersected
with deep and rapid rivers; that they have penetrated
two hundred miles into the enemy's territory, destroyed
two hundred stand of arms, together with five of their
most valuable mills, paroled or dispersed the greater portion of the efficient militia of that part of Upper Canada
west of Grand river; and the whole detachment has returned in safety to this place, with the exception of one
killed.

" The ardor which the troops always evinced when
they expected to meet the enemy, was not more conspicuous or praiseworthy, than the cheerfulness with
which they conformed to the rules of military propriety.
The officers and privates of the detachment, with a very
few exceptions, merited my warmest approbation.

" I was much indebted to the zeal and intelligence displayed on all occasions by Major Dudley, commanding
the Kentucky battalion, and was ably assisted by the
zeal and assiduity of Doctor Turner, of the seventeenth
infantry. Captain Bradford, of the nineteenth infantry,
my brigade-major, already distinguished at fort Meigs
and Tehoopcaw, is entitled to my sincere thanks for his

exertions under every difficulty, and I have the support of the troops in assuring you, sir, that to the military talents, activity, and intelligence of Major Todd, who acted as my adjutant-general, much of the fortunate progress and issue of the expedition is attributable; and I cheerfully embrace this occasion to acknowledge the important services which he has at all times rendered me whilst in command of the district. His various merits justly entitle him to the notice of the government.

" I have the honor to be, very respectfully,

" Your obedient servant,

" DUNCAN McARTHUR,

" *Brig. Gen. U. S. Army Com.*

" To the Hon. JAMES MONROE, Sec. of War."

After returning from this successful expedition, the war languished in the north-west. The Indian tribes had mostly sued for peace; but it was still necessary to garrison the exposed posts along our frontier. This was done by a few companies of militia. At Detroit, a few companies of regular troops and a regiment of Ohio militia, guarded that place. At fort Malden, a regiment of Kentucky militia and a battalion of regular troops were stationed.

During the winter 1814–15, McArthur, now commander of the eighth military district, was straining every nerve to prepare a large force, to be in readiness to take the field as early in the season as the state of the roads would permit the moving of armies. The government had, by fatal experience, discovered the impropriety of sending small detachments (such as General Hull had commanded), to do the work which could only be effected by large armies. War is a trade which requires experience to learn it, as any other trade. " The greatest masters in the art of war may err: he that wars walks in a mist, through which the keenest eyes cannot always discern the right path." The plan in preparation

by the war department, was that General McArthur
should cross from Detroit into Canada, with an army of
seven thousand men from Ohio and Kentucky, and
sweep Upper Canada to York on lake Ontario ; and
there unite with the northern army, and proceed down
the lake Ontario and the river St. Lawrence, and at one
determined sweep break up all the enemy's strong holds
to Quebec. While the generals of our armies were ma-
turing ways and means, to carry these grand and splendid military projects into execution, the news of a treaty
of peace, happily for our country, reached our ears. The
bustle, toils, and vexations, incident to preparing armies
for the "tented field," were abandoned. The clangor
of the horsemen's trumpet, the rolling of the drum, nor
the shrill whistle of the fife, was scarcely heard in our
land. The militia and volunteers were discharged, and
returned to their homes ; and peace again blessed our
land. Congress being in session, when the treaty of
peace was brought from Europe, a law was passed directing the president of the United States to disband the
army.

Our country stood in need of repose, especially the
north-western frontier. The inhabitants on the shores
of lake Érie, on the river Raisin, upon the river Detroit,
and up lake St. Clair, and up the river Thames in Upper
Canada, had suffered more than the pen can describe.
This district of country was alternately occupied by the
American and British armies. The suffering soldiers
paid little respect to the right of property : provision.
clothing, and shoes, were taken wherever they were
found ; and in many instances, the dwellings of the inhabitants were torn down by the soldiers and used for
fuel ; whilst the miserable inhabitants were left without
subsistence, clothing, or even a roof, under which to
shelter from the storm. General McArthur represented
the sufferings of the citizens of this district of country to

the government of the United States. He stated that the sufferings and privations of these wretched inhabitants, were brought about by causes over which they had no control; that humanity required of the government to extend to them relief. His representations had the desired effect: the president directed that half rations should be distributed to these suffering inhabitants. Had it not been for this relief, many of these unfortunate people must have perished of famine during the severe winter of 1814–15. In giving a relation of the sufferings of the inhabitants of Detroit, Sandwich, and Malden, the author is not drawing upon his imagination for fanciful pictures of distress, nor trusting to hearsay: he was upon the spot, a witness to their sufferings; he commanded a regiment of Ohio troops, that was stationed in Detroit, when the grateful news of peace was sounded in our ears.

The inhabitants of the city of Detroit, and the citizens of the town of Sandwich in Upper Canada, before the war took place, although under different governments, were as social, and as friendly in their daily intercourse with each other, as are the citizens of Cincinnati in Ohio, and Covington of Kentucky. The war had for a time estranged them from each other; but as soon as peace was proclaimed, all antipathy created by the war was dissipated, as if by magic. The inhabitants were seen running in groups across the river Detroit on the ice, and in tears of joy embracing each other in the most affectionate manner.

The sound of war, to warm spirits, has something captivating in its thrilling various freaks of fortune; but let its frightful front come stalking to our homes, and then to witness the horrible sight of dwellings in flames, wives, and children, and feeble old age, fleeing to the woods and swamps, for concealment and protection from the destroying hand of their fellow man. Such scenes are the constant companions of war. May our country never engage in any other than defensive war; and let all the people say, amen.

CHAPTER XI.

In the course of the summer 1815, the regular army was disbanded, and General McArthur bade adieu to the "tented field," and returned to his family and home, to attend to the domestic affairs of private life.

Previous to the war, he had deeply engaged in land speculations, as well as in locating land warrants, and in surveying. During the time he was employed in the army his speculations stood still; others had taken the field, he now found himself in the rear of other land speculators; he was now determined, by renewed vigor, to make up, by unceasing industry in that business, for the time he had lost in the war.

Although immersed in business, he could not refrain from taking a part in the politics of the day. In the fall of the year 1815, he was again elected a member of the general assembly; and was upon all occasions the leader of the party with whom he acted.

He had now been acting on the public stage for a number of years, in various responsible situations, and his talents and business habits were found upon all occasions equal to any draft which was made upon him. What confidence the then administrators of government had in his capacity and integrity, the following letter will explain.

"*Department of War*, 14th *Feb*. 1816.

"Sir—Information has been received, that the principal chief of the Wyandotts of lake Erie, has lately died; and that the whole nation is disposed to sell their present possessions, and remove into other regions.

"It is an object of considerable importance to obtain the cession of their lands, if, as it has been represented, they will connect the settlements of Ohio with those of the Michigan territory. It is, at the same time, desirable to avoid all appearance of solicitude to make this, or any other purchase from the Indians in that quarter; as such an impression could not fail to be injurious to the interests of the United States.

"Before any attempt to negotiate for the cession of their lands, is made, it is proper that their disposition to sell, should be distinctly ascertained. If they are willing to sell, it is extremely desirable that the proposition for that purpose should come from them.

"As it has been represented to this department, that the person who has been chosen in the room of the late chief, is personally attached to you, I have been induced to believe, that this service can be more effectually rendered by you than any person. I will thank you, therefore, immediately after the receipt of this letter, to adopt the necessary measures to accomplish the views of the government. Information of the situation and extent of their possessions, the manner in which the cession would connect the settlements of Ohio with those of Michigan, will be of great importance in deciding the question of ultimate negotiation upon this subject.

"If the limits of their possessions should be found to be indistinct, and require the intervention of other tribes in its adjustment, the presence of those tribes at the contemplated treaty, will be necessary. It is also desirable to ascertain where they intend to settle, as that fact may have some influence, not only upon the price, but the mode in which it shall be paid. Should the information which you shall obtain and communicate to this department, lead to a treaty for the cession of those lands, you will be appointed one of the commissioners.

"For any expenses which you may incur in executing

the requests contained in this letter, you are authorised to draw on this department.

"I have the honor to be,
"Your most obedient servant,
"WM. H. CRAWFORD.
"Gen. DUNCAN McARTHUR."

In pursuance of the authority delegated in the foregoing letter, General McArthur took immediate measures to ascertain the views of the Indians on the subject. The belief was, that the Indians were disposed to make a cession of part of their land. Commissioners were appointed, he being one, to negotiate with the Indians. The treaty was held at a place called Springwell, three miles below the city of Detroit. The commissioners succeeded in confirming former treaties, which were made with the Indians previous to the late war, and in a cession of some of their lands, but not to the extent the government wished. This treaty was approved by the president, and ratified by the senate of the United States.

During the summer 1817, General McArthur, and Governor Cass of Michigan territory, were appointed commissioners to hold a treaty with the western Indians. Fort Meigs, at the lower end of the Maumee rapids, was appointed the place to hold the treaty. An immense number of Indians assembled, and a large scope of country was ceded by them. This treaty was concluded on the 29th of September, 1817. In order to induce some of the principal chiefs to accede to making large cessions of land, the commissioners had stipulated, that these chiefs should hold separate tracts in fee simple, and exclusive of the general reservations around their towns. When this treaty was laid before the senate of the United States for their ratification, the senate passed the following resolution.

13

"*In senate of the United States, Feb.* 5, 1818.

"Resolved by the senate, that the further consideration of the treaty, concluded at the foot of the rapids of the Miami of Lake Erie, on the 29th day of September, 1817, with the Wyandotts, Seneca, Shawnee, Delaware, Potowatimy, Ottaway, and Chippeway tribes of Indians, be postponed; and that it be recommended to the President of the United States, to proceed to further negotiation with the said tribes, or either of them, in order that the provisions, whereby it is stipulated that the United States shall receive from the said tribes a cession of certain lands, and grant the same in fee simple to the said tribes, for the uses therein described; and also the articles and schedule of the said treaty, which provide for the division and grant of the said lands, by the chiefs of the said tribes, to individuals thereof, and so that the grantees may convey the same to any person whatever, be expunged from the said treaty; and that such portion of the lands belonging to the said tribes, as shall not be ceded to the United States, be reserved to the said tribes, in like manner as has been practised in other and similar cases.

"Attest,   (Signed)   CHARLES CUTTS, *Sec.*"

As the consequence of this resolution of the senate was to set aside the late treaty, the president of the United States again appointed General McArthur and Governor Cass, commissioners to revise the former treaty with the Indians. The Indians were requested to convene at St. Mary's, early in the month of September. The Indians met the commissioners at the time and place appointed. A treaty was held, and further cession of their land was made, and concluded on the 17th of September, 1818. This treaty and cession of land, was approved by the president, and ratified by the senate of the United States.

In the fall of the year 1817, General McArthur was again elected a member of the general assembly in the house of representatives. The competitors for the speaker's chair were General McArthur, and Mr. Charles Hammond, the present able editor of the Cincinnati Gazette. McArthur succeeded by a small majority. The political war against the bank of the United States, commenced this session of the assembly. Mr. Hammond, who is a man of energy and talents, was the leader of those who were opposed to the United States bank locating branches in the state, without first obtaining the consent of the state. McArthur defended the right of the bank to place branches wherever it should think proper; as the bank had paid fifteen hundred thousand dollars as a bonus for that privilege. Mr. Hammond was much the best speaker, and assailed the bank and its supporters with every argument calculated to make proselytes to his cause: sarcasm, irony, and ridicule, were resorted to. General McArthur made no pretensions to a display of oratory, yet he was by no means a silent member. He spoke often, and with effect; his home-spun speeches thwarted the eloquence of Mr. Hammond. The bill for taxing the branches of the United States bank to death, was defeated this session of Assembly.

The summer of 1818, party strife on the bank question was violent. Every man that was able to scribble a paragraph for the newspapers, was engaged on one side or the other of this momentous question. McArthur used his pen and his tongue without avail. He was a candidate for re-election, and was defeated. A considerable majority of the members elected this year, were opposed to the United States bank. Mr. Hammond was again elected a member of the assembly, and by his talents, and readiness in wielding his pen, together with his strong and confident manner of speaking, was able to dictate law to this assembly. A law was passed at this

session of the legislature, taxing each branch of the United
States' bank located in the state of Ohio, fifty thousand
dollars. When the time arrived for collecting this tax,
the branch banks refused to pay. Mr. Hammond had
provided in the law for a case of this kind: the colletor
was authorized, in case the bank refused to pay the tax,
to employ armed force, and enter the banking house, and
seize on the money; and this was actually done. The
collector, with an armed force, entered the branch bank
in the town of Chillicothe, and took what money he
thought proper.

The bank brought suit in the United States' circuit
court against all the state officers concerned in this forcible collection.

Mr. Hammond, who is a distinguished lawyer, with
other eminent counsel, were employed by the state of
Ohio to defend this important cause. The district court
decided the law of Ohio, levying the tax, unconstitu-
tional, and, of course, null and void; and made a decree,
directing the state to refund to the bank the money thus
forcibly taken. The cause was appealed to the supreme
court of the United States. Mr. Hammond defended the
suit, in all its stages. The supreme court decided this
cause against the state of Ohio. Thus was settled this
knotty and vexatious question, which for a time, threatened the peace of the Union.

Although the bank question estranged the majority of
the citizens of Ross county against General McArthur,
for a time, yet the many important services he had rendered the country, could not be forgotten: he was again
elected, in 1819, a member of the assembly, by his usual
majority.

In the summer of 1822, General McArthur's friends
placed him in nomination as a candidate for a seat in the
house of representatives in congress. Some illiberal and
ungenerous efforts were used to prejudice the public

mind against him, on account of some deserters, whom he had permitted to be shot, in pursuance of the decision of a general court-martial during the late war. These deserters had been previously condemned by a court-martial, and pardoned by General Harrison, and again had deserted, were taken, and brought in to head quarters. General Harrison's disposition was such a mixture of sympathy, kindness, and humanity, that he was like my Uncle Toby—he would not hurt, even a fly, unless it was in self-defense : indeed, the facility with which pardons were procured from him, had a pernicious effect on such soldiers as were discontented with the service. They concluded, if they deserted and effected their escape it was well; if they should be apprehended and condemned by a court-martial, General Harrison would save them by his pardoning power. Under this state of things, the public service suffered, and some examples were called for, to check the daily desertions which were taking place. McArthur was a man of sterner mould. When the command of the western army devolved upon him in 1814, he convened a general court-martial in the town of Chillicothe, for the purpose of trying the numerous deserters that had been apprehended and brought to head-quarters. The court-martial was in session more than a month. At the close of this session, twenty six of the deserters were condemned to be shot. All were pardoned but four. These four had deserted several times, and were retaken. On these four General McArthur permitted the sentence of law, as expressed by the court-martial, to be executed. For this, during the canvass of the election, he was bitterly assailed. He was charged with being a cruel tyrant—a monster, thirsting for blood. Although these charges were rung against him in the bitterest language of malice and envy, and with all the changes that the genius of his opposers could invent—and some of them were men of talents—yet all their abuse did not avail them : he was elected by a triumphant majority.

He now took part in a scene that was new to him. The congress of the United States was generally made up of men of the first talents in the nation. McArthur was a new man, who, without education or influential friends, by the force of his own genius, had slowly but steadily wormed his way out of the deepest obscurity to distinction among his fellow-citizens. In his politics, he was an enthusiastic republican of the Jeffersonian school. His oldest son he named Thomas Jefferson. He was an admirer of Presidents Madison and Monroe. In congress, he was a firm, undeviating supporter of what was then termed the American System. This system of policy was mainly introduced and supported in congress by Mr. Henry Clay. The object of those politicians, who supported the American System, appeared to be to engage the general government in a system of internal improvements ; and to carry out those measures, that congress should levy taxes for the purpose of making roads and constructing canals, for the convenience of commercial transport between the states : and secondly, to levy heavy duties on all articles of foreign importation, which could be manufactured within our own country, in order to prevent foreign manufacturers from coming in competition with American manufacturers. This was called the high tariff. Of this plan of policy McArthur was a devoted and efficient supporter. Although he was slow and deliberate in forming opinions, when formed, he never yielded to opposition.

Whilst General McArthur remained a member of congress, he had considerable influence in that body. His persevering industry, his energetic mind, his sound judgment, and practical business habits, rendered him a very efficient member. He would sometimes make short pithy remarks on the business before the house, but made no attempts at those flourishes of eloquence, which tickle the fancy and please the ear. After having served two sessions in congress, he declined a re-election, being determined to devote all his efforts to arrange his domestic concerns. He left the field of politics to others, and engaged with an unremitted attention to settle his land business.

Having at all times prided himself in the adroitness and dexterity with which he could take the advantage of any defects in the locations or surveys of other land speculators, he was involved in a labyrinth of litigation. He appeared to take as much pride in overreaching other land speculators, as ever ambitious general did in outmaneuvering his adversary on the field of battle. Although he has succeeded in amassing a large fortune, mostly by land speculation, yet, the evening of his days is clouded by turmoil, vexation, and the uncertainty of the law. If wealth, generally, affords no more peace of mind than it has to General McArthur, it is not worth the coveting. Although he has been successful in his land speculations, his conduct in this line of business is not worthy of imitation, but rather reprehensible, and has created him more vexation and enemies, than all the other acts of his life.

The summer of 1830, General McArthur's friends, against his inclination, placed his name in nomination as a candidate for the office of governor of the state of Ohio. At this time, General Jackson had come into power, and his partizans were well organized. It was well known, that General McArthur was a supporter of the internal improvement system ; he was also in favor of what was called the high tariff ; and what was more odious to the Jackson party, he was in favor of rechartering the United States bank. The Jackson party assailed his character with all the animosity and virulence that party strife engenders. The affair of permitting the deserters to be shot, was again brought forward in a new, extended and frightful edition. The party, in their zeal, depicted General McArthur, as a monster, whose delight was in blood: they had forgotten, that their own chief was, at least, equally, if not more, obnoxious to censure in this respect. Perhaps both were actuated by a sense of duty for the good of their country. McArthur's land speculations were depicted in the most horrid colors. From these publications, it would appear, that he had dispossessed of their homes almost every widow and orphan within his reach. So far from this being a true representation of his land law suits—he generally contended with none but other land speculators ; and this was a war of " Greek to Greek." All the weapons of the party, though well aimed and dexterously handled, did not avail them : he was elected by a considerable majority.

His duty, as Governor of the state, was discharged with fidelity. No party clamor was raised against him. The pardoning power, intrusted to the Governor of the state, is a delicate trust. Every criminal has friends, who will use every means to procure pardons—by petitions, letters, and personal applications by mothers, by wives, by fathers, by sisters and brothers. To resist such applications, requires some firmness. Governor McArthur was applied to for the pardon of two criminals in such a courtly manner, that the petition itself will be interesting. The petition is dated " October 25th, 1832," and reads in the following courtly words : " To his excellency, Duncan McArthur, commander in chief of the state of Ohio—Sir, we are sorry that we are necessitated to address you at present, but your executive acts have been such that compels us to do so. You have pardoned John Murry a most notorious villain, and has left Lawrence Lynch in prison, who is an innocent man who happened to be in company with Murry when he was arrested. To be plain with you, you have been in the habit of pardoning those who were most guilty, and suffering those who were innocent to remain in prison. We know you to be a soldier, who has risked your life in defence of your country, and some of us was soldiers in the war and fought in the same battles, we are sorry to have recourse to harsh means therefore as you have the power you will release Lawrence Lynch and Owen McCormack, who is another innocent man—if you do not we are sufficiently numerous and fully determined and will bring fire and destruction on your property first and if that fails we will in the end take your life— Remember we are soldiers and sworn to do it or die. Remember." It is unnecessary to say this modest petition had no effect on a man of McArthur's nerve; neither did these courteous petitioners make an unmeaning and empty threat. On the night of the tenth of November (only fifteen days after the date of the above letter) about nine o'clock at night, his large barn, being full of grain, was discovered wrapped in flames. As the citizens of Chillicothe had not then retired to rest, and the barn being in full view of the town, the citizens, with praiseworthy activity, rushed to the fire. As a Mr. John Harly was running to the fire on foot, he saw a horse with a bridle on, near the road side. Harly mounted the horse and rode him to the conflagration. This horse must have belonged to the incendiary who put the fire to the barn. Mr. Harly advertised the horse in several newspapers, but no person ever appeared to claim him. Some months after the burning of the barn, an elegant saddle was found in a deep hollow below the barn. The horse was exhibited at public meetings in several counties, but no one knew him. The incendiary must have come from a distant place, or the horse would have led to his discovery.

General McArthur's term of Governor expired without any thing further occurring worthy of notice. He was again a candidate for a seat in the house of representatives of congress, and lost his election by one vote. Here, then, is closed the history of his public life.

I have omitted to notice, in its progressive date, a circumstance that befell Gen. McArthur, which accident has been the ultimate cause of clouding the evening of his days in misery. On the 6th day of February, 1830, as he was passing in the street of the city of Columbus, on a side walk with a covering like a porch projecting twelve feet into the street, the roof of this projection being covered with a heavy fall of snow, the slight frame-work gave way just as McArthur came under it, and crushed him on the pavement. The roof was moved from him as soon as possible. In one of his knees all the joints were broken; and he was otherwise horridly bruised in every part of the body—so much so, that his life was despaired of for some time. He, at length, partially recovered: the broken knee still remains crippled, and gives way as easy backwards as forward. From the severe crushing his body received in this melancholy accident, his bodily powers have been constantly on the decline. His once powerful and energetic mind appears to sink and give way with his bodily strength. The once athletic and ambitious Duncan McArthur, is now neither an object of envy to his enemies, nor much attended to by those who formerly professed to be his devoted friends. Almost ever since the accident happened him, he has been confined to his room, only occasionally taking a little exercise in his carriage. Instead of being that strong, athletic man, that exposure nor hardship could weary, nor danger appal, he is now a helpless old man, that requires assistance to rise or lie down. Such a contrast as is exhibited in this man, should humble the pride of strength and ambition.

Although it is but a few years since the fatal accident took place, he appears to be already almost forgotten by all, but more especially by the gay and fashionable, who in the days of health and prosperity, fluttered around him,

like satellites around a brilliant planet. He is now almost
a stranger, where, a short time since, his word was law.
Such are the changeful vicissitudes in human affairs. It
is in the time of adversity that the value of a real disinterested friendship proves its worth. He had one friend
who clung to him in his afflictions, and used every means
in her power to sooth his mind and anticipate his wants
—his wife, the partner of his fortune, stood by him in
his time of suffering ; and diligently watched over his
couch, night and day, till her frail frame gave way by
constant watching and fatigue. She sickened, and died
on the 23d of October, 1836, in the fifty-seventh year of
her age. She was an exemplary and religious woman,
well versed in business, and whose prudence and care
over her husband's domestic affairs, contributed largely
to his happiness and interest. No woman, in Chillicothe
or its vicinity, more generously relieved the necessities
of the poor. By her wealth she was enabled to be liberal ; and her strong and discriminating mind could clearly
discover the proper objects of charity. May her children imitate her moral, prudent, and industrious example,
and prove themselves worthy of such a mother !

Since the death of his wife, General McArthur remains
with but little change : the lonely occupant of his room,
he is indeed " solitary and almost alone." His mind is
in such a morbid state, that it presents no picture of what
it once was. Absent and indifferent on most subjects,
it can only be occasionally roused to reflection on his
own affairs.

General McArthur's private character, in many respects,
was worthy of imitation. His energy and untiring industry in whatever pursuit he engaged, deserves the
highest praise. Wherever he came across an old
frontier man in distress, his purse was open for his
relief. His hospitality at his own mansion, was bor-

dering on extravagance; no one left him hungry or thirsty. Notwithstanding that he was liberal in feeding the hungry, and clothing the naked, he was admitted to be a close and severe dealer.

[Face 183.]   General Wayne.

A SKETCH OF THE LIFE

OF

CAPTAIN WILLIAM WELLS

OF GEN. WAYNE'S ARMY, IN 1794.

CHAPTER I.

It is possible that the author claims more merit for the achievements of the old frontier men, than the men of the present day are willing to admit. However that may be, he here presents to the reading public a few acts, which took place on the campaign with Gen. Wayne, in 1794.

Gen. Wayne had a bold, vigilant, and dexterous enemy to contend with. It became indispensable for him to use the utmost caution in his movements, to guard against surprise. To secure his army against the possibility of being ambuscaded, he employed a number of the best woodsmen the frontier afforded, to act as spies or rangers. Captain Ephraim Kibby, one of the first settlers at Columbia, eight miles above Cincinnati, who had distinguished himself as a bold and intrepid soldier, in defending that infant settlement, commanded the principal part of the spies. The writer of this article, and his brother Thomas, were attached to Captain Kibby's company of rangers. This will account for the author's intimate knowledge of the subject of which he is giving a relation. A very effective division of the spies was commanded by Captain William Wells.

183

Captain Wells had been taken prisoner by the Indians when quite a youth; he grew to manhood with them, and consequently was well acquainted with all their wiles and stratagems. From causes not now remembered, about eighteen months previous to the time of which I am writing, he left the Indians, and returned to his relatives and friends in civilized life. Being raised by the Indians, well acquainted with the country which was about to be the theater of action, talking several of their languages fluently, and withal desperately brave, such a soldier was a real, effective acquisition to the army. Captain Wells was the same gentleman named by the Rev. O. M. Spencer, in the narrative of his capture by the Indians, and release from captivity. It was to Capt. Wells that Mr. Spencer was primarily indebted for his liberty. (See Spencer's Narrative, page 105.) I am particular in describing this corps of the army, as they performed more real service than any other.

Attached to Captain Wells' command were the following men : Robert M'Lelland (whose name has been since immortalized by the graphic pen of Washington Irving, in his " Astoria"), was one of the most athletic and active men on foot, that has appeared on this globe. On the grand parade at Fort Greenville, where the ground was very little inclined, to show his activity, he leaped over a road-wagon with the cover stretched over; the wagon and bows were eight and a half feet high. Next was Henry Miller. He and a younger brother, named Christopher, had been made captives by the Indians when young, and adopted into an Indian family. Henry Miller lived with them till he was about twenty-four years of age ; and although he had adopted all their manners and customs, he at that age began to think of returning to his relatives among the whites. The longer he reflected on the subject, the stronger his resolution grew to make an attempt to leave the Indians. He communicated his intention to his brother Christopher, and used every reason he was capable of, to induce his brother to accompany him in his flight. All his arguments were ineffectual. Christopher was young when made captive—he was now a good hunter, an expert woodsman, and in the full sense of the word, a free and independent Indian. Henry Miller set off alone through the woods, and arrived safe among his friends in Kentucky. Captain Wells was well acquainted with Miller during his captivity, and knew that he possessed that firm intrepidity which would render him a valuable companion in time of need. To these were added a Mr. Hickman, and Mr. Thorp, who were men of tried worth in Indian warfare.

Captain Wells and his four companions were confidential and privileged gentlemen in camp, who were only called upon to do duty upon very particular and interesting occasions. They were permitted a *carte blanche* among the horses of the dragoons, and when upon duty went well mounted ; whilst the spies commanded by Captain Kibby went on foot, and were kept constantly on the alert, scouring the country in every direction.

The head quarters of the army being at Fort Greenville, in the month of June, Gen. Wayne dispatched Captain Wells and his company, with orders to bring into camp an Indian as a prisoner, in order that he could interrogate him as to the future intentions of the enemy. Captain Wells proceeded with cautious steps through the Indian country. He crossed the river St. Mary, and thence to the river Auglaize, without meeting any straggling party of Indians. In passing up the Auglaize they discovered a smoke : they then dismounted, tied their horses, and proceeded cautiously to reconnoiter the enemy. They found three Indians camped on a high, open piece of ground, clear of·brush, or any underwood. As it was open woods, they found it would be difficult

14

to approach the camp without being discovered. Whilst they were reconnoitering, they saw not very distant from the camp, a tree which had lately fallen. They returned and went round the camp, so as to get the top of the fallen tree between them and the Indians. The tree-top being full of leaves, would serve as a shelter to screen them from observation. They went forward upon their hands and knees, with the noiseless movements of the cat, till they reached the tree-top. They were now within seventy or eighty yards of the camp. The Indians were sitting or standing about the fire, roasting their venison, laughing and making other merry antics, little dreaming that death was about stealing a march upon them. Arrived at the fallen tree, their purpose of attack was soon settled ; they determined to kill two of the enemy, and make the third prisoner. McLelland, who it will be remembered, was almost as swift on foot as a deer of the forest, was to catch the Indian, whilst to Wells and Miller was confided the duty of shooting the other two. One of them was to shoot the one on the right, the other the one on the left. Their rifles were in prime order, the muzzles of their guns were placed on the log of the fallen tree, the sights were aimed for the Indians' hearts—whiz went the balls, and both Indians fell. Before the smoke of the burnt powder had risen six feet, McLelland was running at full stretch, with tomahawk in hand, for the Indian. The Indian bounded off at the top of his speed, and made down the river ; but by continuing in that direction he discovered that McLelland would head him. He turned his course and made for the river. The river here had a bluff bank, about twenty feet high. When he came to the bank he sprang [down into the river, the bottom of which was a soft mud, into which he sunk to the middle. While he was endeavoring to extricate himself out of the mud, McLelland came to the top of the high bank, and without hesitation sprang upon him, as he was wallowing in the mire. The Indian drew his knife—McLelland raised his tomahawk—told him to throw down his knife, or he would kill him instantly. He threw down his knife, and surrendered without any further effort at resistance.

By the time the scuffle had ceased in the mire, Wells and his companions came to the bank, and discovered McLelland and the Indian quietly sticking in the mire. As their prisoner was now secure, they did not think it prudent to take the fearful leap the others had done. They selected a place where the bank was less precipitous, went down and dragged the captive out of the mud, and tied him. He was very sulky, and refused to speak either Indian or English. Some of the party went back for their horses, whilst others washed the mud and paint from the prisoner. When washed, he turned out to be a white man, but still refused to speak, or give any account of himself. The party scalped the two Indians whom they had shot, and then set off with their prisoner for head quarters. Whilst on their return to Fort Greenville, Henry Miller began to admit the idea that it was possible their prisoner was his brother Christopher, whom he had left with the Indians some years previous. Under this impression he rode alongside of him, and called him by his Indian name. At the sound of his name he started, and stared round, and eagerly inquired how he came to know his name. The mystery was soon explained—their prisoner was indeed Christopher Miller! A mysterious providence appeared to have placed Christopher Miller in a situation in the camp, by which his life was preserved. Had he been standing on the right or left, he would inevitably have been killed. But that fate which appears to have doomed the Indian race to extinction, permitted the white man to live, whilst the Indians were permitted to meet that " fate they cannot shun."

Captain Wells arrived safely with their prisoner at Fort Greenville. He was placed in the guard house, where Gen. Wayne frequently interrogated him as to what he knew of the future intentions of the Indians. Captain Wells and Henry Miller were almost constantly with Christopher in the guard house, urging him to leave off the thought of living longer with the Indians, and to join his relatives among the whites. Christopher for some time was reserved and sulky, but at length became more cheerful, and agreed, if they would release him from confinement, that he would remain with the whites. Captain Wells and Henry Miller solicited Gen. Wayne for Christopher's liberty. Gen. Wayne could scarcely deny such pleaders any request they could make, and without hesitation ordered Christopher Miller to be set at liberty ; remarking, that should he deceive them and return to the enemy, they would be but one the stronger. Christopher was set at liberty, and appeared pleased with his change of situation. He was mounted on a fine horse, and otherwise well equipped for war. He joined the company with Captain Wells and his brother, and fought bravely against the Indians during the continuance of the war. He was true to his word, and upon every occasion proved himself an intrepid and daring soldier.

CHAPTER II.

As soon as Captain Wells and company had rested themselves and recruited their horses, they were anxious for another *bout* with the red men. Time, without action, was irksome to such stirring spirits. Early in July they left Greenville ; their company was then strengthened by the addition of Christopher Miller ; their orders were to bring in prisoners. They pushed through the country, always dressed and painted in Indian style; they passed on, crossing the river St. Mary, and then through the country near to the river Auglaize, where they met a single Indian, and called to him to surrender. This man, notwithstanding that the whites were six against one, refused to surrender. He leveled his rifle, and as the whites were approaching him on horseback, he fired, but missed his mark, and then took to his heels to effect his escape. The undergrowth of brush was so very thick that he gained upon his pursuers. McLelland and Christopher Miller dismounted, and McLelland soon overhauled him. The Indian, finding himself overtaken by his pursuers, turned round and made a blow at Mc-Lelland with his rifle, which was parried. As McLelland's intention was not to kill, he kept him at bay till Christopher Miller came up, when they closed in upon him, and made him prisoner without receiving any injury. They turned about for head quarters, and arrived safely at Fort Greenville. Their prisoner was reputed to be a Potawotamie chief, whose courage and prowess was scarcely equaled. As Christopher Miller had performed his part on this occasion to the entire satisfaction of the brave spirits with whom he acted, he had, as he merited, their entire confidence.

It is not my intention to give a detailed account of the various actions performed by the spies attached to Gen. Wayne's army, although it would be a narrative most interesting to western readers. I have selected only a few of the acts performed by Captain Wells, and his enterprising followers, to show what kind of men they were. History, in no age of the world, furnishes so many instances of repeated acts of bravery as were performed by the frontier men of western Pennsylvania, western Virginia, and Kentucky; yet these acts of apparent desperation were so frequently repeated by numbers, that they were scarcely noticed at the time as being any other than the common occurrence of the day.

I have no doubt, that during General Wayne's campaign, Captain Wells, and the few men he commanded, brought in not less than twenty prisoners, and killed more than an equal number. Desperate as they were in combat, that bravery was only a part of their merit, is demonstrated by the following circumstance.

On one of Captain Wells' peregrinations through the Indian country, as he came to the bank of the river St. Mary, he discovered a family of Indians coming up the river in a canoe. He dismounted, and concealed his men near the bank of the river, whilst he went himself to the bank, in open view, and called to the Indians to come over. As he was dressed in Indian style, and spoke to them in their own language, the Indians, not expecting an enemy in that part of the country, without any suspicion of danger went across the river. The moment the canoe struck the shore, Wells heard the cocks of his comrades' rifles cry, " nick, nick," as they prepared to shoot the Indians; but who should be in the canoe but his Indian father and mother, with their children! As his comrades were coming forward with their rifles cocked, ready to pour in the deadly storm upon the devoted Indians, Wells called upon them to hold their hands and desist. He then informed them who those Indians were, and solemnly declared, that the man who would attempt to injure one of them, would receive a ball in his head. He said to his men, " that that family had fed him when he was hungry, clothed him when he was naked, and kindly nursed him when sick; and in every respect were as kind and affectionate to him as they were to their own children."

This short, pathetic speech, found its way to the sympathetic hearts of his leather-hunting-shirt comrades. Although they would have made but a shabby appearance on being introduced to a fashionable tea-party, or into a splendid ball-room, amongst polished grandees, or into a ceremonious levee, to pass through unmeaning becks, bows, and courtesies—the present was a scene of nature, and gratitude the motive; they all, at once, entered into their leader's feelings. I never knew a truly brave man, who could hold back the tear of sympathy at the joy, grief, or sorrow of his fellow man: it is the timid coward who is cruel when he has the advantage. Those hardy soldiers approved of the motives of Captain Wells' lenity to the enemy. They threw down their rifles and tomahawks, went to the canoe, and shook hands with the trembling Indians in the most friendly manner. Captain Wells assured them they had nothing to fear from him; and after talking with them to dispel their fears, he said, " that General Wayne was approaching with an overwhelming force; that the best thing the Indians could do was to make peace; that the white men did not wish to continue the war. He urged his Indian father for the future to keep out of the reach of danger." He then bade them farewell: they appeared grateful for his clemency. They then pushed off their canoe, and went down the river as fast as they could propel her.

Captain Wells and his comrades, though perfect desperadoes in fight, upon this occasion proved they largely possessed that real gratitude and benevolence of heart, which does honor to human kind.

CHAPTER III.

EARLY in the month of August, when the main army had arrived at the place subsequently designated as fort Defiance, General Wayne wished to be informed of the intentions of the enemy. For this purpose, Captain Wells was again dispatched to bring in another prisoner. The distance from fort Defiance to the British fort, at the mouth of the Maumee river, was only forty-five miles, and he would not have to travel far before he would find Indians. As his object was to bring in a prisoner, it became necessary for him to keep out of the way of large parties, and endeavor to fall in with some stragglers, who might be easily subdued and captured.

They went cautiously down the river Maumee, till they came opposite the site on which fort Meigs was erected by General Harrison, in 1813. This was two miles above the British fort, then called fort Campbell. On the west bank of the Maumee was an Indian village. Wells and his party rode into the village, as if they had just come from the British fort. Being dressed and painted in complete Indian style, they rode through the village, occasionally stopping and talking to the Indians in their own language. No suspicion of who they were was excited, the enemy believing them to be Indians from a distance, coming to take a part in the battle which they all knew was shortly to be fought. After they had passed the village some distance, they fell in with an Indian man and woman on horseback, who were returning to the town from hunting. This man and woman were made captives without resistance. They then set off for fort Defiance.

As they were rapidly proceeding up the Maumee river, a little after dark, they came near a large encampment of

Indians, who were merrily amusing themselves around their camp-fires. Their prisoners were ordered to be silent, under pain of instant death. They went round the camp with their prisoners, till they got about half a mile above it, where they halted to consult on their future operations. After consultation, they concluded to gag and tie their prisoners, and ride back to the Indian camp, and give them a rally, in which each should kill his Indian. They deliberately got down, gagged, and fastened their prisoners to trees, rode boldly into the Indian encampment, and halted, with their rifles lying across the pummels of their saddles. They inquired when last they had heard of General Wayne, and the movements of his army; how soon, and where it was expected the battle would be fought. The Indians who were standing around Wells and his desperadoes, were very communicative, answering all their interrogatories without suspecting any deceit in their visitors. At length, an Indian, who was sitting some distance from them, said in an under tone, in another tongue, to some who were near him, that he suspected that these strangers had some mischief in their heads. Wells overheard what he said, and immediately gave the preconcerted signal, and each fired his rifle into the body of an Indian, at not more than six feet distance. The Indian who had suspected them, the moment he made the remark, and a number of others, rose up with their rifles in their hands, but not before Wells and his party had each shot an Indian. As soon as Wells and his party fired, they put spurs to their horses, laying with their breasts on the horses' necks, so as to lessen the mark for the enemy to fire at. They had not got out of the light of the camp-fire, before the Indians shot at them. As McLelland lay close on his horse's neck, he was shot, the ball passing under his shoulder-blade, and coming out at the top of his shoulder Captain Wells was shot through the arm on which he

carried his rifle; the arm was broken, and his trusty
rifle fell. The rest of the party and their horses received
no injury.

What confidence, what self-possession was displayed
by these men, in this terrific encounter! They beat
General Marion and his sergeants hollow! They had
come off unscathed in so many desperate conflicts, that
their souls were callous to danger. As they had no
rivals in the army, they aimed to outdo their former exploits. To ride into the enemy's camp, and enter into
conversation with them, without betraying the least appearance of trepidation or confusion, proves how well
their souls were steeled. This action of real life even
rivals the fictious, though sublime muse of the Grecian
poet. Homer sends forth his invincible hero, protected
by the invulnerable panoply of Jupiter, to make a night
attack upon the enemy. Diomede makes the successful
assault upon sleeping foes. Not so our western heroes;
they boldly went into the midst of the enemy, while
their camp-fires were burning bright, and openly commenced the work of death.

After having performed this act of military superero-
gation, they rode at full speed to where their captives
were confined, mounted them on horses, and set off for
fort Defiance. Captain Wells and McLelland were severely wounded; and to fort Defiance, a distance of about
thirty miles, they had to travel, before they could rest or
receive the aid of a surgeon. As their march would be
slow and painful, one of the party was dispatched at full
speed to fort Defiance, for a guard and a surgeon. As
soon as Captain Wells' messenger arrived at fort Defiance, with the tidings of the wounds and perilous situation of these heroic and faithful spies, very great sympathy was manifested in the minds of all. General
Wayne's feeling for the suffering soldier, was at all times
quick and sensitive: we can then imagine how intense

was his solicitude, when informed of the sufferings and perils of his confidential and chosen band. Without a moment's delay, he dispatched a surgeon, and a company of the swiftest dragoons, to meet, assist, and guard these brave fellows to head-quarters. Suffice to say, they arrived safely in camp, and the wounded recovered in due course of time.

As the battle was fought, and a brilliant victory won, a few days after this affair took place, Captain Wells and his daring comrades, were not engaged in any further acts of hostility, till the war with the Indians was auspiciously concluded by a lasting treaty of peace.

A new and happy era was about dawning on the west. A cruel and exterminating war, of nearly fifty years' continuance, was closed by a general peace with the red men of the forest. The names and memories of these brave men, whose march was in the front of danger, should be held in veneration by the millions who now repose in peace and quiet on the territory they acquired at the risk of their lives, in a thousand battles.

It is very natural for the reader to inquire, what became of these men after the war terminated? What became of Thorp, Hickman, and the two Millers, I have never learned; but, if alive, they probably reside in some smoky cabin in the far and distant west, unknown and unhonored. The last I heard of the brave, hardy, and active McLelland, he had just returned to St. Louis, in 1812, from an expedition across the Rocky mountains. He had been to the Pacific ocean, at the mouth of the Columbia river. Such a tour, through uncultivated, unpeopled oceans of prairie, and then to labor through the tempestuous bursts of snow and sleet, which whirl in almost continual storms around the heights of the frightful world of rocks which compose the dreary Rocky mountains, where winter eternally reigns—this enterprise was equal to the daring genius of the man.

The fate of the brave and lamented Captain Wells was sealed during the late war, on the 15th of August, 1812, near fort Dearborn, at the mouth of the Chicago river, on the bank of lake Michigan, where he was slain in an unequal combat; where sixty-four whites were attacked by upwards of four hundred Indian warriors. Then fell as bold a spirit as ever shouldered a rifle or wielded a tomahawk.

A SKETCH OF THE LIFE

OF

GENERAL SIMON KENTON,

OF KENTUCKY.

For the benefit and gratification of those who may come after us, it is right to preserve, for future inspection, records of the actions of men, who have been instruments to prepare the way for settling the Western Country.

To dispossess the barbarous occupants of the almost boundless wilds of the west, required men of resolute minds; and whose bodily composition contained more than the usual quantity of lime and iron, to enable them to endure the fatigue and hardships they had to encounter.

It is a remarkable fact, of nearly all the old frontier-men, that although their trade was war, their hospitality was boundless. They relieved the wants of the stranger, fed the hungry, and clothed the naked. No traveller was permitted to pay for meat, drink, or lodging at their cabins.

General Simon Kenton was born in the month of March, A. D. 1755, in the county of Fauquier, state of Virginia. His father was a native of Ireland; his mother, whose maiden name was Miller, was of Scotch descent, her ancestors being among the first immigrants to Virginia. His parents being poor, he was, to the age of sixteen, employed chiefly in the culture of corn and to-

197

bacco. At this period, our country being governed by a kingly aristocracy, which lorded over the laboring classes in all the pride of a superior caste, the poor—having no motive for exertion—were not ashamed to be ignorant. Learning was then almost exclusively in possession of the clergy, lawyers, and commercial men, or the wealthy farmers, whose estates were entailed. Common schools were then almost unknown in the southern states. As the Kenton family were poor, Simon grew to manhood without learning his A B C.

Notwithstanding man is a free agent, and his future character and usefulness depend on his own choice, yet we see, on some occasions, uncontrollable circumstances fix his destiny : an invisible influence appears to guide his fate. In the sixteenth year of Kenton's age, an incident occurred, which gave a new direction to his mind, and apparently changed the destiny of his life.

The neighborhood in which he was brought up was sparsely inhabited, and implements of husbandry, not required for constant use, such as broad-axes, whip and crosscut saws, were purchased and used as common property. As was common, under such circumstances, social intercourse prevailed, and they were in the constant habit of assisting each other at house-raisings, log-rollings, corn-huskings, &c. Old Mr. Kenton had a neighbor by the name of Veach, with whom he lived on the most friendly terms. At this time, one of Mr. Veach's sons married a girl to whom Simon was much attached. The truth was, although he was only turned of sixteen years of age, he was deeply in love. There are few but know something of the frenzied feelings occasioned by disappointment in this passion. He, like most unfortunate lovers, felt himself exquisitely injured. Being of a warm temperament, and in his first love, his mind was in a tempest. He thought himself undone, and, in the heat of his passion, unbidden, went to the wedding, where mirth and good-humor prevailed till his intrusion. As soon as he entered the room, he looked round and saw the new-married pair seated on the side of a bed, and without hesitation, went forward and obtruded himself between the married couple. A brother of the bridegroom saw the intrusion, and inticed Simon away under the pretence of wishing to treat him, and while in the act of drinking, William Veach struck him a blow which laid him prostrate on the floor—followed it with a severe beating, and sent him home with black eyes and sore bones. As this affair was looked upon as a boyish freak, it did not interrupt the general harmony and good feeling of the two families ; but Simon, who lost his girl, and got a severe flogging into the bargain, viewed the affair in a different light. He felt his future prospects ruined and his character disgraced, and in sullen silence determined on revenge, for which an opportunity soon offered.

His father sent him to old Mr. Veach's for a crosscut saw. Mr. Veach had rived some timber in boards about one hundred and fifty yards from his house, and William Veach was engaged in carrying them to his father, who was covering a small outhouse. After Simon had procured the saw, he and William walked together to the place where the boards had been made. Here they stopped, and Simon laid down the saw, and said to William, " You and your friends had fine sport the other night, in beating me at the wedding : now, we are alone, and can have a fair fight."   William replied, " that they had been raised boys together, and never had a difference, except the one mentioned, which was a foolish, drunken frolic ; that he wished to say no more about it., that he had no desire to fight, and would prefer to live in peace and friendship." But, as Simon would admit of no apology, they threw off their coats and went to work. Victory for some time hung in a doubtful balance. Simon, at length, threw his antagonist to the ground, and as quick

as thought, drawing his queue of long hair round a small
sapling, had him completely in his power. There he
beat him until his strength began to fail; then, letting go
the hair, he kicked him on the breast and stomach till
no further resistance was offered. Simon, having now
gratified his vindictive feelings, desisted from further
abuse. William attempted to rise, but immediately sunk,
and began to puke blood. As Simon had not intended
to kill him, he now raised him up, and spoke kindly to
him, but received no answer, and beheld him sink to the
ground, apparently lifeless. After standing by him for
some time, without perceiving any signs of returning
life, he started for home, under the most poignant and
awful sensations. By the time he had traveled half way
home, he began to reflect, seriously, on the rash act he
had committed. He knew that young Veach would soon
be missed, and that his father had seen them walk together; and consequently, it was impossible for him to
think of concealing or denying the murder. The horror
of being hanged then rushed upon his guilty soul, and he
resolved upon immediate flight. He laid down his saw
on the path, and without stopping to see or consult
parents or friends, he fled to the woods, and made for
the Allegheny mountains. This was on the 6th of April,
A. D. 1771. Lying concealed by day, he traveled by
night. In this way, he passed over the mountains, and
came to a place called Ise's Ford, on Cheat river, a
branch of the Monongahela. When he arrived at this
place, he was nearly exhausted with fatigue and famine.
Here he changed his name to that of Simon Butler.
While he remained in this neighborhood, his mind was
a continual prey to bitter remorse and fear; fancying
that every one he saw was in pursuit of him.

What heart could fail to pity the situation of the unfortunate youth, who, by one rash act, was driven from his
friends and home—a fugitive from justice—under a ficti-

tious name, a solitary wanderer: illiterate, pennyless and friendless. And the act, too, which had plunged him into this forlorn condition, seems to have been entirely foreign from his nature. In subsequent life, he manifested a mild and forgiving disposition, and maintained a character entirely the reverse of what his early conduct seemed to prognosticate.

That Providence, who so overruled the wickedness of Joseph's brethren, as to make it productive of blessings to him and to them, seems to have used the circumstance above mentioned, for the purpose of forcing into active service, one whose athletic frame and fortitude, and decision of character, were admirably adapted to the toils and dangers to which he was exposed, and which qualities were indispensable in preparing the way for the settlement and civilization of the almost boundless West. Well it is for man, that he can only see the present. He is too apt to anticipate evil; and could he penetrate the veil which conceals the future, how often would despair banish hope, and paralize his efforts. God, in mercy to his creatures, keeps the future out of sight. If it had been possible for Kenton, at this time, to have foreseen the thorny path through which he was doomed to pass, his soul, though large and fearless, would have shrunk from the appalling prospect, and the western country been deprived of the prince of pioneers.

I will now return to my narrative. He had been occasionally laboring and sauntering about Cheat river for some months, when he fell in company with William Grills, Jacob Greathouse, and two men by the name of Mahon, who were preparing to descend the river Ohio, on a hunting tour. Having previously, by his labor, procured a good rifle, he was willing to go on any expedition that would take him farther from home. He joined this party, and assisted in making a canoe. This being completed, they embarked, and went down the stream

15

till they came to Fort Pitt, (now the city of Pittsburgh). At this place they met with an Indian trader, by the name of David Duncan, who informed the Mahons, that their father (whom the Indians had taken captive some time previous) was still alive, and where and how he could be found, and for what sum he could be ransomed. The two young Mahons immediately left the hunting party, and went in search of their father, to release him from captivity. To the mortification of Kenton, the hunting tour was abandoned.

As there was then a small garrison maintained at Fort Pitt, Kenton turned in to hunt for that garrison. At this place he first became acquainted with the notorious renegado, Simon Girty. Girty was a man of talents, had great influence in the garrison, and with the Indians, and showed Kenton all the kindness and attention that was in his power, and subsequently saved his life.

In the fall of the year, he fell in with John Strader and George Yeager, who were going down the Ohio, on a hunting tour. Yeager had been raised by the Indians, and could talk several of their languages. He had passed a part of his time on the south side of the river Ohio in the cane land in Kentucky. With these men our wanderer agreed to proceed down the Ohio, he knew not and did not care whither. At that time a small trading establishment with the Indians was kept by one John Gibson, at a place called Log's Town, which was the only settlement of the whites below Pittsburgh. Here they halted a day or two. From thence they proceeded down the Ohio to the Mingo town, which is about seventy miles below Pittsburgh, and three miles below Steubenville. As it was a time of peace here, they frolicked and danced with the young Indians. From thence they proceeded down the Ohio to a Delaware town, three miles below the mouth of the Little Kanawha. Here they passed a few days very agreeably, fishing, hunting, and dancing with the Indians.

As none of these friendly Indians had been down the Ohio to the cane land, they could afford no intelligence on the subject; and Yeager, when there, was young, and had gone either from Detroit, or past Vincennes, and did not know at what point he had crossed the Ohio. As the principal object of their expedition was to explore the cane country, and being ignorant at what point to land for this purpose, they descended the Ohio to near the mouth of Kentucky river, stopping occasionally, without finding any. It is a remarkable fact that, though there was abundance of cane in the country, it did not grow near the bank of the river any where above the mouth of Kentucky river. Being disappointed in the main object of their expedition, they commenced a retrograde movement, and proceeded leisurely up the Ohio. On their return, they examined Licking river, Locust, Bracken, Salt Lick, and Kinnikinnick creek, and Tiger and the Sandy rivers, without finding any cane. By this time, the winter season had commenced. They engaged in hunting, until they arrived at the mouth of the Big Kanawha river, and thence up that river to the mouth of Elk river, where they built a camp, and remained for the winter. During the winter, they had good success in trapping. Beaver, otter, and other game were plenty. In the spring of 1772 they went down the Kanawha to the Ohio, where they met a French trader, to whom they sold their peltry, and procured ammunition, clothing and other articles necessary for hunters.

The summer and fall of 1772 were spent by him and his two companions in roaming and hunting along the Ohio, between Big Kanawha and Big Sandy rivers. He describes this as the most happy season of his life. They were blessed with health, found plenty of game and fish; and free from the cares of the ambitious world, and the vexations of domestic life, they passed their time in that happy state of ease, indolence, and independence, which is the glory of the hunter of the forest. Late in the fall, they returned to their old camp on the Big Kanawha, and spent the winter in hunting and trapping.

About this time the clouds of the American revolution began to appear, and many of the Indians espoused the cause of the mother country, and commenced their depredations upon the frontier settlements. In the month of March, 1773, as Kenton and his companions were lolling about their camp, in the dusk of the evening, not thinking of danger, a party of Indians fired upon them, and killed Yeager. Strader and Kenton fled, with only their lives and their shirts; and in this naked and helpless condition, they wandered for six days and nights, without fire or food. It will be recollected, that the month of March affords none of the casual subsistence of nuts, berries, or pawpaws, that may be found in the forest at other seasons; consequently, they were entirely without sustenance. Add to this, their barefooted and naked condition, exposed day and night, to the bleak winds, and " the peltings of the pitiless storms," compelled to travel through briars, and over rough stones and frozen ground, and we have a scene of sufferings that baffles description. Their legs and bodies became lacerated and torn, and their feet cut, bruised, and inflamed to such a degree, that they were more than two days in traveling the last six miles. It seems almost a miracle, that they did not sink in despair, and put an end to their miserable existence. But such is the love of life implanted in our nature, that we cling to it under the most gloomy and appalling circumstances.

> " Hope, like the glimmering taper's light,
> Adorns and cheers the way ;
> And still, as darker grows the night,
> Emits a brighter ray."

Protected by the guardian care of a merciful Providence, and still hoping for relief, they reached, on the sixth day a point on the Ohio river, within six miles of the mouth of the Kanawha, where, to their great joy, they met with Joel Rease, Jacob Greathouse, William Grills, and the two Mahans, who were of the party, it will be recollected, with which Kenton first united on Cheat river. They had returned from searching for their father, and were now descending the Ohio, with a view of exploring the country bordering upon it. When they came in view of the camp of these men, Strader was so exhausted, that it seemed impossible for him to travel another mile, and Kenton was not in much better condition. Friendship and hospitality were, at that time, universal among western adventurers: consequently, Kenton and his companion were received with much kindness, and had their wants supplied, and their sufferings alleviated as far as circumstances would admit.

Under this treatment, their strength returned, and their spirits revived, and uniting with the party upon which they had so fortunately fallen, they began to think of new adventures. After deliberating some time, it was concluded to return up the Ohio, till Kenton and Strader should meet with some opportunity of supplying themselves with arms, to enable them the better to meet the danger with which they were threatened by the hostile Indians. The whole party then ascended to the mouth of the Little Kanawha, where they found a Dr. Briscoe, who was attempting to make a settlement at that place. The doctor was a man of wealth, and had a number of slaves and some white persons with him. While the rest of his party proceeded higher up the river, Kenton bought a rifle, and hired himself as a hunter for Briscoe, till he should pay for it. About this time, settlements were commenced on the Ohio, at Wheeling, Grave creek, and at the head of the Long Reach.

By the time Kenton had paid for his rifle, and procured a few other necessary articles, Michael Tyger, and
some others, from Virginia, came down the river, on their
way to the country below. With them Kenton united,
and proceeded to the mouth of Scioto, where they halted,
to wait the arrival of Captain Bullit, who had promised
to join them at that place. After waiting some time, and
seeing nothing of Bullit, who had, probably, passed them
in the night, or in a thick fog, they left the Scioto, and
returned up the river, surveying, and making tomahawk
improvements, as far as the mouth of Big Sandy. At
Big Sandy they were overtaken by some men, who informed them that Bullit had gone down, and was lying
at the mouth of the Big Miami, at a place they called
Bullitsburgh; that they had gone out with him, and were
then on their return. Tyger and his party immediately
turned, and proceeded to the place designated, but found
Bullit's camp vacated, and could gain no intelligence con-
cerning him. Concluding that Bullit and his party had
been killed or taken by the Indians, and apprehending a
similar fate to await themselves, they became alarmed,
and commenced an immediate retreat. Halting opposite
the Three Islands, they called a council, whose deliberations pronounced it hazardous to attempt a return by
water. Hence, they destroyed their canoes, and with
Kenton as a pilot, took up the line of march through the
wilderness, for the settlements on Green Briar, where
they arrived in safety, after a fatiguing journey, over
mountains, across rivers, and through thickets, where the
foot of civilized man had never before trod. Thus, was
the first trip from Kentucky to Virginia, by land, performed under the guidance of our young adventurer.

At Green Briar, Kenton left the party, and again directed his steps towards the Monongahela country, where
he met William Grills and Jacob Greathouse, two of his
former companions, who were subsequently joined by

Samuel Cartwright and Joseph Lock. Casting in his lot
with these, Kenton prepared once more to descend the
Ohio, and winter in the wilderness. Having provided
themselves with the necessary articles for the excursion,
the party embarked and descended to the mouth of Big
Sandy, where they continued to hunt and trap till the
next spring. This spring, 1774, an Indian war appeared inevitable. The Indians had robbed some, and killed
others, and continued to manifest so much insolence, that
the hunters and traders took the alarm, and retreated to
Fort Pitt. Kenton's party sold the proceeds of their
winter's hunt, to a French trader, and following the example of others, ascended the Ohio. All the settlements
which had commenced the previous year, were now
evacuated. Some of the adventurers took shelter at a
place called Thomas's Fort, at the mouth of Ten-mile
creek; others, at Fort Pitt; so that no settlement remained on the Ohio, below the latter place.

Lord Dunmore, Governor of Virginia, early this spring,
raised an army, to proceed to the Indian country, and
chastise the aggressors. Kenton entered the army, and
was employed as a spy, to go in front and save the troops
from the snares and ambuscades of the enemy; a service
which requires steady nerve, and cool, deliberate courage. For this service Kenton was well qualified, and
acquitted himself with credit. The army moved through
the wilderness, crossed the Ohio at the mouth of Hock-
hocking, and cautiously proceeded to the Pickaway towns,
on the Scioto river. On approaching these towns, they
were met by a flag from the Indians, who sued for peace.
A treaty for the restoration of peace was entered into,
the troops returned, and were disbanded, and Kenton,
with a detachment of the army, proceeded to Fort Pitt,
which was then under the command of Major Conley.
But the army had scarcely returned, before the Indians
began again to harass the frontiers, and hence another

expedition was determined upon. The Virginia troops, commanded by Colonel Lewis, were to come down the Big Kanawha to its mouth, and there to remain till they were reinforced. At the time Colonel Lewis was expected at that place, Major Conley sent Mr. Kenton and two others with an express to him. Arriving at the mouth of Kanawha, and not finding Colonel Lewis, they concealed their despatch in a hollow tree, and commenced amusing themselves by strolling about this delightful point. Here they were surprised and fired upon by a party of Indians, which caused their separation. His comrades got together and returned to Fort Pitt, while Kenton, alone, pushed his way to Louder's fort, on the west fork of the Monongahela. Captain Louder, not believing the account Kenton gave of himself, had him arrested on the suspicion of his being a spy from the Indians, and confined him till he should hear from Major Conley, to whom he sent an express. When the messenger returned, Kenton, of course, was set at liberty, who immediately returned to Fort Pitt, received pay for his services, and was discharged from the army.

Being now out of employment, and the proper season for hunting having come, he, in company with a young man by the name of Thomas Williams, prepared a canoe, and, armed and equipped for the winter, they descended the Ohio to the mouth of Big Sandy, and thence up that river some distance, where they formed their camp. Here they remained during the winter, and had good success in hunting. Leaving this place early in the following spring, 1775, and proceeding down the Ohio, they met a French trader, who purchased their skins and furnished them with such things as they needed, to enable them to prosecute their search for the cane country.— Passing down the river, they happened to land for the night, at the mouth of a small creek, near the place afterwards known by the name of Limestone. The next morning, Kenton shouldered his rifle, and went back into the hills to look for game. After traveling two or three miles, to his great joy, he found abundance of cane growing upon the richest land he had ever seen. With this intelligence, he returned to his companion; when they sunk their canoe, gathered up their little property, and proceeded out into the cane lands. Finding a spring of good water, they made themselves a comfortable camp, and with their tomahawks commenced clearing a small piece of ground. Their clearing was finished some time in May, and from the remains of some corn which they had got from the French trader, for the purpose of parching, they obtained seed, and planted, perhaps, the first corn that was ever planted in that country on the north side of the Kentucky river. Here, tending their corn with their tomahawks, they remained the undisputed masters of all they could see, and enjoying as much happiness as circumstances would admit of, till they had the pleasure of eating roasting ears, and of seeing their corn come to perfection. This place, which was called Kenton's station, was about one mile from where the town of Washington, in Mason county, Kentucky, now stands.

When autumn came, and the leaves began to fall, Kenton concluded to take a ramble to the south, and see the extent of his rich domain. Leaving the camp in the care of Williams, he took a southern direction, and after traveling ten or twelve miles, came across some large buffaloe roads, and pursuing one of them, was brought, in a few hours, to a salt lick, on Licking river—afterward, from the color of the water, called the Bluelick. This place, now known by the name of the Lower Bluelick, is in sight of where the Lexington and Maysville turnpike crosses Licking. Here, where for ages the wild beasts of the forest had been in the habit of resorting, Kenton killed a buffaloe, and taking a piece of it to prepare for his supper, encamped on the bank of the river, and spent the night, or so much of it as was redeemed from sleep, in a train of the most pleasing reflections and anticipations. The land appeared to be a paradise. Abundance of salt was now added to an unparalleled fertility of soil, in a country abounding with every variety of game. The hunter could ask for no more—his every wish appeared to be realized.

In the morning, he was so occupied in contemplating the visions of bliss that in future prospect danced before his imagination, that it was mid-day before he left his camp, and on approaching the *lick*, he was much surprised to find a white man standing by it. Knowing that many white men lived with the Indians, and were no less savage than they, he at first hesitated, but finally marched up to him, prepared to meet a friend or to encounter an enemy. On saluting the stranger, he found that he had nothing to fear, and learned, for the first time, that he and Williams were not the only inhabitants of Kentucky. This man's name was Michael Stoner; he had come out with Daniel Boon the year before; had left Boon's station to explore and examine the country, and falling into a buffaloe road, had followed it to the lick. Stoner informed him, that there were several settlements commenced that season near the Kentucky river, and advised him to leave his present camp, and join with one of them. As Kenton relished this advice, Stoner accompanied him to his camp, where they tarried one night; then gathered up their little property, and bidding adieu to their corn patch, Kenton and Williams took up the line of march, with Stoner, for the south.

The settlements referred to above, are the following: The first in order of time, was that of Daniel Boon, now known by the name of Boonsborough, on the Kentucky river; which was followed by the station of Captain Harrod, now Harrodsburgh, on the south side of Kentucky river, and ten miles from it; and on the north

[Face 211.]   Boon the Hunter.

side were M'Clelland's settlement, where Georgetown now stands; Huston's, on the present site of Paris, and Hingston's, afterwards called Ruddle's station. The last two were situated within seven miles of each other, in the bounds of the present county of Bourbon. The inhabitants of these embryo settlements were principally from North Carolina, and had been led to the country by Colonel Boon.

After visiting and examining all the settlements, Kenton united with Hingston's party, where he spent the winer, about forty miles distant from his late residence and corn-patch. This year, and throughout the winter, the Indians remained quiet; but early in the spring of 1776, the scene was changed. The American revolution was then in full progress, and the Indians, stimulated by the British, seemed resolved to break up the infant settlements of Kentucky. Consequently every station was attacked, and few, if any, escaped without the loss of some of their men. The survivors were alarmed, and resolved to seek security by uniting their forces. Huston's station being more exposed than the others, was the first to break up. They took shelter with Captain M'Clelland; and numbers from Hingston, following their example, it was reduced to about ten men, among whom was Kenton—the first to advance, and the last to retreat. But the Indians still continuing to harass them, by killing their cattle and stealing their horses, they also concluded to abandon their fort, and fly to M'Clelland's.

Kentucky, lying within the chartered limits of Virginia, her settlements about this time attracted the attention of that state, and Major (afterwards General) George Clark, and a lawyer by the name of Jones, were sent from Wheeling with five hundred pounds of powder and lead in proportion. They concealed the ammunition on the lower of the Three Islands, and came through the woods to M'Clelland's fort. As ammunition was growing scarce, the intelligence of these timely supplies communicated much joy to the inhabitants, and tended to regive their drooping spirits. Concluding they could not spare from the fort as many men as would be necessary to insure a safe conveyance of the ammunition, Maj. Clark and Kenton set off for Harrod's fort to procure assistance. But so soon as they were gone, Mr. Jones imprudently prevailed on ten men to go with him to the place where the ammunition had been left. This was a rash step, and severely did they pay for it. On the way they were met by a body of Indians, under the command of a celebrated chief called Pluggy; a battle ensued, and the whites were defeated. Jones and William Gradon were killed, and Joseph Rodgers and Josiah Dickson taken prisoners. This happened on christmas day, 1776. When Clark and Kenton returned, they had the mortification to meet the remnant of their defeated friends. And though they were much in need of the ammunition, this unfortunate circumstance frustrated for the present the intended expedition, and the party from Harrod's fort immediately returned.

On the morning of the first day of the year, 1777, Pluggy with a few of his party came in sight of the fort. McClelland and several of his men rushed forth to give them battle, but were defeated. Capt. McClelland and two others were slain, and four wounded. After this the Indians directed their march homeward; and Kenton and Bates Collier cautiously pursued their trail to the place where they had crossed the Ohio, near the present city of Maysville; when finding that the Indians had left the country, they went up to the place where the ammunition was deposited, found it safe, and then returned to the fort. About thirty men were then raised, who proceeded to the Three Islands, and brought off the ammunition without molestation.

When Kenton and his party returned to the fort with

the ammunition, they found every thing in gloom. Panic struck, the occupants had resolved to abandon the settlement; and soon the whole party, men, women, and children, moved in a body to Harrod's fort. This removal is represented by Kenton as the most affecting sight he ever witnessed. The hardy hunters were evidently alarmed; despair sat brooding on the countenance of every female; and the children having caught the infection, vented their terrors in wailing cries, which altogether formed a scene that might have excited the sympathy of even a savage heart. All the settlements in Kentucky, except Boon's and Harrod's, were given up; and at this critical period the first legal officers were appointed in the country. A commission arrived from Virginia, giving the command to Maj. George Clark, with authority to appoint his inferior officers. Consequently, Boon and Harrod, and soon afterwards Logan, were raised to the office of captain.

By the time the spring arrived, the settlers were so much in need of clothing, that Kenton, John Haggin, and four others, started for Hingston's, to break-out some flax and hemp which had been left at that place. On approaching the station, Haggin, riding some distance before the rest, discovered a party of Indians encamped around the block-house. With this information, he returned to his companions. Kenton proposed a retreat, but Haggin rejected the proposal with indignation, and in an insolent tone pronounced that no one but a coward would think of retreating without giving the Indians a fire. To this Kenton replied, that it was not a time for quarreling, that he was ready to prove by his works, a willingness to go as far, and fire as free as any man. The whole party, except a young Dutchman who had sat on his horse listening to the dispute, then dismounted and tied their horses. But it seems that the Indians had observed Haggin when he approached the fort, and cautiously pursued him as he retreated; for scarcely had the party dismounted, when a column of Indians appeared in front, and another party, which had nearly surrounded them, commenced a distant and scattering fire through the brush. As further delay would have brought certain destruction, they instantly fled on foot, and thus escaped with their lives, but lost all their horses except the one occupied by the Dutchman. This was early in March, 1777.

When this party left Harrod's fort, Maj. Clark had directed Kenton so soon as the flax and hemp should be dressed, to take two men and pursue a circuitous route through the country to Boon's station. But on commencing their retreat from Hingston, every appearance induced the conclusion that a large body of Indians were on the march to attack Harrod's fort; Kenton therefore determined to go to Boon's alone, while the others should return and apprise Capt. Harrod of his danger, and aid in defending that place, should it be assaulted. Kenton arrived undiscovered by the enemy, in the neighborhood of Boonsborough; but knowing that the Indians were apt to lie concealed around the forts, for the purpose of destroying those who might attempt to pass to or from them, he concluded not to approach till after dark. After lying by for two or three hours, he grew impatient, left his retreat, and approached the fort, and the first thing he saw was the men of the fort carrying in the bodies of two men whom the Indians had shot an hour or two before. These men had been killed on the very route that Kenton came, and hence it is certain that the pause he had made, had saved his life.

The rest of the party, upon their retreat from Hinkston, made a rapid march for Harrod's fort, and arrived in time to warn the garrison and prepare it for the premeditated attack. Indeed, it appears that the Indians knowing they could not take the place by surprise, now their plans were discovered, moved so leisurely as to give Maj. Clark sufficient time to prepare for defence. Finding in their march a few whites at a place called Shawnee Spring, the Indians fired upon them, killed some, and took one prisoner; but the rest, by flying to the fort, gave additional evidence of the approach of the enemy; so that when the garrison on the next morning was attacked, it was fully prepared for a vigorous and obstinate defence. The siege continued several days and nights; and though the Indians succeeded in reducing the number of their opponents, they also lost many of their own men, and at last withdrew in despair.

Previous to this attack Benjamin Logan had been preparing to make a settlement near the place where Lincoln court-house now stands, and soon as the enemy retreated, he, with a number of others, left Harrod's and proceeded to the new settlement, which formed the third post at that time occupied in the country. These settlements, notwithstanding the dangers to which they were continually exposed, were constantly gaining strength by emigrants, through the wilderness, from Virginia and North Carolina.

But the Indians still continuing troublesome, each of the stations agreed to furnish two spies, to be selected by their captains, and Maj. Clark pledged the faith of Virginia for their payment. This arrangement was carried into effect by the appointment of Simon Kenton and Thomas Brooks, on the part of Boon; Samuel Moore and Bates Collier, by Harrod; and John Conrad and John Martin, by Logan. Thus selected, and having their routes and mode of operation left to their own discretion, these choice spirits were constantly on the alert, and by a faithful discharge of their arduous duties proved themselves worthy of the confidence reposed in them. During the summer their constant weekly practice was for two of them to visit the deserted stations of McClel-

16

land, Hinkston, and Huston, from thence by the Upper
and Lower Bluelicks, and to the Three Islands on the
Ohio, thence down to the mouth of Licking, and then
back to the stations. By this vigilance they were always
able, except in one instance, to give the forts timely notice of the approach of the enemy. During the summer
three different attacks were made upon Boonsborough.
The first came upon them unexpected, and in the following manner: Early one morning Kenton and two others
having loaded their guns for a hunt, were standing at the
gate, when two men who had gone into a field in sight
of the fort to drive in some horses, were fired upon by
four or five Indians. Not being wounded, they fled, and
were pursued to within sixty or seventy yards of the
fort, where an Indian overtook one of them, killed him
with his tomahawk, and commenced the operation of
taking off his scalp. But by this time Kenton was within
a few yards of the spot, and shot the Indian down; and
then in company with his hunting companions, gave
chase to the others, and pursued them into the edge of
the field. In the meantime Boon having heard the report of guns, had taken ten men and come forth to their
assistance. As these were advancing from the fort, Kenton casting his eye to the left, discovered an Indian about
to fire upon them; but Kenton shot first, and the savage
sunk to rise no more. By the time his gun was reloaded,
and Boon had come up, they heard a rush of footsteps
upon their left, and discovered that a number of Indians
had got between them and the gate. Their situation was
now perilous in the extreme. But desperate diseases require desperate remedies: Boon, therefore, gave orders
to charge through the Indian column, which was done by
first firing their rifles upon the enemy, and then beating
down all that stood in their way. But this attempt,
though it proved successful, had like to have cost the
life of their leader. Boon received a ball through the

leg, which broke the bone, and left him on the ground; but when the tomahawk was uplifted to dispatch the fallen captain, Kenton came to his rescue, discharged the contents of his gun through the body of the Indian, and conveyed his leader safe into the fort.   Of the fourteen men engaged in this affray, seven were wounded but none killed.   After they had got in, and the gate was closed, Boon sent for Kenton, and said, " Well, Simon, you have behaved like a man to-day.   Indeed you are a fine fellow."   This simple eulogium was probably as gratifying to Kenton as any thing could have been; and certainly the circumstances that called it forth were more praiseworthy than many acts that have crowned their performers with fame and titles of honor.   The Indians continued around the fort two or three days, and then withdrew.

As has been intimated, this fort sustained two other attacks during the year.   On both occasions Kenton was in the fort, and at his post; and though they were apprised of the approach of the enemy, and consequently better prepared for the assault, yet their sufferings were great.   Their cattle was killed, their horses stolen, and their situation so precarious that neither corn nor other vegetables could be cultivated.   Meat they must have or perish, and this was procured at the risk and even the loss of many lives.   To obtain this, the custom of the hunters was to steal out in the dark, and go to the distance of twelve or fifteen miles from the fort; then after killing their meat and drying it over a fire, to load themselves with as much as they could carry, and approach as near the fort as they could in safety by day, then when night came to creep cautiously to the wall, give a signal and be admitted.   In this hazardous employment many lives were sacrificed, but it was the only means of preserving their existence.   And even this afforded but scanty subsistence; for they were sometimes in want and always compelled to eat their meat without either bread or salt. Kenton was employed as a spy till the close of the year 1777.

In 1778, Capt. Watkins, with a few men, was sent from Virginia to aid in the defence of Kentucky, and was stationed at Boon's fort. It was agreed between Boon and Watkins that they would go alternately to the Blue-lick, and make salt for the settlements. Boon went first, and fell to work with about thirty men; who while thus employed were dependent upon game from the woods for their support. One day Boon having gone out to hunt, was surprised and taken prisoner by a party of Indians under the command of a chief by the name of Black Fish. As the Indians were several hundred in number, Boon capitulated for his men at the lick, who were all taken but Thomas Brooks and another, who were out on a hunting excursion. Brooks and his companion, having thus escaped, fled for Boon's station, with the doleful tidings; and on their way met Capt. Watkins proceeding to the lick, who immediately returned to the fort, and the salt scheme was abandoned. Kenton, Haggin, and a few others, anxious for their captured friends, started for the lick, found the Indian trail, and cautiously followed it to where they had crossed the Ohio, some distance above the mouth of Licking, and then returned to the station. At this time Kenton resumed his occupation of ranging the country as a spy.

In the course of the preceding winter, Maj. Clark had gone to Virginia to solicit aid in defence of the country; and having obtained a few men, he descended the Ohio about the first of June, and encamped on an island at the falls. From thence he dispatched messengers to Boon's and Harrod's stations for as many men as could be spared, to join him in an expedition against the British settlements on the Mississippi, This, with those who had families in the forts, was an unpopular movement. They were of opinion that no man ought to leave them; and consequently Kenton and Haggin were all that did go. Clark was mortified at receiving so small a reinforcement; but hearing that Capt. Montgomery, with a party of men, was making salt at Drenning's lick, he sent Kenton to solicit aid from him. Montgomery was an Irishman, "full of fight," and immediately with his whole party, ten or twelve men, proceeded to the falls. Clark's force now amounted to one hundred and fifty-three men; and seeing no prospect of increasing it, he left his camp and moved down the Ohio. What a handful of men for an expedition so hazardous. Landing at a place called Cherokee fort, below the mouth of Tennessee, they sunk their boats, and taking their baggage, provisions, and camp equipage upon their backs, marched through the wilderness one hundred and twenty miles, to Okaw, or Kaskaskia. This town and fort, commanded by one who was called the Governor, Clark determined to take by surprise. The first object was to get possession of the fort, and then he concluded the town would make no resistance. The hour of midnight was chosen for the attack. On approaching the fort they saw a light in a small house near it, and a few men were sent to surround it. They found it occupied by a Pennsylvanian, who disliked the French and was ready to aid in taking the place. He informed them that the fort kept no sentinels, and led the way to a place where the pickets were so rotten as to be easily broken down. Here the whole party entered, and being shown the Governor's room, Kenton and a few others went into it, and gently waked him out of a sound sleep. Resistance being then useless, he at once surrendered himself and his sleeping comrades, prisoners of war. This conquest, effected without the aid of artillery, wagon, or horse, was maintained to the close of the revolutionary struggle, and was of much advantage to our infant settlements in the west.

A few days after the surrender of this place, Kenton and a few others were dispatched with an express to Col. Bowman, who then commanded at Harrodsburg. He was directed to take Vincennes in his way, and endeavor to ascertain whether it could be easily taken; also, to destroy his papers, and trust to his memory for their contents, if he should be likely to fall into the hands of the enemy. Approaching Vincennes, he tore up his papers, and lying concealed by day and reconnoitering at night, continued round the town for three days. Having thus satisfied himself of the strength and situation of the place, he sent one of his companions with the intelligence back to Clark, while he and the other prosecuted their journey, and arrived at Harrodsburgh in thirteen days.

By this time Boon had made his escape from the Indians, and on Kenton's return he proposed to him to join in an expedition against a small Indian town on Paint creek. The proposal was accepted, and taking nineteen men, they set off for the town. When they had approached within five or six miles of the place, they were met by about forty Indians, whom they attacked and put to flight without receiving any injury. Knowing now that the Indians were aware of their approach, and consequently that the town could not be taken by surprise, Boon thought it advisable to return. But Kenton and another man by the name of Montgomery determined to remain, and learn something more of the Indians, and if possible, secure some of their horses. Hence, concealing themselves near the path leading from the town, they watched the whole day without discovering any Indians; and when night came they approached the town, but could not discover that the Indians were at all alarmed at the affray of the morning. The next day they lay concealed near a cornfield, but saw no Indians except some children that did not approach near enough to discover them. On the second night they caught two horses and made a start for home. Discovering, after crossing the Ohio, a large Indian trail leading in the direction of Boonsborough, they turned their course and went to Logan's. They afterwards learned that the Indians whose trail they had seen, were at that time besieging Boon. This siege they kept up for several days; but after killing one white man and a negro, and suffering considerable loss themselves, they retired in despair; and on the next day Kenton and Montgomery rode into the fort upon their Indian horses.

Kenton lay about Boon's and Logan's stations till ease became irksome to him. About the first of September of this same year, 1778, we find him preparing for another Indian expedition. Alexander Montgomery and George Clark joined him, and they set off from Boon's station for the avowed purpose of obtaining horses from the Indians. They crossed the Ohio, and proceeded cautiously to Chillicothe (now Oldtown.) They arrived at the town without meeting any adventure. In the night they fell in with a drove of horses that were feeding in the rich prairies. They were prepared with salt and halters. They had much difficulty to catch the horses; however, at length they succeeded, and as soon as the horses were haltered, they dashed off with seven—a pretty good haul. They traveled with all the speed they could to the Ohio. They came to the Ohio near the mouth of Eagle creek, now in Brown county. When they came to the river, the wind blew almost a hurricane. The waves ran so high that the horses were frightened, and could not be induced to take the water. It was late in the evening. They then rode back into the hills some distance from the river, hobbled and turned their horses loose to graze; while they turned back some distance, and watched the trail they had come, to discover whether or no they were pursued. Here they remained till the following day, when the wind subsided.

As soon as the wind fell they caught their horses, and went again to the river; but their horses were so frightened with the waves the day before, that all their efforts could not induce them to take the water. This was a sore disappointment to our adventurers. They were satisfied that they were pursued by the enemy; they therefore determined to lose no more time in useless efforts to cross the Ohio; they concluded to select three of the best horses, and make their way to the falls of the Ohio, where Gen. Clark had left some men stationed. Each made choice of a horse, and the other horses were turned loose to shift for themselves. After the spare horses had been loosed, and permitted to ramble off, avarice whispered to them, and why not take all the horses. The loose horses had by this time scattered and straggled out of sight. Our party now separated to hunt up the horses they had turned loose. Kenton went towards the river, and had not gone far before he heard a whoop in the direction of where they had been trying to force the horses into the water. He got off his horse and tied him, and then crept with the stealthy tread of the cat, to make observations in the direction he had heard the whoop. Just as he reached the high bank of the river, he met the Indians on horseback. Being unperceived by them, but so nigh that it was impossible for him to retreat without being discovered, he concluded the boldest course to be the safest, and very deliberately took aim at the foremost Indian. His gun flashed in the pan. He then retreated. The Indians pursued on horseback. In his retreat, he passed through a piece of land where a storm had torn up a great part of the timber. The fallen trees afforded him some advantage of the Indians in the race, as they were on horseback and he on foot. The Indian force divided; some rode on one side of the fallen timber, and some on the other. Just as he emerged from the fallen timber, at the foot of the hill, one of the Indians

met him on horseback, and boldly rode up to him, jump-
ed off his horse and rushed at him with his tomahawk.
Kenton concluding a gun-barrel as good a weapon of defence as a tomahawk, drew back his gun to strike the Indian before him.   At that instant another Indian, who
unperceived by Kenton had slipped up behind him,
clasped him in his arms.   Being now overpowered by
numbers, further resistance was useless—he surrendered.
Whilst the Indians were binding Kenton with tugs,
Montgomery came in view, and fired at the Indians, but
missed his mark.   Montgomery fled on foot.   Some of
the Indians pursued, shot at, and missed him ; a second
fire was made, and Montgomery fell.   The Indians soon
returned to Kenton, shaking at him Montgomery's bloody
scalp.   George Clark, Kenton's other companion, made
his escape, crossed the Ohio, and arrived safe at Logan's
station.

The Indians encamped that night on the bank of the
Ohio.   The next morning they prepared their horses for
a return to their towns with the unfortunate and unhappy
prisoner.   Nothing but death in the most appalling form
presented itself to his view.   When they were ready to
set off, they caught the wildest horse in the company,
and placed Kenton on his back.   The horse being very
restif, it took several of them to hold him, whilst the
others lashed the prisoner on the horse.   They first took
a tug, or rope, and fastened his legs and feet together under the horse.   They took another and fastened his arms.
They took another and tied around his neck, and fastened one end of it around the horse's neck ; the other end
of this same rope was fastened to the horse's tail, to answer in place of a crupper.   They had a great deal of
amusement to themselves, as they were preparing Kenton and his horse for fun and frolic.   They would yelp
and scream around him, and ask him if he wished to steal
more horses.   Another rope was fastened around his

thighs, and lashed around the body of the horse; a pair
of moccasons was drawn over his hands, to prevent him
from defending his face from the brush. Thus accoutered
and fastened, the horse was turned loose to the woods.
He reared and plunged, ran through the woods for some
time, to the infinite amusement of the Indians. After
the horse had run about, plunging, rearing, and kicking,
for some time, and found that he could not shake off, nor
kick off his rider, he very quietly submitted himself to
his situation, and followed the cavalcade as quiet and
peaceable as his rider.   The Indians moved towards
Chillicothe, and in three days reached the town.   At
night they confined their prisoner in the following manner : He was laid on his back, his legs extended, drawn
apart, and fastened to two saplings or stakes driven in
the ground.   His arms were extended, a pole laid across
his breast, and his arm lashed to the pole with cords.
A rope was tied around his neck, and stretched back just
tight enough not to choke him, and fastened to a tree or
stake near his head.   In this painful and uncomfortable
situation, he spent three miserable nights, exposed to
gnats, and musketoes, and weather.   O, poor human nature, what miserable wretches we are, thus to punish and
harass each other.   (The frontier whites of that day,
were but little behind the Indians, in wiles, in cruelty,
and revenge.)   When the Indians came within about a
mile of the Chillicothe town, they halted and camped for
the night, and fastened the poor unfortunate prisoner in
the usual uncomfortable manner.   The Indians, young
and old, came from the town to welcome the return of
their successful warriors, and to visit their prisoner.   The
Indian party, young and old, consisting of about one hundred and fifty, commenced dancing, singing, and yelling
around Kenton, stopping occasionally and kicking and
beating him for amusement.   In this manner they tormented him for about three hours, when the cavalcade

returned to town, and he was left for the rest of the night, exhausted and forlorn, to the tender mercies of the gnats and musketoes. As soon as it was light in the morning, the Indians began to collect from the town, and preparations were made for fun and frolic at the expense of Kenton, as he was now doomed to run the gauntlet. The Indians were formed in two lines, about six feet apart, with each a hickory in his hands, and Kenton placed between the two lines, so that each Indian could beat him as much as he thought proper, as he ran through the lines. He had not ran far before he discovered an Indian with his knife drawn to plunge it into him ; as soon as Kenton reached that part of the line where the Indian stood who had the knife drawn, he broke through the lines, and made with all speed for the town. Kenton had been previously informed by a negro named Cæsar, who lived with the Indians and knew their customs, that if he could break through the Indians' lines, and arrive at the council-house in the town before he was overtaken, that they would not force him a second time to run the gauntlet. When he broke through their lines, he ran at the top of his speed for the council-house, pursued by two or three hundred Indians, yelling and screaming like infernal furies. Just as he had entered the town, he was met by an Indian leisurely walking towards the scene of amusement, wrapped in a blanket. The Indian threw off his blanket ; and as he was fresh, and Kenton nearly exhausted, the Indian soon caught him, threw him down. In a moment the whole party who were in pursuit came up, and fell to cuffing and kicking him at a most fearful rate. They tore off all his clothes, and left him naked and exhausted. After he had laid till he had in some degree recovered from his exhausted state, they brought him some water and something to eat. As soon as his strength was sufficiently recovered, they took him to the council-house, to determine upon his fate. Their manner of deciding his fate, was as follows : Their warriors were placed in a circle in the council-house ; an old chief was placed in tne center of the circle, with a knife and a piece of wood in his hands. A number of speeches were made. Kenton, although he did not understand their language, soon discovered by their animated gestures, and fierce looks at him, that a majority of their speakers were contending for his destruction. He could perceive that those who plead for mercy, were received coolly ; but few grunts of approbation were uttered when the orators closed their speeches. After the orators ceased speaking, the old chief who sat in the midst of the circle, raised up and handed a war-club to the man who sat next the door. They proceeded to take the decision of their court. All who were for the death of the prisoner, struck the war-club with violence against the ground ; those who voted to save the prisoner's life, passed the club to his next neighbor without striking the ground. Kenton, from their expressive gestures, could easily distinguish the object of their vote. The old chief who stood to witness and record the number that voted for death or mercy, as one struck the ground with the war-club, he made a mark on one side of his piece of wood ; and when the club was passed without striking, he made a mark on the other. Kenton discovered that a large majority were for death.

Sentence of death being now passed üpon the prisoner, they made the welkin ring with shouts of joy. The sentence of death being passed, there was another question of considerable difficulty now presented itself to the consideration of the council ; that was, the time and place, when and where, he should be burnt. The orators again made speeches on the snbject, less animated indeed than on the trial ; but some appeared to be quite vehement for instant execution, whilst others appeared to wish to make his death a solemn national sacrifice. After a long de-

bate, the vote was taken, when it was resolved that the
place of his execution should be Wapatomika (now
Zanesfield, Logan county.) The next morning he was
hurried away to the place destined for his execution.
From Chillicothe to Wapatomika, they had to pass
through two other Indian towns, to wit: Pickaway and
Machecheek. At both towns he was compelled to run the
gauntlet; and severely was he whipped through the course.
While he lay at Machecheek, being carelessly guarded,
he made an attempt to escape. Nothing worse than death
could follow, and here he made a bold push for life and
freedom. Being unconfined, he broke and run, and soon
cleared himself out of sight of his pursuers. Whilst he
distanced his pursuers, and got about two miles from the
town, he accidentally met some Indians on horseback.
They instantly pursued, and soon came up with him, and
drove him back again to the town. He now, for the first
time, gave up his case as hopeless. Nothing but death
stared him in the face. Fate, it appeared to him, had sealed
his doom; and in sullen despair, he determined to await
that doom, that it was impossible for him to shun. How inscrutable are the ways of Providence, and how little can
man control his destiny! When the Indians returned with
Kenton to the town, there was a general rejoicing. He
was pinioned, and given over to the young Indians, who
dragged him into the creek, tumbled him in the water,
and rolled him in the mud, till he was nearly suffocated
with mud and water. In this way they amused themselves with him till he was nearly drowned. He now
thought himself forsaken by God. Shortly after this his
tormentors moved with him to Wapatomika. As soon
as he arrived at this place, the Indians, young and old,
male and female, crowded around the prisoner. Amongst
others who came to see him, was the celebrated and notorious Simon Girty. It will be recollected that Kenton
and Girty were bosom companions at Fort Pitt, and on

the campaign with Lord Dunmore. As it was the custom of the Indians to black such prisoners as were intended to be put to death, Girty did not immediately recognize Kenton in his black disguise. Girty came forward and inquired of Kenton where he had lived. Was answered Kentucky. He next inquired how many men there were in Kentucky. He answered, he did not know; but would give him the names and rank of the officers, and he, Girty, could judge of the probable number of men. Kenton then named a great many officers, and their rank, many of whom had honorary titles, without any command. At length Girty asked the prisoner his name. When he was answered, Simon Butler. (It will be recollected, that he changed his name when he fled from his parents and home.) Girty eyed him for a moment, and immediately recognized the active and bold youth, who had been his companion in arms about Fort Pitt, and on the campaign with Lord Dunmore. Girty threw himself into Kenton's arms, embraced and wept aloud over him—calling him his dear and esteemed friend. This hardened wretch, who had been the cause of the death of hundreds, had some of the sparks of humanity remaining in him, and wept like a child at the tragical fate which hung over his friend. "Well," said he to Kenton, "you are condemned to die, but I will use every means in my power to save your life."

Girty immediately had a council convened, and made a long speech to the Indians, to save the life of the prisoner. As Girty was proceeding through his speech, he became very animated; and under his powerful eloquence, Kenton could plainly discover the grim visages of his savage judges relent. When Girty concluded his powerful and animated speech, the Indians rose with one simultaneous grunt of approbation, saved the prisoner's life, and placed him under the care and protection of his old companion, Girty.

The British had a trading establishment then at Wapatomika. Girty took Kenton with him to the store, and
dressed him, from head to foot, as well as he could wish;
he was also provided with a horse and saddle. Kenton
was now free, and roamed about through the country,
from Indian town to town, in company with his benefactor. How uncertain is the fate of nations as well as that
of individuals! How sudden the changes from adversity
to prosperity, and from prosperity to adversity! Kenton
being a strong, robust man, with an iron frame, with a
resolution that never winced at danger, and fortitude to
bear pain with the composure of a stoic, he soon recovered from his scourges and bruises, and the other severe
treatment he had received. It is thought probable, that
if the Indians had continued to treat him with kindness
and respect, he would eventually have become one of
them. He had but few inducements to return again to
the whites. He was then a fugitive from justice, had
changed his name, and he thought it his interest to keep
as far from his former acquaintances as possible. After
Kenton and his benefactor had been roaming about for
some time, a war party of Indians, who had been on an
expedition to the neighborhood of Wheeling, returned;
they had been defeated by the whites, some of their men
were killed, and others wounded. When this defeated
party returned they were sullen, chagrined, and full of
revenge, and determined to kill any of the whites who
came within their grasp. Kenton was then the only
white man upon whom they could satiate their revenge.
Kenton and Girty were then at Solomon's town, a small
distance from Wapatomika. A message was immediately
sent to Girty to return, and bring Kenton with him. The
two friends met the messenger on the way. The messenger shook hands with Girty, but refused the hand of
Kenton. Girty, after talking aside with the messenger
some time, said to Kenton, they have sent for us to attend

a grand council at Wapatomika. They hurried to the town; and when they arrived there the council house was crowded. When Girty went into the house, the Indians all rose up and shook hands with him; but when Kenton offered his hand it was refused, with a scowl of contempt. This alarmed him; he began to admit the idea that this sudden convention of the council, and their refusing his hand, boded him some evil. After the members of the council were seated in their usual manner, the war chief of the defeated party rose up and made a most vehement speech, frequently turning his fiery and revengeful eyes on Kenton during his speech. Girty was the next to rise to address the council. He told them that he had lived with them several years; that he had risked his life in that time more frequently than any of them; that they all knew that he had never spared the life of one of the hated Americans; that they well knew that he had never asked for a division of the spoils; that he fought alone for the destruction of their enemies; and that he now requested them to spare the life of this young man on his account. The young man, he said, was his early friend, for whom he felt the tenderness of a parent for a son, and he hoped, after the many evidences that he had given of his attachment to the Indian cause, they would not hesitate to grant his request. If they would indulge him in granting his request to spare the life of this young man, he would pledge himself never to ask them again to spare the life of a hated American.

Several chiefs spoke in succession on this important subject; and with the most apparent deliberation, the council decided, by an overwhelming majority, for death. After the decision of this grand court was announced, Girty went to Kenton, and embracing him very tenderly, said that he very sincerely sympathized with him in his forlorn and unfortunate situation; that he had used all the efforts he was master of to save his life, but it was now decreed that he must die—that he could do no more for him. Awful doom!

It will be recollected, that this was in 1778, in the midst of the American revolution. Upper Sandusky was then the place where the British paid their western Indian allies their annuities; and as time might effect what his eloquence could not, Girty, as a last resort, persuaded the Indians to convey their prisoner to Sandusky, as there would meet vast numbers to receive their presents; that the assembled tribes could there witness the solemn scene of the death of the prisoner. To this proposition the council agreed; and the prisoner was placed in the care of five Indians, who forthwith set off for Upper Sandusky. What windings, and twistings, and turnings, were seen in the fate of our hero.

As the Indians passed from Wapatomika to Upper Sandusky, they went through a small village on the river Scioto, where then resided the celebrated chief Logan, of Jefferson memory. Logan, unlike the rest of his tribe, was humane as he was brave. At his wigwam the party who had the care of the prisoner, staid over night. During the evening, Logan entered into conversation with the prisoner. The next morning he told Kenton that he would detain the party that day—that he had sent two of his young men off the night before to Upper Sandusky, to speak a good word for him. Logan was great and good—the friend of all men. In the course of the following evening his young men returned, and early the next morning the guard set off with the prisoner for Upper Sandusky. When Kenton's party set off from Logan's, Logan shook hands with the prisoner, but gave no intimation of what might probably be his fate. The party went on with Kenton till they came in view of the Upper Sandusky town. The Indians, young and old, came out to meet and welcome the warriors, and view the prisoner. Here he was not compelled to run the gaunt-

17

let. A grand council was immediately convened to determine upon the fate of Kenton. This was the fourth council which was held to dispose of the life of the prisoner. As soon as this grand court was organized and ready to proceed to business, a Canadian Frenchman, by the name of Peter Druyer, who was a captain in the British service, and dressed in the gaudy appendages of the British uniform, made his appearance in the council. This Druyer was born and raised in Detroit—he was connected with the British Indian agent department— was their principal interpreter in settling Indian affairs ; this made him a man of great consequence among the Indians. It was to this influential man, that the good chief Logan, the friend of all the human family, sent his young men to intercede for the life of Kenton. His judgment and address were only equaled by his humanity. His foresight in selecting the agent who it was most probable could save the life of the prisoner, proves his judgment and his knowledge of the human heart. As soon as the grand council was organized, Captain Druyer requested permission to address the council. This permission was instantly granted. He began his speech by stating, " that it was well known that it was the wish and interest of the English that not an American should be left alive. That the Americans were the cause of the present bloody and distressing war—that neither peace nor safety could be expected, so long as these intruders were permitted to live upon the earth." This part of his speech received repeated grunts of approbation. He then explained to the Indians, " that the war to be carried on successfully, required cunning as well as bravery —that the intelligence which might be extorted from a prisoner, would be of more advantage, in conducting the future operations of the war, than would be the life of twenty prisoners. That he had no doubt but the commanding officer at Detroit could procure information from

the prisoner now before them, that would be of incalcu-
lable advantage to them in the progress of the present
war.   Under these circumstances, he hoped they would
defer the death of the prisoner till he was taken to Detroit, and examined by the commanding general.   After
which he could be brought back, and if thought advisable, upon further consideration, he might be put to death
in any manner they thought proper."   He next noticed,
" that they had already a great deal of trouble and fatigue
with the prisoner without being revenged upon him ; but
that they had got back all the horses the prisoner had
stolen from them, and killed one of his comrades ; and to
insure them something for their fatigue and trouble, he
himself would give one hundred dollars in rum and to-
bacco, or any other articles they would choose, if they
would let him take the prisoner to Detroit, to be examined by the British general."   The Indians, without hesitation, agreed to Captain Druyer's proposition, and he
paid down the ransom.   As soon as these arrangements
were concluded, Druyer and a principal chief set off with
the prisoner for Lower Sandusky.   From this place they
proceeded by water to Detroit, where they arrived in a
few days.   Here the prisoner was handed over to the
commanding officer, and lodged in the fort as a prisoner
of war.   He was now out of danger from the Indians,
and was treated with the usual attention of prisoners of
war in civilized countries.   The British commander gave
the Indians some additional remuneration for the life of
the prisoner, and they returned satisfied to join their
countrymen at Wapatomika.

Although Kenton was still a prisoner, he was now in
no danger from the faggot or the tomahawk ; when he reflected on the many dangers and hair-breadth escapes
through which he had passed in such rapid succession,
it looked to him like some terrible dream, which made
his hair stand on end.   He was taken prisoner about the

first of September, and arrived at Detroit about the beginning of November. During the two months he was in possession of the Indians, his life was in perpetual and imminent danger, and consequently his mind harassed with incessant suspense, and fluctuations between hope and fear ; no situation could be more appalling or distressing to the human heart. Notwithstanding the corporeal abuses and privations which he had so repeatedly to experience, together with the anguish of mind, inseparable from his perilous situation as to life, his health was uninterrupted during his dangerous and severe trials. From the sufferings through which he passed, it is almost miraculous that he had not sunk in despair, or that the privations and exposures he was forced to undergo, had not brought on diseases which would put an end to his miserable existence ; but such was his confidence in the protection of an all-seeing eye, that he was buoyed up to bear the sufferings by which he was encompassed, with resignation. As soon as his mind was out of suspense and at ease, his robust constitution and iron frame enabled his body to recruit in a few days, from the most trying exposures and privations, such as the want of sleep, subsistence, and the many and severe flagellations which he had so repeatedly to undergo during his painful captivity.

The next day after Kenton had passed into the possession of the British at Detroit, the commanding officer sent for him and had a long conference with him, on the subject of the strength and number of the inhabitants in the infant settlements of Kentucky. He next inquired of the prisoner what he knew of the strength, and designs of the movements of General McIntosh, who, it was understood, was on the way, or preparing to invade the Indian country. To all of which interrogatories, Kenton gave such answers as a patriot might be expected to give. He told the truth where the truth would not injure his country; evaded direct answers where the information might afford advantage to the enemy. After the British commander had interrogated him as long as he thought proper, he dismissed him, and gave an order on a Captain McGregor, the commissary of clothing, for two suits of clothes, which were furnished forthwith. He was now permitted the liberty of the city of Detroit, but was charged not to leave the town; if he did, the Indians, in all probability, would kill him. Here he did some work, and drew half rations from the British, and lived pretty much at his ease; but the town and suburbs of Detroit were too confined a range for a man like him, who thought the valley of the grand Ohio too small a theater for his active, enterprising genius. He was like the bird confined in a cage, always longing for more space, that he might take his flight east, west, north or south. Here he passed the winter of 1778 and '79. Early in the spring of 1779, the Indians brought to Detroit several prisoners whom they had taken from Kentucky. Amongst them were some of Kenton's old associates. These prisoners had also the liberty of the town, and Kenton and they strolled about at pleasure. Among these prisoners were Captain Nathan Bullit and Jesse Coffer. With these two men Kenton began to meditate an escape. They had frequent conferences on the subject; but the enterprise was almost too appalling for even these hardy, enterprising pioneers. If they should make this bold push, they would have to travel nearly four hundred miles through the Indian country, where they would be exposed to death by starvation, by flood, by the tomahawk, or to capture, almost at every step. But the longer they brooded over the enterprise the stronger their resolutions grew to make the attempt. They could make no movement to procure arms, ammunition, or provision, without exciting suspicion; and should they be once suspected they would be immediately confined.—

In this situation they could only brood over their wished flight in secret and in silence. Kenton was a fine looking man, with a dignified and manly deportment, and a soft, pleasing voice, and was everywhere he went a favorite among the ladies. A Mrs. Harvey, the wife of an Indian trader, had treated him with particular respect ever since he came to Detroit, and he concluded if he could engage this lady as a confidant, by her assistance and countenance ways and means could be prepared to aid them in their meditated flight. Kenton approached Mrs. Harvey on this delicate and interesting subject, with as much trepidation and coyness as ever maiden was approached in a love affair. The great difficulty with Kenton was to get the subject opened with Mrs. Harvey. If she should reject his suit and betray his intentions, all his fond hopes would be at once blasted. However, at length he concluded to trust this lady with the scheme of his meditated flight, and the part he wished her to act for him. He watched an opportunity to have a private interview with Mrs. Harvey; an opportunity soon offered, and he, without disguise or hesitation, in full confidence informed her of his intention, and requested her aid and secrecy. She appeared at first astonished at his proposal, and observed that it was not in her power to afford him any aid. Kenton told her he did not expect or wish her to be at any expense on their account—that they had a little money for which they had labored, and that they wished her to be their agent to purchase such articles as would be necessary for them in their flight—that if they should go to purchasing it would create suspicion, but that she could aid them in this way without creating any suspicion; and if she would be their friend, they had no doubt they could effect their escape. This appeal from such a fine looking man as Kenton, was irresistible. There was something pleasing in being the selected confidant of such a man; and the lady, though a little coy at

first, surrendered at discretion. After a few chit chats,
she entered into the views of Kenton with as much
earnestness and enthusiasm as if she had been his sister.
She began to collect and conceal such articles as might
be necessary in the journey: powder, lead, mocasons,
and dried beef were procured in small quantities, and
concealed in a hollow tree some distance out of town.
Guns were still wanting, and it would not do for a lady
to trade in them. Mr. Harvey had an excellent fowling
piece, if nothing better should offer, that she said should
be at their service. They had now every thing that they
expected to take with them in their flight ready, except
guns. At length the third day of June, 1779, came, and
a large concourse of Indians were in the town engaged
in a drunken frolic; they had stacked their guns near
Mrs. Harvey's house; as soon as it was dark, Mrs. Harvey went quietly to where the Indians' guns were stacked, and selected the three best looking rifles, carried them
into her garden, and concealed them in a patch of peas.
She next went privately to Kenton's lodging, and conveyed to him the intelligence where she had hid the Indians' guns.—She told him she would place a ladder at
the back of the garden (it was picketed,) and that he
could come in and get the guns. No time was to be
lost; Kenton conveyed the good news he had from Mrs.
Harvey to his companions, who received the tidings in
ecstacies of joy; they felt as if they were already at
home. It was a dark night; Kenton, Bullit and Coffer
gathered up their little all and pushed to Mrs. Harvey's
garden. There they found the ladder; Kenton mounted
over, drew the ladder over after him, went to the pea-
patch, found Mrs. Harvey sitting by the guns; she handed him the rifles, gave him a friendly shake of the hand
and bid him a safe journey to his friends and countrymen. She appeared to Kenton and his comrades as an
angel. When a woman engages to do an action, she

will risk limb, life, or character to serve those whom she respects or wishes to befriend. How differently the same action will be viewed by different persons : by Kenton and his friends her conduct was viewed as the benevolent action of a good angel ; while if the part she played in behalf of Kenton and his companions had been known to the commander at Detroit, she would have been looked upon as a traitress, who merited the scorn and contempt of all honest citizens. This night was the last time that Kenton ever saw or heard of her.

A few days before Kenton left Detroit, he had a conversation with an Indian trader, a Scotchman, by the name of McKinzie, who was well acquainted with the geography of the country, and range of the Indians, between the lakes and the Ohio and Mississippi. The Scotchman slyly observed to Kenton, that if he was going to Kentucky, and did not wish to meet with the Indians, he would steer more west than the common route, and get into Wabash prairies as soon as possible. Kenton did not know what to think of the remarks of the Scotchman. He began to think that perhaps Mrs. Harvey had divulged his secret to this man, and that he was pumping Kenton ; or probably he wished to aid him, and this was offering friendly advice. As no more was said, he did not pretend to notice what the Scotchman said, but treasured the remarks in his mind.

As soon as Kenton and companions took their leave of their friend and benafactress, Mrs. Harvey, they made their way to the little store in the hollow tree, bundled up, and pushed for the wood, and steered a more westerly, than the direct course to Kentucky. They had no doubt but every effort would be made to retake them ; they were, consequently, very circumspect and cautious in leaving as few traces, by which they might be discovered, as possible. They went on slowly, traveling mostly in the night, steering their course by the cluster, call-

Kenton killing the Buck.

[Face 239]

ed the seven stars, till they reached the prairie country, on the Wabash. In this time, though they had been very sparing of their stock of provision, it was now exhausted, and their lives depended on their guns. In these large prairies there was but little game, and they were days without provision. They, like the Hebrews of old, began to wish themselves again with the flesh pots at Detroit. One day as they were passing down the Wabash, they were just emerging out of a thicket of brush-wood, when an Indian encampment suddenly presented itself to their view, and not more than one hundred and fifty or two hundred yards from them. No ghastly visit could have set their hair on end sooner. They immediately dodged back into the thicket, and concealed themselves till night. They were now almost exhausted with fatigue and hunger—they could only travel a few miles in a day. They lay still in the thicket, consulting with each other the most proper measures to pursue in this their precarious situation. Bullit and Coffer thought the best plan to save their lives, would be voluntarily to surrender themselves to the Indians. The Indians who had taken them had not treated them so roughly as Kenton had been handled. Kenton wished to lay still till night, and make as little sign as possible, and as soon as it was dark they would push ahead, and trust the event to Providence. After considerable debate, Kenton's plan was adopted. As soon as it was dark they made their way farther from the river, into those large prairies. They kept a slow and painful jog till morning. In the morning they made for a piece of timber land, which was not a great distance from them. Kenton was a small distance in advance. As they entered the wood a fine red buck presented itself close to him. Kenton took deliberate aim—his rifle fired clear, and down fell the buck. They immediately made a fire and went to cooking ; and never did food eat more delicious. How

little do the men of the present age, who live sumptuous-
ly every day, sympathize with the sufferings of the war-
worn, weather-beaten pioneers, who braved death and
misery in every form which can be imagined—want, fatigue, starvation, exposure in the night, exposure to the
heat and the cold; added to these, the exposure to the
wily Indian by day and by night. All these difficulties
and privations were cheerfully met by a set of men who
thought but little of wealth, their whole object appeared
to be either prompted by patriotism or love of danger.
The small remnant of these weather-beaten woodsmen,
who are still amongst us, are generally poor, and treated
with neglect by their more polished and fortunate successors.   Notwithstanding that Kenton and his party
were now in the neighborhood of an Indian encampment,
they remained at their fire till they roasted the greatest
part of their buck.   After their feast was over, they again
took up their slow, weary, and toilsome march.   They
made the best of their way to the falls of the Ohio, and
arrived there after a painful and tedious march of thirty-
three days, from the time they left Detroit.   Here Kenton remained a few days with his old companions.   This
was in the month of July, 1779.   It required only a few
days of plentiful living, when his mind was free from suspense, to recruit both his body and mind.   The account of
the captivity and release of our hero is now related.   It
might naturally be expected that after his narrow and
providential escapes, severe trials, and his long and painful march for freedom, and to again enjoy the pleasure of
the company of his countrymen, that he would take some
repose; but not so: danger and fame were the food
which afforded him most enjoyment.   The many dangers, trials, and hair-breadth escapes, through which he
had passed, only whetted his appetite to engage in more
perils.   As soon as his health and strength were recruited he began to cast his active mind about for further ad-

venture. The indolence of a stationary life became irksome to our bold adventurer. It was in the clangor of arms, and in the din of battle, that he appeared at home.

It will be recollected that in the spring of the preceding year, 1778, he went with Gen. Clark to the Mississippi, and aided in capturing Ocho, or Kaskaskia; that Gen. Clark sent him with dispatches to Kentucky; that on his way he had reconnoitered Post Vincent, and sent one of his comrades back to inform Gen. Clark of the weak situation, and careless manner in which Post Vincent was guarded by the enemy. As soon as Kenton's messenger arrived at Kaskaskia with this intelligence, Gen. Clark moved a detachment from Illinois, across the grand prairie, and took Post Vincent by surprise, as cheap as he had before taken the Ocho station. Gen. Clark still remained at Post Vincent in 1779, when Kenton had made his escape from captivity. After loitering about the falls of Ohio some time, he concluded he would now push for Vincennes, and join his old companion in arms, Gen. Clark. There was then neither settlement nor house between the falls of Ohio and Vincennes; but that did not deter, it rather invited him to the enterprise. Our wandering hero went to Vincennes without meeting any adventure worth relating. As there was no prospect of immediate skirmishes or battles on the Wabash, the times appeared too dull for him to remain long in " inglorious ease." He shouldered his rifle, came back to the falls of Ohio, and then to Harrod's station, on the Kentucky river. The winter, 1779–80, passed off without any particular occurrence to our hero worth notice.

* * * I will now notice occurrences which took place in Kentucky in 1779, while Kenton was in captivity. During this year a number of new settlements were formed. Some settlements were made on Bear Grass, near the falls of the Ohio. Bashear's and Martin's sta-

tions were settled. McLelland's, Riddle's, and Hinkston's stations were again occupied; and every prospect appeared favorable for the speedy filling up of the country with inhabitants.

How deceitful are appearances in times of war! What short sighted beings we are! We cannot know what a day may bring forth! Although in the summer and fall of 1779, every thing appeared favorable to the views of the inhabitants of the infant settlement of Kentucky, the spring of 1780 ushered forth in melancholy forebodings of the future. The Kentuckians were then isolated in the wilderness, some hundred of miles from where any friendly aid could be procured to relieve in their distress. Under these circumstances they had to rely principally upon their own energies for defence. At this time a large British and Indian force invaded Kentucky. The enemy were well equipped for war, having with them several pieces of artillery from Detroit. They brought their artillery and munitions of war, by water from Detroit, up the Maumee, and thence by land to Big Miami; down the Miami to the Ohio; up the Ohio to the mouth of Licking, and up Licking to the forks. From thence they proceeded by land; and simultaneously invested Martin's and Riddle's stations. As these stations had only for defence log block-houses and pickets, resistance against artillery would be a useless risk and waste of life, the inhabitants capitulated, and surrendered themselves prisoners of war. When this disaster took place, Kenton was at Harrod's station. The news soon spread from station to station. Kenton was ever on the alert; went in company with Charles Gatiffs, and cautiously followed the Indian trail, to ascertain the direction which the enemy had taken, and their probable future movements. They found the enemy encamped at the forks of Licking river. Here they hovered about them for a day or two, when the Indians broke up the camp, and proceeded down

the river to the Ohio. What urged them to move off
without delay, was, the Licking river was falling very
fast, and should they delay much longer they would not
be able to take their artillery by water; and if they should
be pursued and beaten they would lose the effect of their
successful enterprise. As soon as the Indians commenced their retrograde movements from the forks of Licking,
Kenton returned to Harrod's station. As soon as Gen.
Clark, who was still at Post Vincent, heard of the disaster which had taken place in Kentucky, he returned to
the falls of the Ohio, with all the force that could be safely spared; thence he proceeded to Harrod's station, to
consult on ways and means to be revenged on their enemies. An expedition being determined on against the
enemy, all who were able to bear arms were called upon.
The mouth of Licking was appointed the place of general rendezvous. Kenton was appointed a captain, and
commanded an active and numerous company of volunteers from Harrod's station. At the mouth of Licking
river, was now concentrated Kentucky's united strength,
amounting to about eleven hundred men, commanded by
Gen. Clark, a man of intrepidity and talents; who was
seconded and aided by numerous spirits, no way inferior
to himself. They had with them one brass twelve
pounder, which the state of Virginia had sent to the falls
of Ohio. The provisions furnished at the expense of
the public, was three quarts of corn to the man. In addition to this, each man brought with him as much dry
jirk as he could conveniently carry. Thus scantily supplied, this intrepid band commenced their march. The
object of this grand expedition, was the destruction of
the Chillicothe town, on the Little Miami. Although
Kenton was now a captain of a company, as he had been
several times at Chillicothe town, he was selected as the
pilot to direct their march. This army went through the
unbroken wilderness, with Kenton for their guide; made

their own roads, and moved rapidly for the Indian towns, in order to take them by surprise if possible, and not to afford the enemy time to concentrate all their force at any one point. When the army arrived at the Chillicothe town, the Indians had just left the place, and set the town on fire. The Indians had retreated to the Pickaway town, and were collecting their force as fast as possible to give the whites battle. Gen. Clark commenced an immediate pursuit. When he arrived at the Pickaway town, he found the Indians embodied and prepared for defence. Gen. Clark immediately made the necessary arrangements, and the battle commenced. The Indians fought like *furies*, but being overpowered by numbers, were compelled to leave the field of battle, with their dead and wounded to the whites. The whites destroyed several of their towns without meeting any further resistance. A vast quantity of corn and other vegetables were consumed, and otherwise destroyed. This was a severe blow on the Indians. It was the first visit the Kentuckians had paid the Indians in mass. The northwestern Indians were as brave and full of prowess, and skilled in stratagem, as any men that ever lived. The Kentuckians were only their equals.

Gen. Clark remained at Pickaway town three days, destroying every thing that could be found which might render either aid or comfort to the Indians. In this work of destruction, Kenton's knowledge of the situation of this part of the Indian country was of immense service. Let it be recollected, that while he was a prisoner, he rode with Girty to nearly all the Indian towns on the Miamies and head of the Scioto. The army returned to the Ohio opposite to the mouth of Licking, now the city of Cincinnati, and there disbanded, and every man returned to his home, without the formality of a written discharge. There was no muster-roll. No pay received or expected. Every man fought for himself. This was a real democratic army, where every man went when he pleased, staid as long as he pleased, and returned when he pleased; but wo to the man who dodged in time of danger.

From the mouth of Licking, Kenton returned to Boon's station, and went occasionally to Logan's and Harrod's, sometimes acting as a spy or ranger, and sometimes on hunting excursions, and sometimes attending with locaters and surveyors to land business. In this way he passed off his time till the fall of the year 1782. During all this time his days and nights were passed in tedious sameness, without being once enlivened by the thrilling animation of an Indian fight. Such is the force of habit, that the dull pursuits of civil life soon become irksome to the soldier.

About this time he first heard from his parents. His parents or friends could not hear from him, as he had changed his name, and till now had been known by the name of Simon Butler. He now for the first time learned that he had not killed Veach! that Veach had recovered and was still living. He now for the first time since he came to Kentucky assumed his proper name.

In the fall of the year 1782, the Kentuckians determined on paying the Indians another visit, and endeavor to overwhelm them in destruction their troublesome neighbors. For this purpose, George R. Clark was again appointed, by general consent, commander of their forces. When we take a retrospect of the intrepidity and fortitude of those pioneer fathers of the west, we are almost lost in astonishment at the daring achievements, and the discouraging difficulties which they so nobly overcame. When we see them collecting and forming themselves into armies, traversing large tracts of country without roads ; no friendly garrison to retreat to in case of disaster ; with no other subsistence but what every man furnished himself with ; where every man found

18

his own arms, ammunition, tents, and baggage, without
any of the equipments which constitute the strength of
armies, we are lost in wonder at the fortitude and resolution of those men, that did not quail or fall into despair
at the appalling dangers and difficulties by which they
were encompassed.

(1782.)   The mouth of Licking was again appointed
the place of rendezvous.   On this expedition Kenton
again commanded a company, and was looked upon by
both officers and privates as one of the pillars of their
force.   His knowledge of the country intended to be invaded, his cautious yet fearless courage, his tact and in-
vention for forming stratagem, for ambuscading the enemy, rendered him popular with these pioneers.   These
hardy soldiers would hesitate to obey or execute any plan
or order, which did not meet the approbation of Simon
Kenton.   The troops having arrived on the ground where
Cincinnati now stands, they immediately prepared for an
expeditious march.   Their number was about fifteen
hundred men.   They directed their march for the Indian
towns on the Great Miami.   So sudden and secret was
the expedition, that they fell upon the first Indian town
without being discovered previous to the attack.   In this
town a large number of Indians were killed, and between
thirty and forty made prisoners.   The alarm being given,
the Indians deserted their other villages and fled to the
woods.   The whites without further resistance, burnt
their towns, destroyed their corn, with every other thing
that fell in their way, that could render the Indians aid
or comfort.   The army then returned to the Ohio, opposite the mouth of Licking, where they disbanded.   On
the morning that the troops disbanded themselves, Col.
Floyd, from the falls of the Ohio, made a proposition to
the army: that all of them who should be living fifty
years hence, should meet at that place, and talk over the
affairs of the campaign, and of the various improvements

which might by that time take place in the country. This resolution was adopted with shouts of acclamation. There was something grand and sublime in the proposal; and Col. Floyd must have had correct notions of the probable population which might by that time be in quiet, peaceable possession of this, then, western wilderness. He must have observed, too, the probability of a large city growing up at, or opposite the mouth of Licking, and the many advantages that this site possessed, from its contiguity to several rivers, together with the fine country by which it was surrounded. The revolutionary war was about this time ended; the colonies were acknowledged sovereign, independent states, and the prospects of a happy and long peace, was, as they believed, dawning upon them. The Indians were the only enemies with whom they had to contend; and as they had, unaided kept them in check, they hoped now, that as their brethren of the Atlantic states were relieved from the horrors of war, that they might count upon receiving a helping hand from their fellow citizens east of the mountains. They had some doleful feelings, too, about the small remnant of them who should probably be alive when the fifty years should expire. Although the settlements of Kentucky went on rapidly, they continued to be harassed by Indian wars much longer than was anticipated by any. Col. Floyd, who brought forward the resolution for the fifty years' meeting, was killed by the Indians on Bear Grass, near the falls of the Ohio, a few years afterwards. As the fifty years would expire on or about the 10th day of November, 1832, intense were the feelings of the few remaining of those hardy men, as the time of the meeting approached. When the fifty years were about expiring, almost all the western newspapers gave notice of the expected meeting. It would have been a scene which men indeed would gaze and wonder at with awe and astonishment. To see and converse with the weather-beaten pioneers who had marched in the front of war fifty years before, would have excited sensations that the pen is unable to describe. The imagination can only picture to itself some pleasant, gloomy, scene, in which the ghosts of some long-gone-by generation were called upon to act a part, in the presence of living men. At the time of the proposed fifty years' meeting, a goodly number of those ancient heroes were still remaining upon the stage of action. Amongst others, Simon Kenton. He was as anxious for the meeting as ever a bridegroom was for the wedding night. It was his day and night dream. The ways of Providence are inscrutable. When the 10th of November, 1832, came, Cinninnati and the whole surrounding country was covered in gloom. The dreaded cholera had made its appearance, and thousands were falling before its awful and pestilential strides. This awful visitation postponed the fifty-years' meeting forever.

To return to the narrative: When the army was disbanded, Kenton returned to Harrod's station, and attended to his private concerns. He had by this time acquired some valuable tracts of land, and as the country was rapidly filling up with inhabitants, he concluded that he too would make a settlement. For this purpose, he selected a fertile spot of land on Salt river. During the winter and spring of 1782 and '83, a few families joined him, reared up some block-houses, surrounded with pickets for defence, cleared some land, and planted corn. The woods furnished them with an abundant supply of meat, and he went on for the present, improving his estate, without interruption from the Indians. After having laid by his corn, he concluded to visit his father, mother, brothers, and sisters, who still remained in his native land, Virginia. He had now been absent nearly thirteen years, the greater part of which time was passed in perils, privations, and sufferings, almost too great for human nature to survive; but his iron frame, and unyielding disposition, bore him through his difficulties in triumph.

When he returned to the home of his childhood, he had the exquisite satisfaction to find his father and all his family living. This meeting had something in it like the meeting of the old patriarch Jacob with his son Joseph, except that Kenton showed himself the most dutiful and filial son of the two, as he went, whilst Joseph sent for his father's family. Kenton now associated with the friends of his childhood. This was to him a real mental feast, as his soul was a storehouse of friendship and sympathy. Those whom he had left children thirteen years before, were now the active business men and women of the country. As he passed through the country, some hill or hollow, some tree or rivulet, would recall to his mind some fun or freakish event of his childhood or youth. He visited his old friend Veach, whom he thought he had killed. They mutually forgave each other, and buried the tomahawk, and smoked the pipe of peace.

Simon Kenton described to his father and family, the fertility and the advantages of the new country of Kentucky, in such glowing colors, that the whole family agreed to accompany him to Kentucky. The whole tribe set off; their baggage was placed on a few pack-horses, and moved to Redstone fort (now Brownsville). Here they made what was called a Kentucky boat. While engaged in constructing their boat, his father sickened and died, and was buried on the bank of the Monongahela. No stone or marble points to the place where lie the bones of the father of the celebrated Simon Kenton. Their boat was soon finished; and men, women and children, together with the little stock of animals, were crowded on board, and they floated down the stream to the falls of the Ohio. By this time winter was setting in. From the falls they made their way to Kenton's station, on Salt river, where they found themselves at the end of their wearisome journey. Here Kenton remained till July, 1784. Nothing took place worth noticing. Peace appeared to bless the country, and immigrants came pouring in. From the falls of the Ohio up Bear Grass, on Salt river, on Kentucky river up to Boon's and Logan's stations, on Elkhorn, and through the country, as far as the neighborhood of. where Paris now stands, was checkered with stations.

It will be recollected by the reader, that Kenton and Thomas Williams had cleared and planted a small piece of ground near Maysville, in 1777, and from this place they went and joined Col. Boon and his friends on the Kentucky river. In July, 1784, Kenton once more collected a party of adventurers, and went to his old camp near Limestone, now Maysville. The Indians were then spread over that part of the country. Kenton and his party thought it too dangerous to remain here, and they returned again to his station on Salt river. In the fall of this year, 1784, he returned to his old camp near Limestone; built some block-houses; and, in the course of the winter 1784–5, many families joined them. This station was erected about three miles from Limestone, and one mile from where Washington, in Mason county, now stands. This was the first permanent settlement made on the northeast side of Licking river. As the Indians made no disturbance this winter, many new settlements were commenced in Mason county, in the following spring. Limestone, now Maysville, was settled by old Ned Waller. Lee's, Warren's, and Clark's stations were made; and new comers were constantly pouring in. During the whole of the year 1785, no interruption was given by the Indians to this infant settlement. The chastisement given them on the late expedition by General Clark, had in some measure broken their spirits.

1786. The country round Kenton's station continued to receive a throng of emigrants: numerous new stations

were made, and Limestone (Maysville) became one of
the principal landing places. This year Kenton sold, or
rather gave, Arthur Fox and William Wood, one thousand acres of land, on which they laid out the present
town of Washington, which town soon received a great
number of inhabitants. Although the Indians stole, occasionally, some horses from this infant settlement, yet they
did nothing serious enough to check the growth of the
country.

As it was supposed that they were the Indians from
Mochacheek and Pickaway, who had been stealing their
horses, an expedition was resolved upon to chastise them.
The inhabitants from all the stations sent on a good many
men, and the new town of Washington was appointed
the place of rendezvous.   Col. Logan had the chief command.   The detachment consisted of about 700 men,
armed and equipped at their own expense, as usual.
They crossed the Ohio at Limestone.   Kenton commanded a fine company, and was the pilot to direct their
march.   So secret and expeditious were their movements, that they arrived at the Indian towns without being discovered.   These towns were about a mile from
each other.   The whites were divided into two columns,
and attacked both towns about the same time.   A number of Indians were killed, and a number of prisoners
made.   Their wigwams and other property were destroyed.   As some of the Indians escaped, the alarm was
given to the other towns, and the Indians made for the
woods.   This little army marched through the Indian
country without further resistance ; they burnt four other
towns, destroyed their corn and every thing which might
render the Indians aid or comfort.   On this expedition,
which had done the enemy a great deal of harm, they
lost about ten men.

1787. This year the Indians kept the inhabitants
around Kenton's station in perpetual alarm, with their

predatory incursions; sometimes stealing horses, at other times killing some of the inhabitants. As Kenton's settlement was a kind of outpost for the settlements around Paris and Lexington, the people of the latter settlements always lent them a helping hand. Kenton sent word to Col. Tod, that if he would come on with as many men as he could bring with him, that he, Kenton, would raise what men he could, and that with their joint force, they could destroy the Indian town on the north fork of Paint creek, now Oldtown, then Chillicothe. This detachment rendezvoused in Washington. Col. Tod commanded. They crossed the Ohio at Limestone. Kenton, as usual, commanded a company, and piloted the expedition to the Chillicothe town. On their route out, about five miles south of Oldtown, on a place now called poplar-ridge, the advance guard, commanded by Kenton, met four Indians. Kenton and one Helm fired, and killed two of the Indians. The other two were taken prisoners. Had either of those Indians escaped, the Indians in the town and country would have been alarmed and fled. Kenton was now surrounded by a set of young men of his own training, and fearful was the doom of enemies of equal numbers who came in their way. From the two prisoners they had taken, they learnt that there was a large Indian encampment between them and old Chillicothe, about three miles from the latter place. On this intelligence the army was halted on poplar-ridge, and Kenton and his company went forward, to reconnoiter the situation of the enemy. Kenton proceeded near the Indian camp, lay by till night, and then with a few men reconnoitered the place, and made himself acquainted with the situation of the enemy. He then sent an express to Col. Tod, informing him of their probable number and situation. Before day Maj. Hinkston came on and joined Kenton. Prompt measures were immediately taken. The Indian camp was surrounded. The whites were too impatient for delay; the attack was made before it was light enough. Two Indians only were killed, and seven made prisoners. Many in the darkness made their escape. Col. Tod, with the main body of the troops, lingered behind, and did not reach the place where the Indians were defeated, till the sun was at least two hours high in the morning. The Indians who escaped from camp, alarmed the town. Their men, women, and children, took naked to the woods, and by the time Col. Tod reached the town, they had all fled. The town was consumed to ashes, and every thing around was destroyed. The army camped on the north fork of Paint creek that night, and next day made their way for home, without the loss of a man killed or wounded.

1788. The settlements continued to increase around Kenton's station, although the Indians continued to harass them. The scouting parties of the whites occasionally fell in with straggling parties of Indians, and frequent skirmishes ensued during the year. On one occasion the Indians came near Kenton's station, and stole a great number of horses. Kenton raised a party and pursued them. The Indians crossed the Ohio near the mouth of Locust. Kenton and his party pursued them with unerring tact, and the speed of a well trained pack of hounds. They overtook the Indians as they were preparing to camp for the night. As Kenton and party lay concealed some small distance from the camp, one of the Indians straggled to where the whites were concealed. The Indian was shot. The whites rushed upon the Indian camp, but a gun being fired, the Indians got alarmed, and took to the woods; and it being the dusk, or twilight of the evening, the rest of the Indians made their escape Kenton recovered all the horses, and some of their guns, and all their camp equipage, and returned in triumph home.

During the years 1789, '90, and '91, Kenton was not

engaged in any particular scrape worth detailing. He now became rich in land, and stock of every kind; reared up near Washington, a fine brick building, upon the site where his block-house had formerly stood in times of peril. His hospitable mansion was the welcome retreat of his friends and relatives. His hospitality was as boundless as space—his manners easy and pleasing. All his visitors (and they were numerous) felt themselves perfectly at home at his friendly dwelling. In the year 1789, the writer of these sketches first became acquainted with Kenton; and although young, was with him on many excursions after Indians. Notwithstanding the many difficulties and dangers which the early settlers had to encounter, they, in the general, were as happy and merry people as ever lived. Their times of security and plenty (they sometimes enjoyed both) was a real feast of body and mind.

1792. In the spring of this year the Indians were very troublesome, occasionally killing some of the inhabitants, and stealing their horses. In April a party of Indians crossed the Ohio some distance below Limestone, and took off a number of horses. The alarm was given, and Kenton raised a party of thirty-seven men, who immediately went in pursuit. These were all young men of intrepidity, of his own training, bold, dextrous, and cautious. The Indians took the direction towards the head of the Little Miami. Kenton pursued; and when near the east fork of the Little Miami, silently pursuing the Indian trail, he heard a bell at a distance. He immediately stopped his party, and as was his custom, he went in person to reconnoiter. He took with him three others. Among those he selected, was Cornelius Washburn, a young man whose nerves and pulse were as steady and regular while taking aim at an Indian, as when he was practicing with his rifle at a target. He had been with Kenton on several expeditions, and always distinguished himself as a bold soldier. Kenton and his companions went cautiously forward towards the bell. After they had gone some distance, they saw an Indian riding, nearing toward them. (The Indian was hunting with his bell open, as deer are not alarmed at the sound of a bell; on the contrary, they stand and gaze at the horse on which the bell hangs.) As soon as Kenton saw the Indian approaching, he concealed his little party, till the Indian came as near them as the direction he was traveling would admit. He selected Washburn to shoot the Indian. When he came into an open space in the wood, Kenton called, or made a noise. The Indian, as was expected, stopped to listen. The moment the Indian stopped his horse, Cornelius Washburn drew his bead upon him—drew his hair trigger—the rifle fired clear, and down fell the Indian. Kenton then returned to his main party, and a consultation was held on the subject of their future operations. They were satisfied this Indian was not alone in the woods—that his comrades were not far distant. As they were satisfied they were in the neighborhood of the enemy, circumspection in their movements was indispensable. They were still on the trail of the Indians who had stolen the horses. Cornelius Washburn, with another choice and confidential spirit, moved on the trail some distance in advance. They had not traveled far before Washburn was seen returning hastily to meet the party. He gave Kenton intelligence that about a mile ahead, he had heard a vast number of bells, and that he was convinced the bells were near the Indian camp, as they appeared to be scattered as if the horses were feeding in different directions. A council was immediately held, to make arrangements for the coming combat. It was now late in the evening and drizzling rain. Kenton, after placing his detachment in a proper situation to defend themselves should they be attacked, took Cornelius Washburn, and went to ascertain by personal observation the situation of the enemy. About the dusk of the evening he came in view of the Indian encampment. With the stealthy and watchful tread of the cat, he approached as near their camp as prudence would dictate. The Indians were camped on the bank of the east fork of the Little Miami, about five miles above where Williamsburg now stands. They had a number of tents and marquees, which it is probable they had taken at St. Clair's defeat. The number of Indians he could not ascertain; but he had no doubt there was three or four times the number there was of whites. Kenton returned and reported to his comrades their situation, and probable number; and after consultation, it was determined to trust to fortune and attack them boldly. Kenton moved on his party near to the enemies' camp, and then divided them into parties of four men each, and each party was to attack a separate tent or marquee. He chose midnight for the attack, lest he might have to retreat, and in that case he wished a good part of the night to get the start, as they could not be pursued in the dark. As soon as his arrangements were made, they moved cautiously forward to the unequal contest. So cautious and noiseless was their approach, that every party was within five or six paces of the line of tents, without being discovered. They rushed upon the Indian tents with tremendous yells, and each fired his rifle against an Indian as they slept. The Indians who were uninjured, broke through the backs of the tents. Kenton's party were so small that not near half the tents were fired into. At the first fire nearly all the Indians who had left the tents, seeing the small number of the whites, boldly rallied, returned to the tents that were not attacked, gathered up their arms, and returned the fire. There was on a lower bottom, a second line of tents, which Kenton had not discovered when he reconnoitered the camp. The Indians from this low ground run up the bank to the aid of their comrades. Kenton perceived this movement, and seeing the Indians attempting to surround him, ordered a retreat. The whole skirmish lasted but a few minutes. Just as the retreat was commenced, John Barr (the father of Maj. William Barr, of Cincinnati, and John T. Barr, of New York) was killed, and Alexander McIntire was taken prisoner, and the next day killed. The residue of Kenton's little band arrived in safety at home. From information received from a Mr. Riddle, a white man, who lived with the Indians, their numbers were two hundred; some of whom were women. There were about thirty of them killed, and a number wounded. This is very probable, from the advantage the whites had in the attack, and while the fight lasted. The celebrated Tecumseh commanded the Indians. His caution and fearless intrepidity made him a host wherever he went. In military tactics, night attacks are not allowable, except in cases like this, where the assailing party are far inferior in numbers. Sometimes in night attacks, panics and confusion are created in the attacked party which may render them a prey to inferior numbers. Kenton trusted to something like this on the present occasion, but was disappointed; for where Tecumseh was present, his influence over the minds of his followers, infused that confidence in his tact and intrepidity, that they could only be defeated by force of numbers.

1793. As Mason county was filling up with inhabitants very rapidly, they felt themselves strong in numbers. They kept spies constantly ranging the country, and if the Indians crossed the Ohio, they had to do it very slyly, or they would be discovered by these ever watchful spies. Kenton had, this season, made an arrangement with a Col. Enoch Smith, of Strode's station, that should the Indians show themselves in his (Smith's) neighborhood, that Kenton, with his select corps, would endeavor to head the Indians about the Ohio. A party of Indians had crossed the Ohio about the mouth of the Scioto, went back, attacked and took Morgan's station. Col. Smith, pursuant to the arrangement, sent an express to Kenton, informing him of the disaster which had befallen Morgan's station, and the course the Indians had taken. Kenton immediately raised a party of about thirty men, crossed the Ohio at Limestone, and moved rapidly through the woods to endeavor to head the Indians about the mouth of Paint creek, on the Scioto. When he came to Paint creek, at the place now known as Reeve's crossing, he came on a fresh trail of Indians going down the creek. It was then late in the evening. He pursued the trail till nearly dark : Kenton then left his party, and took Michael Cassady, and went forward to make observations. They had not proceeded far before they heard bells. They cautiously went forward to reconnoiter. They found the Indians encamped on the bank of Paint creek. They had three fires; some of them were singing and making other merry noises, showing that they felt in perfect security. Kenton and Cassady returned to their party, and it was concluded to lay still till daylight, and then surround and attack the Indians. Kenton's party were all on horseback. They tied their horses, and laid still till nearly day, when they moved on for the Indian camp. When they got near the camp, a halt was made, and they divided into three divisions : Captain Baker, with one division, was directed to proceed to the creek above the camp; Cassady, with another division, was ordered to make to the creek below the camp ; and Kenton, with the remaining division, was to attack the camp in front. Strict orders were given that no attack was to be made till it was light enough to draw a clear bead. The divisions took their several stations promptly. Daylight began to appear—the Indians had risen, and some were standing or sitting about their fires. Captain Baker, seeing the Indians, soon became impatient to commence the action ; and before it was light enough to draw a clear sight, he made the attack. All the divisions then rushed upon the Indian camp and fired. The Indians dashed through the creek, and scattered through the woods, like a flock of young partridges. Three Indians, only, and a white man by the name of Ward, were killed. Ward was taken prisoner by the Indians when young, and in every respect was an Indian. This Ward had two brothers, James and Charles, who were near neighbors to Kenton, and who were respectable men. Kenton's party lost one man in this rencounter, a Mr. Joseph Jones. The party now returned home without any further adventure.

In the course of this summer, the spies who had been down the Ohio below Limestone, discovered where a party of about twenty Indians had crossed the Ohio, and sunk their canoes in the mouth of Holt's creek. The sinking of their canoes, and concealing them, was evidence of the intention of the Indians to recross the Ohio at the same place. When Kenton received this intelligence he despatched a messenger to Bourbon county, to apprise them that Indians had crossed the Ohio, and had taken that direction ; whilst he forthwith collected a small party of choice spirits, whom he could depend upon in cases of emergency. Among them was Cornelius Washburn, a man who had the cunning of the fox for ambuscading, and the boldness of the lion for executing. With this party, Kenton crossed the Ohio at Limestone, and proceeded down to opposite the mouth of Holt's creek, where the Indian canoes lay concealed. Here his party lay concealed four days, before they heard or saw any thing of the Indians. On the fourth day of their ambuscade, they discovered three Indians come down the bank, and drive six horses into the river. The horses swam over. The Indians then raised one of the canoes they had sunk, and crossed over. When the Indians came near the shore, Kenton discovered that of the three men in the canoe, one was a white man. As he thought the white man was probably a prisoner, he ordered his men to fire alone at the Indians, and save the white man. His men fired : the two Indans fell. The headway which the canoe had, run her on the shore. The white man in the canoe, picked up his gun, and as Kenton ran down to the water's edge to receive the man, he snapped his gun at the whites. Kenton then ordered his men to kill him. He was immediately shot. About three or four hours afterwards, on the same day, two more Indians and another white man came to the river, and drove in five horses. The horses swam over; and the Indians raised another of their sunk canoes, and followed the horses across the Ohio. As soon as the canoe touched the shore with the Indians, Kenton's party fired upon them, and killed them all. The white man who was with this party of Indians, had his ears cut, his nose bored, and had all the marks which distinguish the Indians. Kenton and his men still kept up their ambuscade, knowing there were still more Indians, and one canoe yet behind. Sometime in the night, the main body of the Indians came to the place where their canoes were sunk, and hooted like owls ; but not receiving any answer, they began to think all was not right. The Indians were as vigilant as weasels. The two parties who had been killed, the main body expected to find camped on the other side of the Ohio ; and as no answer was given to their hooting like owls, which hooting was doubtless the agreed upon countersign, one of the Indians must have swam the river, to reconnoiter, or discover what had become of heir friends. The Indian, who had swam the river, must have discovered the ambuscade. He went up on a high hill, or knob, which was immediately in Kenton's rear, and gave three long and loud yells ; after which he informed his friends that they must immediately make their escape, as there were a party of whites waylaying them. Kenton had several men who understood the Indian language. Not many minutes after the Indian on the hill had warned his companions of their danger, the Bourbon militia came up. It being dark, the Indians broke and run, leaving about thirty horses, which they had stolen from about Bourbon. The next morning some attempts were made to pursue the Indians, but they had straggled and scattered off in such small parties, that the pursuit was abandoned, and Kenton and his party returned home, without this affair making any more noise or eclat, than would have taken place on the return of a party from a common hunting tour. Although Kenton and his party did not succeed as well as they could wish, or was expected by their friends, yet the Indians were completely foiled and defeated in their object, six of them were killed, and all the horses they had stolen were retaken, and the remainder of the Indians scattered, to return home in small squads. This was the last inroad the Indians made in Kentucky; from henceforward they lived free from alarms.

This same season, 1793, Gen. Wayne came down the Ohio with the regular army, and was camped on a piece of ground just below Cincinnati, called Hobson's choice. Gen. Wayne made a requisition for men on Kentucky, which was promptly afforded. Gen. Scott commanded the Kentucky troops. Of these Kenton was a major, and placed at the head of a battalion of as choice spirits as ever settled on the frontier. Wayne, with his army, went on, and built Fort Greenville. By this time the season was too far advanced, and Gen. Wayne concluded to suspend his principal operations for the present. He sent a detachment, and erected Fort Recovery, on the ground where Gen. St. Clair had been defeated. While Fort Recovery was building, Gen. Wayne permitted

19

Kenton of the Kentucky troops, and Maj. McMahan of the regulars, to take an excursion towards the lakes. This Maj. McMahan was one of the first settlers about the Mingo bottom, on the Ohio, above Wheeling. He was about the same age and experience with Kenton. McMahan and Samuel Brady were the admitted chiefs among the frontier men, from Wheeling to Beaver creek. When among the pioneers, McMahan was sure to be obeyed, let who would hold the commission. Kenton and McMahan were both now with Gen. Wayne, and both were majors. These men, though the bravest of the brave, knew nothing about the slow, cautious movements of armies, whose intention was to maintain the conquest they might make. They bitterly complained of Gen. Wayne's dilatory movements; declared they might flog the Indians much easier, and with less labor, than build forts. Gen. Wayne apprised of their discontent, concluded that he would permit these two distinguished and celebrated majors, to have a detachment of about three hundred men, and let them push forward till they would find a fight. Kenton's and McMahan's detachment consisted of 150 men each—150 regulars, and 150 volunteers. This detachment went on till they were near the mouth of the Auglaize, near Fort Defiance, where they began to find Indian signs plenty. Though McMahan was equally brave, Kenton was far the most cautious and discreet soldier. The scouting parties from this detachment, found numerous large trails of Indians, coming from different directions, and appearing to center not far from them. Kenton did not like the signs about him, and thought it would be most prudent to retire. McMahan, who was very brave, and very obstinate in his opinion, said he could not think of retiring without fighting. Kenton told him that he thought it very imprudent and very hazardous to go farther; but if it were determined to have a fight at all hazards, that he would juin him ; that all should be done that men could do; that if a rapid retreat became necessary, he (Kenton) and his men were mounted, and consequently would have some advantage in a rapid retreat. Nothing was concluded that night. Next morning before day, McMahan went to Kenton, and said, that after weighing all the circumstances in relation to the apparent concentration of the Indians, that appeared to be gathering around them, that he thought his (Kenton's) course of proceeding the best, at least the safest. This detachment then returned to Greenville, without having struck a blow. General Wayne said that he thought more of his two majors now than he did before ; that he now found they had some conduct with their courage. Kenton lay at Greenville with Gen. Wayne till winter set in, when he was discharged, and returned home. Thus closed Kenton's military career, till 1813. Maj. McMahan commanded Fort Recovery when the Indians attacked that place. Not content with defending the fort, he rushed out upon the Indians and was slain, 1794.

The Indian war being now happily terminated, the emigration to Kentucky pushed forward in a constant stream. Land became valuable; and as there was great irregularity, and want of precision, in the first entries and surveys, the late locaters made their entries and surveys of land very special. Although Kenton was then thought to be one of the richest men in Kentucky, in land, yet one of his land claims failed after another, till he was completely bewildered in a labyrinth of litigation. As Kenton was unlettered, and consequently unacquainted with legal proceedings, every advantage was taken of his ignorance, and in a few years the glorious technicalities and uncertainty of the law, stripped this honest man of his blood-bought earnings, and sent him in the evening of his days, pennyless and dejected, to spend his few remaining years in poverty and want.

About the year 1802 he settled in Urbana, Champaign county, Ohio; where he remained some years, beloved and respected by all who had any regard for patriotic worth. While in Champaign county, he was elected a Brigadier-general of the militia. About 1810, he became a member of the methodist church, of which he remained a respected member till the day of his death.

In 1813, when Governor Shelby came to Urbana, at the head of the Kentucky troops, Kenton would not remain in "inglorious ease," when his country required defenders. He shouldered his rifle, mounted his horse, and joined the army as a private, but a privileged member of the Governor's military family. He crossed the lakes, and accompanied General Harrison to Malden in Upper Canada; from thence up lake St. Clair and the river Thames. He was present at the glorious battle of the Moravian Town, and played his part with his usual intrepidity. Here ends the military career of the famous Simon Kenton—a man who, it is probable, passed through more hair-breadth escapes than any man living or dead.

About 1820, he moved to the head of Mad river, in Logan county, near to the site of Old Wapatomika, one of the places where he passed through scenes of suffering, indescribable, while a captive with the Indians in his youth. Here, in the midst of a beech forest, was passed, in humble poverty, the evening of the life of this illustrious man. If a long life of hardy adventures—with a courage that never quailed at danger, and patriotism that never ceased its exertion in his country's cause, deserves the title of illustrious, then stands the name of General Kenton in the first rank of worthies.

About 1824, through the exertions of Judge Burnet of Cincinnati, (then a member of the United States senate) and of General Vance, the present Governor of Ohio, (then a member of the house of representatives, in congress) a pension of twenty dollars a month was obtained for him. This sum, though small for such services as he rendered to his country, secured his declining age from actual want.

In the month of April, 1836, this great and good man* breathed his last. In the Western Christian Advocate, of June 24, 1836, I find the following appropriate and graphic notice of his death, by Mr. W. I. Ellworth.

" After the din of war had ceased, and savage barbarity was no longer dreaded by the peaceful emigrants, General Kenton retired to private life, to enjoy the sweets of domestic happiness. He settled a few miles north of Old Wapatomika, (now Zanesfield) Logan county, Ohio, where he spent the last of a long and, we trust, a useful life. The frosts of more than eighty winters had fallen on his head, without entirely whitening his locks. During the last few years, he declined rapidly ; not so much from the effects of disease, as by the influence of early hardship and toil. He was for more than eighteen years a respectable member of the Methodist church; and a regular attendant on the ministry of the word. When his trembling limbs would no longer perform their wonted functions, he would solicit some kind friend to lead him to the house of God. I visited him a few hours before his decease, and found him perfectly willing to die. His death, though not triumphant, was peaceful; and we trust he has exchanged a world of care and grief, for a state of holy and uninterrupted joy."

He lived to hear the " din of war hushed," and gentle peace returning. He lived to see changes more extraordinary. He lived to see farms, towns, and schools of learning, and temples of worship constructed, where

---

* I am aware, that, by too many of the present day, none are considered *great*, but such as are adepts in procuring and retaining wealth. Such men as Cincinnatus, Epaminondas, or Miltiades, would now be sneered at as poor drivelers.

the solitary hunter in days past pitched his lonely camp; and in the silent and dark forest pursued his game. What a change! He was permitted to live a long life as a connecting link, to illustrate the manners of two ERAS as dissimilar as if they were one thousand years distant from each other. He had lived to see moral revolutions as surprising as these extraordinary changes. These mutations in manners and in morals have been gradual in their progress, but most important in their results: and they have been introduced in our country in less than fifty years. Every sketch of them, however slight or detached, should be treasured with pious care.

General Kenton was of fair complexion, six feet one inch in height. He stood and walked very erect; and, in the prime of life, weighed about one hundred and ninety pounds. He never was inclined to be corpulent, although of sufficient fulness to form a graceful person. He had a soft, tremulous voice, very pleasing to the hearer. He had laughing, grey eyes, which appeared to fascinate the beholder. He was a pleasant, good-humored, and obliging companion. When excited, or provoked to anger (which was seldom the case) the fiery glance of his eye would almost curdle the blood of those with whom he came in contact. His rage, when roused, was a tornado. In his dealing, he was perfectly honest; his confidence in man, and his credulity, were such, that the same man might cheat him twenty times; and if he professed friendship, he might cheat him still.

I have now related the principal incidents in the eventful life of this extraordinary man; with truth only for my guide. I am aware that my composition will require the indulgence of my readers; and it is believed that those who know me best, will not hesitate to pardon my want of method, and the coarse style of my writing. Although I am ambitious to please the reader, vanity, or a false estimate of my acquirements, or talents, did not induce me to write these sheets. My aim was to be useful, by recording the actions of men, to whom Kentucky and Ohio owe a debt of gratitude. How could the rising generation set a correct estimate on the character of men of whom they had only heard by common fame?

In 1830, I paid a visit to General Kenton, and from his own words, and in his presence, committed to writing the principal incidents related in the foregoing narrative. In a life so long and full of actions, there is no doubt but many interesting events escaped the old hero's recollection. The writer of this narrative, in his youth, accompanied him on several minor expeditions, of which no notice is taken. But enough is written to show the genius and enterprise of the man, who first planted corn on the north of Kentucky.

I will close these narratives, by quoting a few lines from a western bard.

" Say, shall the rough woodland pioneers,
    Of Mississippi's wide-extended vale,
Claim no just tribute of our love and tears,
    And their names vanish with the passing gale?
With veteran arms the forest they subdued,
    With veteran arts subdued the savage foe;
Our country, purchased with their valiant blood,
    Claims for them all that gratitude can do.
Their arduous labors gave us wealth and ease;
    Fair freedom followed from their doubtful strife;
Their well-aimed measures gave us lasting peace,
    And all the social blessedness of life.
Then let their offspring, mindful of their claims,
    Cherish their honors in the lyric band.
O save from dark oblivion's gloomy reign,
    The brave, the worthy fathers of our land."

THE END.

Breinigsville, PA USA
10 November 2010
249114BV00003B/20/P